www.librex.co.uk

# HOW
# TO DRIVE

# HOW TO DRIVE

THE ULTIMATE GUIDE – FROM THE MAN WHO WAS THE STIG

## BEN COLLINS

First published 2014 by Macmillan
an imprint of Pan Macmillan, a division of Macmillan Publishers Limited
Pan Macmillan, 20 New Wharf Road, London N1 9RR
Basingstoke and Oxford
Associated companies throughout the world
www.panmacmillan.com

HB ISBN: 978-1-4472-7283-0
TPB ISBN: 978-1-4472-7285-4

9 8 7 6 5 4

A CIP catalogue record for this book is available from the British Library.

Typeset by Here Design Ltd
Printed by Printer Trento S.r.l.

Visit **www.panmacmillan.com** to read more about all our books and to buy them. You will
also find features, author interviews and news of any author events, and you can sign up
for e-newsletters so that you're always first to hear about our new releases.

# Contents

**Prologue:**

How Not To Drive ................................................ 6

**Introduction:**

How to Drive ...................................................... 8

**Part 1: A Very Short History of Driving**

Roads Aren't Straightforward............................ 14

Burning Rubber ................................................ 16

Road Rage ....................................................... 18

The Driving Test ............................................... 21

King of the Road ............................................... 24

**Part 2: The Basics**

Are You Sitting Comfortably? ............................ 28

The Beast ......................................................... 36

Smooth Operator.............................................. 46

Changing Gear ................................................. 50

Steering............................................................ 60

Braking............................................................. 65

Cornering ......................................................... 91

**Part 3: The Open Road**

Avoiding Accidents ........................................... 116

Junctions ......................................................... 128

Overtaking........................................................ 135

Dual Carriageways ........................................... 150

Motorways ....................................................... 152

In the Zone ...................................................... 169

Free Your Mind ................................................ 174

Vision ............................................................... 180

Night Driving .................................................... 186

Basic Instinct.................................................... 190

Visualization .................................................... 195

**Part 4: Skidding**

The Limits of Grip ............................................ 200

Driving in the Wet............................................. 209

Winter Driving................................................... 220

Worst-case Scenarios ...................................... 232

Stunt Driving .................................................... 240

**Epilogue:**

Drifting through London..................................... 266

Index ................................................................ 270

Credits ............................................................. 272

# Prologue:
## *How Not to Drive*

### 1998. A twisting country lane in the middle of nowhere, travelling at 80 miles per hour.

The sound of 14 tons of metal colliding is almost deafening when you're right next to it. Imagine 100 heavy doors slamming in unison and you're not even close. It's loud enough to summon people from farmhouses half a mile away to search for plane wreckage, but inside the crash … you hardly hear a thing.

That's because your brain is moving – and as it thumps the inside of your skull it disrupts the electrical activity powering things like sight and hearing.

My Toyota Supra cornered like it was on rails. It sat on enormous wide tyres and had a whale-tail wing with enough downforce to leave a dent in the floor. At the time I was a Formula 1 hopeful and one of the fastest men in Formula 3 – even Sir Jackie Stewart said so, and boy did I know it.

I was *so* clever and knew my local roads *so* well that I had a braking plan for every conceivable scenario. One flowing section in particular had a bottleneck into a single-track lane with no passing space. I calculated my velocity precisely to be able to make it all the way through it and out the other side before an approaching car filled the gap, or if there was a car coming through I would throw the anchors to buy enough time for it to emerge.

According to a recent insurance survey there are certain types of music that make you put your foot down and generally drive like a complete moron. The Black Eyed Peas topped this deadly driving chart with 'Hey Mama', a banging tune there's no doubt, but at the time I had the Beastie Boys busting decibels.

I wanged the stereo up a notch and tipped into the familiar dusty right-hander towards the mouth of the funnel at full speed. Over the course of the next second the vanishing point ran into a scene that I hadn't budgeted for.

Thick mud was spread lavishly across the road. Alarm bells were ringing, but the mud was quickly replaced by a more pressing issue. A very large, slow-moving

'Inside the crash you hardly hear a thing.'

## 'Time slowed down, but the car didn't.'

truck was lumbering through the bottleneck, too slowly to clear it at my rate of closure.

Time slowed down, but the car didn't.

I braked. Wide tyres and downforce were powerless on the greasy mud, and my front tyres locked instantly. The trajectory involved a double whammy of hedge and a lethal side impact with the truck. *Think fast*.

0.25 seconds later I released the useless brakes, hoping to recover enough steering to swing across the front of the truck and punch through the gateway into a field.

*Nope.*

The mouth-like radiator grill and the word *VOLVO* filled the screen.

Then it was that big moment. There were no more choices, only consequences. I could have been an accountant. I could have been a yoga teacher. But there I was with no more tricks up my sleeve. It was time to take the hit, and I had no airbag.

I closed my eyes as the hood of the Supra exploded into the truck's bumper and deformed until it met with the Volvo's front axle, which didn't bend much. The Supra's engine and gearbox travelled 2 feet my way as the physics of displacement and momentum did their thing. Stopping a 12-ton truck, fully laden with turf, dead in its tracks put a force of deceleration through my body in excess of sixty times the force of gravity. I did not feel well.

The head-on impact and abrupt stop rearranged all sorts of things inside the Supra, including my kidneys, which ruptured and bled for several days. Pens, loose change and a half-eaten sandwich from the previous owner all relocated themselves to the dashboard.

Temperament has always been a problem for me, and although I've learned to control it I know that there are demons lurking. The track offers me a positive outlet for unleashing that side of my personality in very controlled bursts. But there are certain things I can't combine with driving, and loud music is one of them.

0.2

# Introduction:
## *How to Drive*

### Driving is one of the most pleasurable things that each of us does on a daily basis.

It is also the most dangerous. And it doesn't matter whether you drive on the right or the left, using an automatic gearbox or a stick – the fundamental principles and physics of driving are the same everywhere.

The world population of motor vehicles exceeded 1 billion a couple of years ago. Car crashes kill 50 per cent more people than malaria, and the World Health Organization predicts that road deaths will rise 52 per cent by 2030, overtaking HIV AIDS as a global killer within the decade.

Perhaps that isn't so surprising. Whichever country you're from, you want to go from being a learner to a driver as fast as possible. Having tackled a tough multiple-choice questionnaire, reversed round a corner and successfully navigated a supermarket car park, you tear off your L-plates or probationary stickers, and take a ton of speeding metal out onto the open road. Millions of drivers will receive their licences this year with less than eighteen hours' driving experience under their belt.

A Starbucks barista receives twenty-four hours of training before being handed the keys to an espresso machine.

The robotic syllabus of the driving test itself remains painfully inadequate – not so much in what it contains as how much is left out: controlling a skid, driving on a motorway, tackling a corner, driving at night and overtaking … to name but a few. And of those who pass, less than 1 per cent receives further training.

Governments, road safety groups, even the Green lobby want to wrap us in cotton wool and then pull it over our eyes. They would have us believe that speeding, among other things, is the biggest danger facing modern drivers, but 700,000 police road accident reports gathered over the last five years tell a different story. The real killer is simply poor driving.

'Millions of drivers will receive their licences this year with less than eighteen hours' driving experience under their belt.

A Starbucks barista receives twenty-four hours of training before being handed the keys to an espresso machine.'

# 01

# A Very Short History of Driving

# Roads Aren't Straightforward

The rules of the road inevitably shape the way we travel. Man and cart made their way along the left-hand side of Ancient Roman pathways, and this was no accident.

'I blame Napoleon.'

The vast majority of humans are right-handed and right-eye-dominant; by hanging left, they could most easily identify and wield a weapon against any oncoming threat.

The Romans were a clever bunch; they built straight roads across their burgeoning empire, from the Appian Way in Italy to the trunk roads (like the A5) that still connect Great Britain. With reins in their left hand and a whip in their right, Roman riders were as ergonomically sound as modern-day right-seated drivers whose dominant right hand never leaves the steering wheel. The entire world followed this logic – until the French got involved. I blame Napoleon.

The Frogs began hauling goods in bulk using teams of horses whose master was seated on the rearmost horse to the left, for no good reason other than to be different. In order to jostle their cumbersome wagons past oncoming traffic, they had no choice but to drive past on the right to observe the clearance. Napoleon, who was left-handed and naturally biased, was so impressed that he imposed the system everywhere he went. Wellington's armies prevented this madness spreading to Britain and her colonies, but the rot was setting in.

The Americans started using French pack-horses and adopted the keep-right rule, in large part to defy their former British colonial masters. The Canadians eventually followed suit in 1923 to stave off carnage at their border. Hitler enforced driving on the right across the parts of Europe that Napoleon had unaccountably missed, and China took the plunge in 1946 to accommodate imported US gas-guzzlers.

So today, two-thirds of the world's population drives on the wrong side of the road, using the weaker left eye to check the nearside wing mirror and overtake, all because of a little Frenchman and a disagreement over some tea in Boston. Britain, India, Australia and Japan remain notable exceptions to the global decline in common sense – civilized, tea-drinking nations all.

Research in 1969 (by J. J. Leeming) showed that countries driving on the left have a lower collision rate than countries driving on the right. Cyclists and horse riders typically mount from the left-hand side, placing them safely on the kerb when vehicles are travelling on the left. And if you still don't believe me, then check out the military: all aircraft carriers from American, British to Chinese have their control towers on the right-hand side, so that pilots can approach for landing and take-off from the left, with their dominant eye watching out for the only building they might accidentally crash into for a hundred miles.

'So today, two-thirds of the world's population drives on the wrong side of the road.'

# Burning Rubber

'Modern tyres have become such normal objects of the roadside that the marvel of their existence ceases to excite wonder. Yet it is something of a miracle that a column of compressed air can be bound round a wheel, endowing it with a life and luxuriousness absolutely unknown to a former generation, whose carriage wheels were shod with iron, and whose use of horse power was strictly limited to the equine meaning of that phrase.'

*The Dunlop Book: The Motorist's Guide, Counsellor and Friend, 1920*

The first self-propelled 'automobile' was probably the steam-powered three-wheeler built in 1769 by a Frenchman called Nicolas-Joseph Cugnot. Nic demonstrated the shortcomings of three wheels by crashing into a wall on his first display … at 2 miles per hour. I did so too when I barrel-rolled a Reliant Robin at our Dunsfold test track on *Top Gear* in 2010.

Early vehicles were cumbersome and tricky to control; stopping them on their skinny wagon wheels was an act of faith. Thanks to a little divine intervention in 1839, a bankrupt American inventor by the name of Charles Goodyear was displaying a ball of sulphur-treated gum he had concocted, when it flew out of his hands onto a stove, scorching the surface and creating the world's first weatherproof rubber compound. The air-filled tyre was subsequently invented in 1846 by Scotsman Robert Thomson, a self-taught genius who also invented a machine for drying his mother's laundry. Another Scot – John Dunlop – brought tyres into the mainstream by creating his first factory in 1889.

The 'pneumatic' tyre behaved more like a living organism than the rigid, clunking load-bearers of the previous age. The cushioned ride spared ladies the displeasure of having their rumps tenderized on every journey. The capacity of inflated rubber to absorb energy from multiple directions was the key to its success. It would transform motoring. Even the cream of tyre anecdotes still won't get you invited to dinner parties, but on the racing circuit it's all we talk about. Tyre dynamics is what sticks the car to the road, not the metal bit sitting on top of them. Above all else, the chassis and suspension settings of a racing car are tuned to maximize the performance of the tyres. Some cars are better communicators than others, but every sensation the driver feels, every experience you will ever have on the road, travels along the hotline that connects the tyre to your backside.

The Michelin Company mascot earned his name, Bibendum (Latin for 'let's drink'), in 1903 by literally swallowing the debris littering the course to win the Paris Road Race. Their durability over nails and broken glass was such that Michelin runners occupied eight of the top ten finishing positions, taking the fight to the drawbridge of Fort Dunlop.

The recipe for creating a good tyre is even more complex than the culinary delights promoted in the Michelin Guide. Research and development departments push the physical boundaries by constantly testing new materials to add to the 200 existing ingredients.

The tread pattern we find ourselves studying as we queue for our latest MOT is the bit that works on a wet road. At 50 mph it displaces around 30 litres of water per second – enough to fill fifteen bathtubs every minute.

The black rubber stuff comes in a variety of compounds that determine how sticky the tyre is. But grip is nothing without the strength of the underlying construction: a vulcanized blend of steel cords, polyester and Kevlar tailored to the size, stiffness and performance demanded by each particular vehicle.

There have been a few hiccups along the way. American car manufacturers at first dismissed the innovation of steel-belted radials after World War II. They preferred blancmange for suspension. Radials eventually won out because they were so much more fuel-efficient. The tyre, quite simply, was more important than the car.

'Every experience you will ever have on the road, travels along the hotline that connects the tyre to your backside.'

# Road Rage

## Back in 1865 the Red Flag Act still restricted national speeds to a dizzying 4 mph and

required that a man walk in front of vehicles at all times, brandishing the said ensign (until it was finally put to one side in 1878). The world's first road fatality came in 1896 when Mrs Bridget Driscoll stepped into the path of a Roger-Benz 'horseless carriage' and stood 'bewildered' by the machine as it zigzagged towards her at a 'tremendous pace' (no more than 8 mph). Frozen with fear, she was run over and later died in what was judged to be an accidental death.

Cars were feared because they were different – but there was nothing new about the way people drove them. In 1720 traffic fatalities from 'furiously driven' carts and coaches were claimed to be the leading cause of death in London. In the New York of 1867, horses were killing an average of four pedestrians a week – roughly the same number as are killed by cars today, with denser traffic and a significantly larger population.

In 1817 Lord Byron wrote thus to Thomas Moore:

*Last week I had a row on the road … with a fellow in a carriage, who was impudent to my horse … I wheeled round, rode up to the window, and asked him what he meant. He grinned, and said some foolery, which produced him an immediate slap in the face, to his utter discomfiture. Much blasphemy ensued, and some menace, which I stopped by dismounting and opening the carriage door, and intimating an intention of mending the road with his immediate remains, if he did not hold his tongue. He held it.*

A Texas City Grand Jury recently heard the case of a truck driver tailgating a man's daughter and waving his arms at her, prompting her father to give chase in his Mercedes. 'There was evidentially some swerving between the two vehicles, and the two exchanged words and were cussing at each other,' explained Captain Goetschius of the Texas police force. The men pulled over and faced down. The Merc driver pulled out his pistol, but the truckie was faster on the draw. He floored Merc Man by planting a bowl of oatmeal in his face. Proof, if any was needed, of the perils of regression when in possession of the keys to something shiny. And the benefit of a healthy diet.

'Much
blasphemy
ensued,
and some
menace,
which I
stopped by
dismounting
and opening
the carriage
door.'

We become as stubborn as mules inside our tin cans, even when confronted with the threat of losing more than our licence. On the edge of an otherwise serene Cotswold village one enraged woman rammed another from behind with her Vauxhall Nova. She was so angry that she sat there gunning the engine until the front wheels shredded through to the steel cords. The resulting sparks ignited her engine's fluids and the whole vehicle lit up with her inside it. She threatened would-be rescuers with a clenched fist, preferring to perish in the flames.

The machines we use these days have been through a time warp, but the human psyche hasn't always kept up. It's a jungle out there.

## Motor Racing

In Victorian times health and safety was regarded with a disdainful curl of the stiff upper lip, so there was little serious driving regulation. 'Motor racing' took place on long stretches of dusty country road and so gripped the pioneers and engineers of the age that technology, once triggered, advanced rapidly. By 1900 the world speed record (set by an electric car, no less) topped 65 mph.

In 1903, 2 million enthusiasts lined the route from Paris to Madrid as 274 cars of all shapes and sizes battled for supremacy. British racing ace Charlie Jarrott set the scene:

*Long avenues of trees, top-heavy with foliage and gaunt in their very nakedness of trunk; a long, never-ending white ribbon, stretching away to the horizon; the holding of a bullet directed to that spot on the sky-line where earth and heaven met; fleeting glimpses of towns and dense masses of people – mad people, insane and reckless, holding themselves in front of the bullet to be ploughed and cut and maimed to extinction, evading the inevitable at the last moment in frantic haste; overpowering relief, as each mass was passed and each chance of catastrophe escaped; and beyond all, the horrible feeling of being hunted.*

The first day saw eight fatalities and twenty injured – perhaps unsurprising in an environment where drivers achieved *average* speeds of 65 mph on narrow lanes packed with spectators. The French authorities shut the contest down before it left Bordeaux. Road racing was abandoned, and the pioneers moved to closed circuits at places like Le Mans and Brooklands.

The gruelling, high-speed epics that followed would eventually spawn every piece of technology on the modern car, from disc brakes to power steering. And what's more, it created a set of driving principles that continues to be developed inside the cauldron of competition in Formula 1 and across the spectrum of the sport. These principles involve looking ahead, as well as within – a mental game that requires you to tie up emotional loose ends that might lead to mistakes or influence your ability to make calculated decisions. It is a cold and methodical approach to addressing a fast-developing situation.

'The gruelling,high-speed epics that followed would eventually spawn every piece of technology on the modern car.'

# The Driving Test

## The transition from horse to horseless carriage took the authorities by surprise.

In America the first driving exams were set up by high schools, arguably the best model, before state legislature intervened in order to regulate traffic with a licensing scheme for vehicles and their operators, starting with Chicago in 1899. The red tape started flowing in Europe with authorities looking to everyone from steam boiler associations to car salesmen for guidance and training in how to drive, a test finally materializing in Britain as late as 1934.

The coveted flaps of paper providing motorists their ticket to ride still amount to dubious currency when you take them overseas, with the Germans refusing to recognize American driving licences granted in California or Georgia.

The modern driving test allegedly teaches safe driving for life, but the newly passed are four times more likely to crash than the rest of us. And the majority of 'us' believe we would fail the test if we had to retake it. QED: being 'good' at the test does not equal being a good driver.

The skills we learn to pass the test come from the highest possible authorities – the government and the police. So we might expect to find some answers about our evolution here. The UK's most revered driving credential, the advanced driving licence, is based on the Police System of Car Control and presided over by instructors who hold Police Advanced Driving Certificates. The Police System has been described as the Holy Grail of driving: followers of the system believe that questioning its teachings is tantamount to heresy. But it is not just obsolete – it can be dangerous. In Britain the first words a student hears from his police instructor on the open road are: 'GOLF, LIMA, FOXTROT', or 'Go Like F***.'

Lord Trenchard (1873–1956) was a visionary with a taste for speed. Having lost a lung and been paralysed from the waist down after being shot during the Boer War, he took up bobsleighing during his recuperation in Switzerland. When the impact of a hefty crash on the Cresta Run miraculously cured him, he returned to active duty, became a pilot and laid the foundations for the Royal Air Force with Winston Churchill. He was appointed police commissioner in 1931.

'Being "good" at the test does not equal being a good driver.'

The number of cars in the UK grew from a few thousand at the turn of the century to over 2 million by the mid '30s. People with no formal training and no idea how to operate heavy machinery were discovering new ways to kill themselves – and others – on the roads. They notched up 7,305 fatalities in 1930 alone, and the average police driver had a crunch every 8,000 miles. The new commissioner decided to do something about it.

He picked up the telephone to a man who had been busy writing the history of motoring with his right foot. A Grand Prix winner in the early days of the sport, Sir Malcolm Campbell would take the world speed record to beyond 300 mph by 1935. Having evaluated the fleet, Campbell concluded that the lack of training and experience was the root cause of their attrition rate.

Trenchard recruited Lord Cottenham, the Stig of his time – aka racing driver and MI5 agent Mark Pepys – to oversee the creation of a police driving course. Cottenham set out the Ten Commandments of Motoring in his book *Steering Wheel Papers*, a manual on maintaining control of the cumbersome vehicles of the day. He taught the police:

- since power steering hadn't been invented, to pull the desperately large, heavy wheel with one hand and push it with the other;
- to apply their 10 horsepower gently and continuously through the corner so as not to upset their delicate suspension and hard, skinny tyres;
- to use the brakes independently of changing down gears so that both feet were free to 'double de-clutch': pumping the clutch several times to swing the gears whilst right-footing the accelerator to match the revs.

The results spoke for themselves. His training saw the police accident rate improve to one in 27,000 miles. Cottenham's work was done. He left the Met after just three years, but his gospel of Police Roadcraft was canonized and passed through the generations *unchanged*. Roadcraft's system of car control continues to form the backbone of police driver training and is at the root of the physical skills we learn to pass the driving test. The fundamentals of car control, however, have changed a bit since the 1930s …

Some eighty years on, the number of registered vehicles on UK roads has grown from 2 million to more than 34 million. A Ford Fiesta has ten times the power of a 1930s cop car; it could leave Sir Malcolm's Grand Prix racer dead at

'A Ford Fiesta has ten times the power of a 1930s cop car.'

the traffic lights and hit corners on tyres with twice as much grip. Synchromesh gearboxes don't require double de-clutching. Power steering points the vehicle in whichever direction you want it to go, and braking distances are up to 40 per cent shorter than yesteryear.

And Cottenham wouldn't have expected his 1935 methods to remain unchanged any more than an RAF pilot would expect a Spitfire manual to help him fly a Harrier Jump Jet. Yet with the creaking gospel according to the *Highway Code* in one hand and gear knob in the other, we duly line up to receive the wisdom of these authorities like disciples at the temple. Somewhere during the grinding of gear ratios, burning clutch plates and jarring emergency stops, we stop thinking about what we are doing and sometimes even sacrifice good sense on the altar of *just passing the damn test*.

'Cottenham wouldn't have expected his 1935 methods to remain unchanged any more than an RAF pilot would expect a Spitfire manual to help him fly a Harrier Jump Jet.'

# King of the Road

Not long after obtaining my road licence, after just three lessons, I enrolled at Silverstone's racing academy to apply for a competition licence.

I had to learn the different flags and display proficiency in late braking, tackling a corner at speed and controlling the twitching rocket that was a Peugeot 306 around the Grand Prix circuit. Before I knew it I was flying around the track less than an inch off the ground in a single-seater that was the closest thing to a Formula 1 car, and heaven, that I had ever experienced.

That took me all of a single day, fuelling my conviction that I was Carlos Fandango reincarnated behind the wheel.

My dad decided to take out an insurance policy by having me attend a specialized skid-control course at Silverstone. The course took place using a normal car fitted to a frame that lifted the front or rear tyres off the tarmac to induce a skid. And skid we did. I learned to pulse the brake pedal to unlock a stopped wheel, throw the steering into opposite lock to catch the car as it fishtailed and to perfect the recovery of a 360-degree spin at 70 mph by spotting the desired direction and fixing on it like a ballerina.

Armed with knowledge spanning not just how to execute a three-point turn but also how to nail a chicane and stop the world from turning, I was primed to become an insurance statistic.

I set off on a long trip with a mate to test a single-seater racing car at some far-flung airfield. I returned at the end of the session to discover that my buddy, who was never renowned for his common sense, had locked my keys in the boot. So began the kind of journey of self-discovery they don't teach in classrooms.

The AA had to hotwire the ignition, and the delay meant I was running late to get to Brands Hatch for a season-opening Formula First race. With a gut full of nerves and my friend jabbering in my ear, I ventured onto the M25 for the first time just as it started to rain.

'I was primed to become an insurance statistic.'

My front tyres were on the bald side, due to the extra air pressure I'd cleverly pumped into them for the five minutes of extra grip this afforded on a dry road … until the tread wore away. With the rain lashing at the windscreen and some fascinating radio stations to choose from, I failed to notice the traffic slowing in front.

They stopped.

I didn't.

Crunch: a five-car concertina.

I arrived at Brands late, with what remained of my Honda on the back of a flat-bed truck. Fortunately I was already wearing my racing suit, since my normal clothes were still locked inside the boot with my keys. I qualified on the front row. Then it started to pelt down with rain, and through further ignorance I opted for brand-new, and therefore greasy, tyres for the race.

Having survived the first lap, I took the lead. Then I braked so late for Paddock Hill bend I could see the incredulous look on the flag marshal's face as I shot past him. For the second time in twenty-four hours I locked up my front wheels, and no amount of pulse braking could prevent me firing off the track at 80 mph to an ignominious finish in the gravel trap.

Gutted.

Understanding how my choices had set this disastrous chain of events in motion took me longer than it should have done. In the words of my race team manager, I needed to 'break the cycle before you kick the bucket'.

If only I had paid more attention to that bucket. I destroyed a further three Formula First cars that season, to be awarded the championship's inglorious Bent Wishbone trophy for the hardest hit of the season.

But it finally sank in: I'd been ambushed by sheer ignorance of the real world at the very moment my mind and body were most eager to explore every nuance of it. The desire to tinker with machinery, push personal boundaries and ignore the advice of crusty old men with too much time on their hands is a trap that most of us have fallen into somewhere along the line.

The process that began, very slowly, was a painful one. I desperately needed to understand *why* I was failing on so many levels. Over time, I set about picking apart the patterns that led to my mistakes and began conditioning my responses.

To this day I'm still learning, and because there's so much to discover I'll never claim to be an expert. But that's what makes driving such an art.

# 02

# The Basics

---

# Are You Sitting Comfortably?

Once you get used to whatever car you're driving, it becomes an extension of your body, of your mind even.

When you're completely in tune with it, you lose awareness of rudimentary controls like the pedals. All that is left is your perception as you float through a colourful universe where the present meets the future.

To achieve Zen, the car should fit like a glove. Conversely, a bad seating position can turn a car into a torture chamber on a long journey. Chiropractors rub their hands with glee at the sight of drivers resting their noses on the top of the steering wheel, or with their feet so far from the pedals that only telepathy can link them to the road. Optimizing your driving position is the first step towards optimizing your drive.

## Feet, Not Legs

It's your feet that operate the pedals, not your whole leg. If I'd known this at the age of four, I'd have averted my first major crash. Having achieved terminal velocity aboard a sit-on lawnmower in a neighbouring farmer's field, I realized that I was hurtling towards the chicken pens. Emergency braking alone stood between me and a giant omelette. But my foot could barely reach the pedal. Ditching the machine into some pig wire was the only option – and not one I'd wholeheartedly recommend.

It goes without saying that choice of footwear – whether stilettos or oversized hobnail boots – can present a similar challenge.

Manufacturers spend millions of dollars on ergonomics, and modern vehicles mould the instruments around you. It's worth spending a few minutes to tailor them to your particular needs; you'll be more comfortable, and drive better.

Adjust the seat to position yourself as low down in the car as possible.

'Optimizing your driving position is the first step towards optimizing your drive.'

# 1. Driving Position

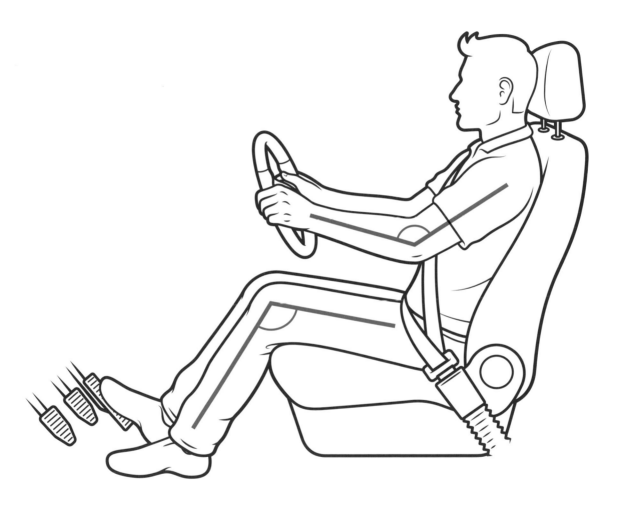

The lower you are, the closer to the centre of gravity you become, and the more you will feel part of the machine. Just make sure you have a clear view above the steering wheel.

If your legs are straight when you press the brake pedal, you won't be able to use it fully. Maximum braking requires a strong continuous force on the pedal, which simply isn't possible without a 15–30-degree bend at the knee. With your heels on the deck you should be able to easily move your feet, not your whole leg, between the pedals.

Most cars have a footrest to keep your left foot out of the way. This enables you to brace yourself in a corner when you need to by pushing on your left leg.

## Arms

You should be able to relax into the back of the seat and find that your arms are still bent when you hold the steering wheel. Driving with straight arms only uses a fraction of their strength, and you won't be able to turn the wheel properly. Sit too close to the wheel and you will a) look ridiculous, and b) break your nose on it some day. Ideally, your hands should be level with your shoulders in the quarter-to-three position on the wheel face. Then relax. And if you can't relax, start over until you can.

## Seat Belts

A third of passengers killed in the UK weren't wearing a seat belt. The lap belt, in particular, prevents your core mass from turning into a projectile and your thick skull from annihilating everyone in the car like a cannonball.

A friend of mine called Tony Harris, who lost half his leg courtesy of the Taliban, was competing in the world's most gruelling rally: Dakar. His team of exhausted former soldiers was commuting between stages on a placid stretch of carriageway connecting the dusty planes between Peru and Chile, when a taxi driver coming the other way decided it would be a great idea to overtake and drove headlong into their vehicle. The lads could have been forgiven for not wearing their belts and catching some shut-eye after all they had been through. But they did wear them, so they all survived, whilst the unbelted occupants of the taxi did not.

'If your butt is rolling around like Beyoncé's husband in an elevator, you've got no chance.'

From a driving perspective the belts offer a convenient way of staying in the chair, especially if you have to swerve to avoid something. In any form of racing, the belts are crucial for feeling what the car is doing through the divining rod that is your backside. If your butt is rolling around like Beyoncé's husband in an elevator, you've got no chance.

---

Are You Sitting Comfortably?

**Hot Tips**

> **The head rest isn't actually a rest – and if you remove it, or it's not lined up with your melon, you're more likely to break your neck if you have a shunt.**
> **Wear comfortable clothing that doesn't restrict your movements, especially your arms.**
> **Keep sunglasses at the ready to handle low-lying sun and glare off a wet road. Avoid at all costs polarized sunglasses. I don't know who invented them or why, but they ruin your ability to judge perspective and are totally unsuitable for driving.**

---

## Mirror, Signal, Manoeuvre … and Reversing

I'm very particular about my mirrors because these are my third eye. I tweak the offside mirror down a fraction towards the kerb for parking, and aim the nearside mirror for a longer view down the side of the car for monitoring traffic. I'm not alone in this.

Jean-Claude Van Damme, legendary martial artist, also respects the angle of dangle. To my knowledge he is the only man to have performed the splits on the wing mirrors of a pair of reversing Volvo trucks without dismembering his undercarriage.

I unleashed my inner Van Damme a few years ago for a Volvo S60 commercial on a similarly wind-streaked airfield. Scott, the director, was an old pal from *Top Gear*, now living the Hollywood dream and looking the part with his Yankees baseball cap and aviator sunglasses. He casually understated the order of events as the 'usual driving stuff'.

I was handed the keys to a prototype vehicle worth $3 million and invited to reverse it at high speed through a slalom of solid metal posts and up a set of ramps onto a moving car transporter with six inches to spare between the tyres and the inner edges of the ramps. The transporter had no sides. If I overcooked it, $3 million was going overboard. Scott wanted to start filming in ten minutes.

Unleashing my inner Van Damme, California 2010

**'If I over-cooked it, $3 million was going overboard.'**

I confessed early that this wasn't something I had done before, and it might be a good idea to do some practice using rubber cones.

I lined up the cones, looked over my shoulder through the rear screen and went for it at 40 mph. The first weave went OK, then the cones disappeared out of sight as soon as the car turned the other way. With the car effectively rear-wheel steering, going from left to right was totally unstable, and before long there was a cone massacre.

The only way to accurately reverse that worked for me was using the door mirrors. I adjusted them a little lower down so that I could see more ground than air, and practised using smaller, more precise steering movements to avoid getting caught out by the tendency for the car to over-rotate. It was seamless.

With the slalom under control we turned our attention to the car transporter. The good news was that my initial approach would be driving forwards. Then they wanted a 180-degree handbrake turn to spin the car backwards, select reverse and drive up the ramps. Easier said than done since Volvo, like many carmakers, did away with handbrakes in favour of a parking button that only worked when stationary.

When nobody was looking, we unplugged the ABS braking chip that would otherwise override what was to come and dialled in the move. The truck was rolling at 40, so I drove towards it at 65 mph to allow for the speed that would scrub off during my pirouette. Then came the hard part.

With the transporter ramps dead ahead, I jinked to the right, then left and thumped the brake pedal whilst accelerating hard. As this was a front-wheel-drive car, the acceleration countered the braking effect on the front wheels, allowing the brakes to act solely on the rears like a handbrake would. The rears locked, and around she went.

I kept my hand in one position throughout the turn so that I could whip the wheel straight as soon as I finished spinning. Then I engaged reverse, checked my position in the broader view of the head mirror and floored it. The nearside mirror was naturally my favourite for the close-quarter reverse, and I used it to line up my rear tyre with a support strut I noticed beneath the on-ramp. I knew that if I hit that mark, I had metal rather than air underneath my other tyres. And as I'd picked out that mark in advance of reversing, it turned a complicated job into a walk in the park.

As soon as the car shot up the ramp, the door mirrors lost their perspective so I switched back to the head mirror to maintain a straight course, alternating with the odd glance to the sides once I levelled out, then back to the head mirror until I closed up to the back of the towing rig.

And *relax*.

'When nobody was
looking, we unplugged
the ABS braking chip.'

# The Beast

You're about to connect your consciousness with a miracle of engineering that will transport you, as far I'm concerned, to the centre of the universe.

The stretching of rubber, connecting of shafts and flanges and all the torque of thrusting is enough to get pulses racing, but let's look at the functions of the equipment before we push analogies too far.

Turn the key and fire the engine: *suck, squeeze, bang, blow*. The pistons deep inside the engine bay circulate like the legs of a cyclist pumping the pedals. As the piston falls within its chamber it *sucks* in a mixture of air and fuel, then *squeezes* it so hard that the fiery cocktail is compressed to a tenth of its original volume. The heat of this molecular crush alone is enough to ignite diesel. With petrol, a spark is introduced, creating an explosion that *bangs* the piston into its next cycle, and exhaust gases are *blown* out along the way.

When the engine is free of the drivetrain, it idles at around 22 piston revolutions every second or 1,300 revs per minute without breaking a sweat. Pressing the 'accelerator' introduces more fuel and power to the system, so the pistons revolve faster. They report their rate of progress with a rising note and rumble, and via the needle within the oft-ignored tachometer next to the speedo.

Somewhere between idle and the point where the needle ventures into the red on the tacho, the engine develops its peak turning force or 'torque'. You wish that sweet spot would last for ever as all that rotational power begs to be harnessed in some way. The clutch has the means to do it by slaving the engine to the gearbox, which in turn connects to the wheels that sit on the road.

The engine spins constantly, whereas the gearbox and the car's wheels do not. The clutch manages the speed differential between the engine and gearbox by holding the gear in one hand and harnessing the engine's spinning flywheel with a high-friction pressure plate in the other.

Think of the flywheel as a spinning merry-go-round and your feet as the

'A spark is introduced, creating an explosion.'

> 'Imagine the gears as being athletes running a relay race with different physiques and specialist skills.'

clutch plate when you climb aboard. When your feet land on the ride, your speeds suddenly match, and round you go.

As you release the clutch pedal with a gear engaged, the clutch plate rubs on the flywheel and begins turning until their speeds match. As the clutch plate turns it delivers drive to the gear and through to the wheels. Forward motion commences. When the clutch is fully released the car's road speed matches the engine speed for that gear.

The gearbox contains a gear for different ranges of road speed from zero all the way up to the car's maximum, enabling the engine to unleash its finest torque again and again as we accelerate from one gear to the next.

Imagine the gears as being athletes running a relay race with different physiques and specialist skills. First gear has short, powerful legs like a weightlifter, delivering maximum force to the wheels to get a ton of metal moving from a standing start. But as the car begins to speed up, our short, fat, hairy man in lycra reaches his top speed and runs out of steam. We need to pass the baton to a new gear with longer legs for faster running, and so on, until we reach top gear with the likes of Usain Bolt.

Handing the baton back to a slower runner when the vehicle is still sprinting at high speed forces short legs to spin much faster than they were designed to. The engine screams, and the tacho sees red.

When the gear exceeds its speed range in this way and is slaved to the engine by a cruel master releasing the clutch, it creates an engine speed so fast that the pistons try to relieve themselves by exploding out of their housing. So you use the gears that marry engine revolutions with road speed to avoid a meltdown.

All the pounding metal and churning fluid within the engine and gearbox creates internal resistance by friction. The faster the engine is turning, the greater the resistance. When you hit the road there are other frictional forces acting on the beast as the tyres meet the road and the bodyshell encounters resistance from the air. These natural forces want to slow the car, so by lifting off the accelerator pedal and cutting power to the engine, you decelerate. So it's time to adopt this pedal's real name: the throttle. Because the throttle can be used to accelerate as well as decelerate by choking the engine.

Last, but by no means least, there is the brake pedal with its near-infinite range of pressure adjustment. This is the primary device for slowing the car.

A mere brush compresses the fluid underfoot, instantly winding its way through a series of pipes to squeeze four sets of clamps onto their respective discs, themselves attached to the rotating wheels. Friction on the discs drags speed from the car and transmits weight to the front tyres.

It sounds like a lot to take in at first, but the engineering quickly synchronizes with biology to make the process as thoughtless as breathing. Being clumsy with any element of the control process is no bad thing; the only mistake would be not to admit it.

For me it was the clutch. I was so insensitive to its powers that passengers were handed neck braces, but a winter racing series forced me to change. 100 mph corners became ice rinks where *every* passage of the clutch pedal would break traction unless it was accompanied by acute patience and feel. I developed my left foot accordingly and in years to come this would prove vital with *Top Gear.*

## Light Touch

Operating a vehicle for the first time is rather like being in an egg-and-spoon race while riding a unicycle. There are bumps and shudders aplenty, a few expletives and grazed knees. Multi-tasking with hands, feet and brain in concert with the way the car is responding is no picnic. Most drivers settle for a mediocre performance, and it stays that way for the rest of their lives.

I was forced to relearn the basics when I drove a Skoda with a helicopter balanced on the roof for *Top Gear*. Any sudden movements would have resulted in a beheading. When I accelerated it tilted up the rotors as the weight of the car moved rearwards, so if I'd tramped the gas pedal it would have fallen off the back. If I slowed too quickly or fumbled a down-change it would send weight forwards, the rotors would dip and threaten to transform the chopper into a lively hood ornament.

A rooftop helicopter is an expensive training device, but what you can do is plant an imaginary glass of water on the dashboard and drive in such a way that you don't spill a single drop. If you can avoid getting wet, you will benefit in three ways:

- You are highly unlikely to be involved in a crash.
- You will save up to 25 per cent on your fuel bill.
- You will be a better driver, on the road *and* the race track.

'I was forced to relearn the basics when I drove a Skoda with a helicopter balanced on the roof.'

> 'When the weight of the car moves and bears down on a given tyre, that tyre generates grip.'

## Balance

The entire business of operating a car revolves around the transfer of weight. You're basically sitting in the middle of a see-saw, with the engine at one end and the passengers and whatever's in the boot at the other.

The see-saw starts out level.

It only moves when you do something, like standing on the brakes, at which point it tips forward and loads its weight onto the front tyres, giving them grip for stopping or turning into a corner. The plank goes level mid-corner and then tips back to load the rear wheels when you press the accelerator. This front-and-back transfer of weight alters the 'vertical load' borne by the tyres.

The plank also leans from one side to the other in the corners, weighing down the outside wheels to create steering grip and cornering thrust. That's lateral load.

The important thing to get your head around is that when the weight of the car moves and bears down on a given tyre, that tyre generates grip. The rubber takes a fraction of a second to respond, which is why it pays to ask politely. If you suddenly dump the accelerator it spins the wheels, but if you moderate the initial touch and then go hard the tyre has time to accept it.

Likewise, when you turn the steering wheel, the weight leans across the vehicle. The rate at which it leans depends on how much *force* you put into the

*Philippe Petit, hands spread equally apart, walks a wire between New York's Twin Towers shortly after their construction in 1974. With every step, he makes tiny adjustments of pressure from his toes to his heels and from side to side to maintain his balance. He remains totally calm. His hands and body are relaxed, bringing enormous accuracy and sensitivity to each step. And he looks ahead, never down.*

# 2. Balance

Static

Braking

Accelerating

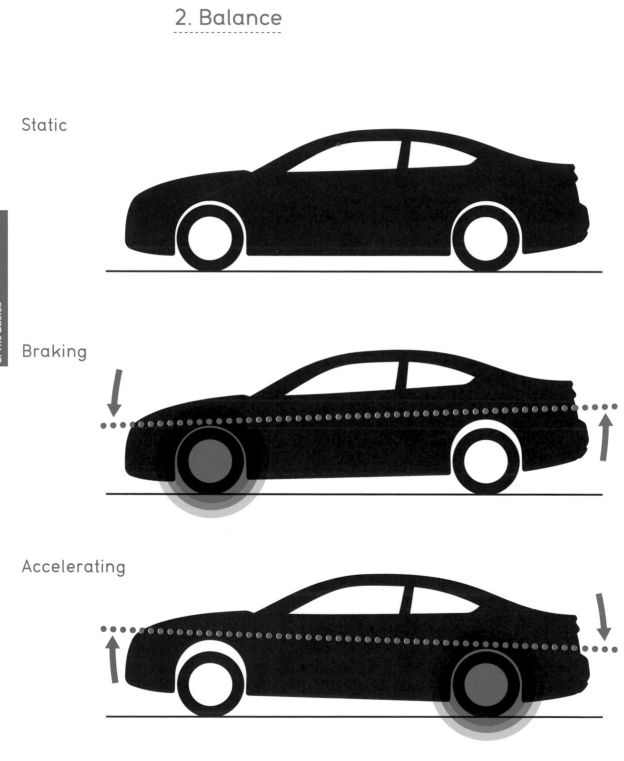

'Like you're lifting a cup of tea rather than smacking Mike Tyson on the kisser.'

steering – i.e.: how much grip *you* put into the front tyres in the first place, coupled with how quickly *you* turn. Yes – *you* create the grip. And once you know how, you can command the weight to be exactly where you want it, when you want it, for perfect cornering.

Balancing a car involves shifting its weight around the tyres at the right time. Each movement flows harmoniously into the next. When driving a car, go for maximum sensitivity. The more you feel at one with the machine, the better you will drive it. When you place your foot on the accelerator or the brakes, feel the pressure through the tips of your toes rather than via the force in your thigh. Control your strength so that you are conscious of the movement in your toes and the pad of your foot as it reaches your ankle. It allows for a far more delicate touch, with power in reserve if you need it.

Likewise, holding the steering wheel with the tips of your fingers provides more sensory feedback. If you clasp it like a vice, your inputs become heavy-handed and decrease the car's stability, reducing your ability to create grip and increasing the likelihood of a skid.

With your hands equidistant from each other, cradling the wheel in the quarter-to-three position, you create a perfect sense of balance. Balance in the palm of your hands makes the physical inputs measured and soft, like you're lifting a cup of tea rather than smacking Mike Tyson on the kisser. It matters because the corresponding weight transfers in the machine amplify your inputs.

The worst kind of weight transfer occurs when the driver creates a violent pendulum effect. This is usually the result of a sudden switch in direction that puts momentum into a weight transfer, causing the suspension to whip one way then another, like a charging elephant swishing its buttocks. The sudden overload can cause a loss of traction and rapid departure from the road.

Ben leading the field in the FIA World Endurance Championship in 2014, aboard the Ferrari 458 Italia GTE. So much weight has shifted across to the outer side of the car that the inner front tyre lifts off the ground.

Cornering Thrust

# Dynamic Handling

## Every car is unique, which is why we end up feeling so at home in the daily steed.

The traits we learn to love or hate are conveniently known as dynamic handling characteristics, which really means how the car throws its weight around. The biggest weight sitting in the car, unless you've spent your life in McDonald's, is the engine, so we tend to notice the effects of weight most during acceleration. All cars fall loosely within the following categories.

### Front-wheel-drive – Front-engine

The garden variety favoured by manufacturers because it's cheaper to build. Front-wheel-drive means that the engine is only delivering rotational power to the front axle; the back tyres are merely freewheeling behind. With the engine weight over the front wheels, the driver senses more inertia through the steering when cornering. The front-loading over the driven wheels is an advantage in snow and ice – an advantage shared by rear-engine/rear-wheel-drive models such as the Porsche 911.

The disadvantage is that the front tyres have two jobs to do in both accelerating and steering the car, which ultimately compromises their adhesion. The resulting loss in steering ability is obvious to the driver (as the hands no longer agree with the vehicle's direction), and equally simple to remedy by reducing speed. The result is that they are perceptibly 'easier' to drive than their rear-wheel-drive cousins.

### Four-wheel-drive (aka All-wheel-drive)

These are nearly always front-engine, with the exception of the Bugatti Veyron. Weight is slightly more evenly split front to rear, but 4x4s generally handle like a front-wheel-drive/front-engine in terms of their steering model. These vehicles are usually heavier and with power output distributed across four tyres rather than two; they benefit from superior traction in slippery conditions, but use more fuel.

### Rear-wheel-drive – Front-engine

The weight is balanced more evenly with the engine in the front and the driven elements spread towards the rear. These models tend to respond eagerly to steering inputs due to their engine weighing down the front tyres, but they can bite or feel nervous when the rear loses traction during acceleration. They suffer most in icy conditions.

### Rear-wheel-drive – Mid-engine

A sports car designed for optimum performance with the weight oriented around the centre and to the rear of where the driver sits, providing a heightened sense of the polar inertia as the car rotates into the corner. The best, but there's not much room for groceries.

# 3. Engine Types

Front-Engine
Front-Wheel-Drive

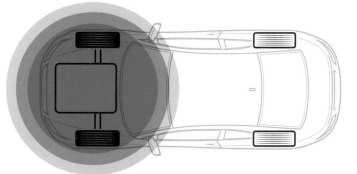

Front-Engine
Rear-Wheel-Drive

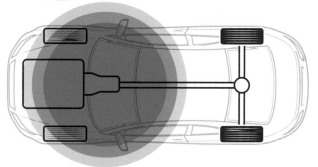

Front-Engine
4 x 4

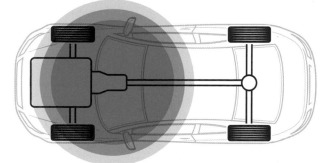

Rear-Engine
Rear-Wheel-Drive

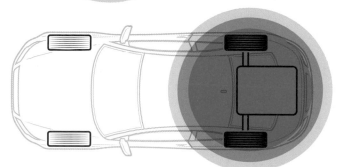

# Smooth Operator

Three-time world champion racing driver Sir Jackie Stewart is a supercool cat, whether sporting fireproof Nomex or his immaculately tailored blazer and tartan strides.

'The smoothest way, the quietest way, the slowest way around Monte Carlo is the fastest way.'

You know he's taken time to think ahead. As a result very little takes him by surprise, on the road or in life. When he coached me as a young driver in his race team (Stewart Racing) I quickly realized that he set the bar very high, and saw us novices coming a mile off.

Balancing a car throughout the transitions of a corner is all about being smooth. Here's what Sir Jackie had to say about it: 'The smoothest way, the quietest way, the slowest way around Monte Carlo is the fastest way.' He won three F1 world championships and countless races by driving 'as slowly as possible'.

The strange irony about going 'fast' on a racing circuit is that your technique is slow and measured. Of the hundred or so celebrities I coached around the *Top Gear* circuit, I never told anyone to steer faster, or to hurry their feet across the pedals. Good driving is smooth driving; everything is under control, and nothing catches you unawares.

Contrary to popular belief, the faster the car is going, the slower your inputs have to become in order to keep the weight of the machine stable. You nurture the precious patch of rubber sticking you to the black stuff. It's as true on the road as it is on the track. Fluid inputs through the steering wheel and pedals permeate through the machine and dictate its road-holding capability. Your perception of the road improves, and you become more accurate.

Jackie exhorted us to drive flat out around the racing track, watching as we lurched and growled our way to the finish line, always at the edge of what the car could take. Whenever he spotted anything remotely untidy with our performance he would begin his sermon thus: 'Don't upset the balance, laddie.'

To achieve this, you had to drive super smooth, which meant you couldn't afford any last-minute corrections for failing to plan ahead. You climbed gently onto the brakes and squeezed, eased the steering towards the corner and then gradually picked up the gas.

Jackie's way taught us discipline and came with several bonuses. It saved the tyres, it saved fuel, and, over the course of a race, that made us faster.

## Pulling Away

'Teach us to pull away, Ben? Have you mistaken the reader for a complete moron?'

I promise I haven't. But every mountain starts with a single grain of sand – and you didn't complain when Delia taught you how to boil an egg.

On a flat road you can pull away in first gear without even pressing the accelerator pedal, and it's a great way to train your left foot. With the engine just ticking over, you slowly release the clutch and feel the plates bite as the car begins to creep forward. By keeping your heel on the carpet and the ball of your left foot on the pedal, your calf muscle can create a powerful, slow and deliberate hinge. With this mastered you might, just might, convince a potential mate that you really are James Bond or Lara Croft in your spare time.

---

**Hot Tip**

> Gently tense your calf muscles and ease up the ball of your foot, or curl your big toe slowly upwards, until you reach the biting point. With only a light weight on the clutch pedal, forward motion will commence. And after you've released it completely, the car will travel at its natural pace for that gear.

> Slowing your clutch foot demonstrates the kind of self-control that is much appreciated in the bedroom. And adding a little extra gas thereafter just makes the whole thing sing.

---

**Common Mistakes**

> Lifting your whole leg – it makes the whole process lumpier than a plastic surgeon's waiting room. Keep your heel on the deck.

> Rushing the clutch up and past the biting point then stalling – slow and steady wins the race.

> Snapping the foot off the last few millimetres of clutch and lurching forward or stalling – Bond does not favour this method.

---

If you're in more of a hurry or on a hill then you add some revs to bolster the process, but don't overdo it or you'll be treated to the acrid waft of burning clutch plate.

Ah, but there's more. Your driving instructor taught you to apply the handbrake and release it whenever you pull away. That doesn't cut it for me because a) it's a pain for anything less than a super steep hill-start, and b) I like to have all four tyres in my vice rather than the one or two rear tyres that the handbrake latches onto. So I use 'heel-and-toe'.

Whoah – an advanced racing technique this early on?

We will explore heel-and-toe as a braking technique later. Suffice to say here that your right foot can cover both the brake and throttle pedals at the same time in most road cars. You use the ball of your foot to hold the car still on the foot brake and swivel your ankle to put some pressure on the throttle and raise the revs if you need to. It's quicker and easier for pulling away.

## 4. Heel and Toe

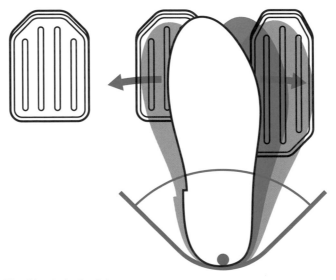

Fixed heel pivot point

## Smooth Acceleration

Once mobile, the idea is to be as smooth with the throttle as possible. The Holy Grail is for your foot to progressively build up to the maximum pressure required for the piece of road you're travelling along before decelerating for the next event. Throttle, once applied, should not need to be released in the middle of the corner, otherwise it implies that you accelerated too soon and have to correct the mistake. You can apply that rule to every aspect of driving because you should always be able to set your speed appropriately.

What that really means is that you don't poke and prod the pedal in a series of clunky encounters. A practical demonstration that you can re-create in the safety of your driveway is to attach a piece of string from your big toe to the six o'clock position on the steering wheel. When the wheel is straight the string is tight at full throttle, but as you turn the wheel in either direction it pulls your foot off the gas and vice versa. It teaches you only to accelerate as the corner opens out and to unwind the steering on departure.

Another feature of acceleration is its relation to speed. The slower you are driving, the faster the car will accelerate and therefore the slower you apply the loud pedal. The faster you're going, the slower it will accelerate and therefore the faster you can apply power.

At low speed this relationship is relevant for maintaining traction and smoothness. At higher speeds your lack of acceleration limits your ability to overtake. As we shall see this fact affects more than just speeding up, it also influences braking.

'Don't poke and prod the pedal in a series of clunky encounters.'

# Changing Gear

## The perfect gear change should neither be felt nor heard.

Look, I'm sure that you can physically change gear. What I'm proposing is the ninja method, smoother than a cashmere codpiece.

The perfect gear change is no less satisfying than a perfectly boiled egg, and just as regularly scrambled. Running roughshod through the gears sends shockwaves through the transmission to the wheels, where it creates unregulated weight transfers and can even cause the tyres to skid.

For pure locomotion – or if you're about to get T-boned – you can change gear any way you like. But I'm hoping to teach you to turn off your lunacy switch and lay down some smooth moves.

### Gear Selection

Every engine has a sweet spot, where its pulling power, or torque, is maximized. In the dead zone at 1,500 rpm it has little to offer, but at peak revs the engine runs out of breath, so your aim is to keep the revs somewhere in between so that the engine can pull you out of the corner. Ignore the textbooks and don't drive around staring at the rev counter. If you listen carefully to the engine and feel the power underfoot you can develop a keen sense of your speed.

Always try to select the appropriate gear for the corner before you get to it. Mid-corner shifts are far more likely to get fumbled.

### How to Hold the Gearstick

Modern engines and transmissions may be pretty macho, but the shrieking protest of cogs and pistons when you accidently graunch into the wrong gear makes for terrible foreplay.

'Palming' – applying pressure to one side of the gearstick or the other – minimizes the risk of wrong gearing. Hold the knob as you would a handshake – that's the thumbs-up position – to cross the gate from second to third and fourth to fifth.

'What I'm proposing is the ninja method, smoother than a cashmere codpiece.'

Invert the hand, so your thumb faces down, to stay left when changing first to second, or to cross back down from third to second and fifth to fourth. In other words: thumbs-up to pull the gear towards you, thumbs-down to push away.

The gearstick sits in a spring-loaded housing. It will naturally find the centre of neutral, the third/fourth axis, so you only need to apply sideways pressure to find lower (to the left) or higher (to the right) gears.

Whenever you get lost, take a breath and pop the thing into neutral, without any side pressure, so that you know where you are. Then take it from there.

Using the spring is also the easiest way to change from second to third. Just push forward into neutral – the stick will flip across to the centre of its own accord – then slip it forward.

Having proven your dexterity beyond question, you are ready for the secret ingredient to a cool gear change: the accelerator.

## Changing Up (i.e. Going Faster)

The hardest change is from first to second while accelerating. You have the most power under your right foot and the engine responds aggressively. It gets easier as you go up the gears, but the same technique applies.

You actually have to guide the gearstick through three phases: pulling out of first, crossing neutral and then taking second.

When you're about to shift gear, release some pressure on the gas pedal first, to reduce the rate of acceleration. Then, as you come off the accelerator you start to depress the clutch, but for those seeking heaven on a gearstick: *leave a tiny touch of accelerator on* – just enough to keep the revs hovering above idle and cushion the flow.

Float the gearstick from first through neutral and, as you move towards second, don't rush it: allow half a second to pass as the next gear engages then gradually release the clutch pedal. It makes all the difference because this fraction of time allows the new gear to start jogging and synchronize with the engine speed, take the baton from the previous gear and run away with it. Once the clutch is fully released you can accelerate away as swiftly as you like, without any bumps.

| Hot Tip | > Cheat. If you're having trouble you can 'short-shift' by changing to second gear early at lower rpm to avoid kissing the dashboard. |
|---|---|

**Common mistakes**

> Holding your knob too tight when cornering. Too much sideways pressure and you'll stick it into the wrong hole. (No sniggering at the back.)

> Impatience with the gear shift. You'll get snagged on the gate. Chill out; less haste means more speed.

> Accelerating between shifts. The engine shrieks, the clutch sizzles; pedestrians crane their necks and stare. Only use a hint of accelerator.

> Most people release the gas altogether when they depress the clutch pedal. The revs drop, then when the clutch is released and you accelerate again, the car jolts forward, or there's a thud as the engine speed suddenly catches up with the road speed, Mr Bean style, in the new gear.

> Rushing the transition. If you whip your foot off the gas prior to the gear change the resulting kangaroo hop will have your passengers head-butting the dashboard. After taking a gear, if you then dump the clutch by suddenly taking your foot off the clutch pedal, everyone gets a second bounce off the dash as the engine abruptly reconnects with the gear. You finally pound your audience into their seatbacks by reapplying the loud pedal. It's like Tarzan's first driving lesson. Slow it down; release the accelerator pressure gently at first, but not all the way, ease the clutch, then gently reapply the power.

'Avoid kissing the dashboard.'

A little patience as you cross the gate goes a long way towards achieving a smooth ride and will save a lot of explaining to your local mechanic as to why the gearbox contains so much shrapnel. Once you're slick with the basics, your changes will speed up by themselves.

## Slowing Down, Braking, Changing Down the Gears
### Engine Braking

On a good road trip when you're cruising around traffic you should hardly need the foot brake at all. When you lift off the throttle in gear it cuts propulsion to the engine, but the internals, the pistons and other gubbins continue spinning, and the friction of these moving parts causes drag known as engine braking. It's a superb tool for controlled deceleration.

Engine braking by itself will not stop the car anything like pressing the brake pedal, but by looking ahead and reading the traffic flow you can just roll off the gas and let engine braking do the work. When you do have to brake, the idea is to operate the pedal once with a consistent pressure, rather than a sequence of kangaroo jumps.

Where engine braking really comes into play is for slowing on hills, in slippery conditions and for stopping in an emergency.

For the boy racers out there – none of the above includes dropping a cog at every opportunity to kick bass from the exhaust. But your garage will welcome you like a lost son when the gearbox collapses at the traffic lights.

### Rev Matching

If you're driving up a hill, for example, you might need to change down from fourth to third gear in order to boost your pulling power. With a speed of 65 mph in fourth the engine might be running at 2,500 rpm, but the corresponding rpm in third at that speed might be 4,000. You already have your right foot on the gas pedal, so all you need to do is leave it there as you depress the clutch. The revs will naturally rise from, say, 2,500 to 4,000 rpm. Slide the gear into third, release the clutch and then continue accelerating. There shouldn't be a jerk, because you've matched the revs.

Conversely if you're driving towards a corner or a downhill section where you don't need to brake, you can control your speed by selecting a lower gear. Depress the clutch, raise the revs with the throttle, engage the gear then gently release the clutch and you will feel the drag of the engine holding back your speed.

## Common Fallacies about Gear Changing

The method prescribed by the British police is 'Gears to go, brakes to slow.' This system forbids the 'overlapping' of braking and down-changing phases; they don't want you doing both at the same time.

In the old days before the invention of synchromesh gearboxes, finding a gear was like stirring tar. To get the cogs to disengage you had to pump the clutch pedal, then blip the throttle to match the engine speed and finally operate the

'You'll be
equally
ready to
drive a Fiat
or a Ferrari.'

clutch again as you selected the gear. Your feet couldn't be everywhere at once, so this necessitated a separation between braking and down-shifting. In short, there might have been a good reason for splitting the phases in the 1930s, digging out the next gear with a stick that resembled a crowbar.

But not now.

The separation of braking and down-changing doubles the distance required to slow down, or, as the police manual neatly explains: 'The problem is that if you brake some distance before the turn to avoid an overlap, you can confuse other drivers … (who) may be tempted to overtake.'

Engine braking gives you more stability in a corner and proves critical in restraining the inertia of the gearbox and engine when you descend a steep hill.

## Skipping Gears

Going up through the box I often skip gears to save fuel. Block changing is when you drop down from say fourth to second in a single leap. If you know ahead of time that second is the gear you ultimately want, then it can be convenient to skip third by leaving your down-change later than if you went through each gear. There's no hard and fast rule on this, but I personally prefer to be in the right gear at all times during braking, with control over the engine and the ability to react to any situation. In traffic a squirt of acceleration can often prevent an accident just as much as a hard brake.

## Down-shifting

Changing down the gears keeps the engine jogging along as you slow down, and the internal resistance complements the braking effort. Going through all the gears means that you always have the power and stability to manoeuvre if you need to.

As you slow down with your right foot on the brakes, it falls on your left foot to work the clutch in order to make smooth transitions from the longer gears to the short-legged ones as you switch from fourth down to third and so on. Smooth clutch work allows the engine revolutions to gradually adjust to the road speed in each new gear.

Most people never operate the clutch pedal at the same time as the brake. They automatically take their foot off the brake whenever they release the clutch pedal. My explaining this might seem about as helpful as getting you to consider which way you swing your arms when you walk … and watching you fall over.

The trick is to start thinking of your right and left feet independently of each other, so that you can modulate brake pressure with one whilst easing the clutch in and out with the other. Then you'll be equally ready to drive a Fiat or a Ferrari …

---

**Common Mistakes**
> Modern gearboxes have a 'synchromesh', a synchronizer that helps the internal gear cogs get up to speed with each other. This only takes a fraction of a second, but if you try to slam the gear lever home it will resist.
> Dumping the clutch by releasing the pedal too quickly. The engine suddenly engages, sending a jarring force to the driven wheels.

---

Braking and changing down simultaneously utilizes engine braking, so your brake pads will last longer. More importantly it keeps the weight consistently on the front tyres during the deceleration phase. That's not only smoother, it also creates additional grip in the front tyres just when you want it for turning into the corner.

Now that you can place the weight of your beast precisely where you want it, it's time to turn and burn.

## Braking and Entering

Dunsfold Aerodrome, 8 a.m. A crisp morning, good for engines, especially ones with giant turbo chargers force-feeding them air like crack to a junkie. I grew up with the poster of the Ferrari F40 on my wall, right next to the brazen image of Cindy Crawford (and, to my twelve-year-old self, just as attractive).

I was jogging on the spot, not so much to keep warm but to give my legs something to do while I waited for Jeremy Clarkson to finish salivating. He called it 'the best car ever' and from where I was hopping he might just have been right.

On closer inspection the car looked like something you might have made from a Corn Flakes packet. It was boxy, with gaps between the blood-red body panels, and protruding through some Perspex was an engine that must have fallen off the back of a truck on its way to the F16 factory. It made a hissing sound just like a jet as it forced air out of the way at 201 mph.

'It flew past again like a stray tracer bullet scorching across the greenbelt.'

Dunsfold was no stranger to that sound. Safely tucked away deep within the wilderness south of Guildford in Surrey, Dunsfold's creaking hangars with their distant echoes of rushing airmen had been host to top secret aviation projects for fifty years. From the dawn of the Spitfire to the revolutionary Harrier Jump Jet, the broad, expansive runways had seen them all.

In track mode we joined Dunsfold's two parallel straights together to form the familiar figure 8 now immortalized as the *Top Gear* circuit. But for pushing maximum velocity we ran it the way that nature and fast jet pilots intended, using the full length of the landing strip.

It flew past again like a stray tracer bullet scorching across the greenbelt. Even after a *Top Gear* diet of double espresso and bacon sarnie, our twitchiest cameraman put his neck out whipping his lens across in hot pursuit.

When it was finally my turn I fell into the bucket seat, my feet thudded into the carpetless floor and *kunk* went the door. To keep the weight down to an anorexic 1,100 kgs, there were no creature comforts onboard. Just a chair, some well-appointed pedals and a gear lever shaped like a Victorian door handle. The steering wheel felt like it was cast from solid iron and was angled forward, challenging the driver to an arm wrestle. The Ferrari F40 was a brute all right.

I limbered up with a few passes through the Hammerhead loop to see how the '80s girl handled. In a word, evil.

The heavy steering lightened up, marginally, once I got going, but it bucked, pulled and bit over every bump and burp in the track's surface. I held on firmly with both hands.

The tight chicane approached. When I pressed the brake pedal I realized that someone had replaced it with an anvil and pushed harder for more response. It eventually came. The nose of the see-saw dipped, and I felt the rear lighten. Then came the moment I feared: the down-change.

I dipped the clutch, grasped the black ball atop the long metal gear lever and ushered it across the tight metal gate towards third. The satisfying brush of metal took longer than expected to find home, by which time the revs had dropped considerably. I needed to keep braking to make the corner, but I also needed to tickle the throttle to raise the revs or face retribution from the motor when it re-engaged …

The obvious solution to a racing driver would be to 'heel-and-toe'. The term was coined during the days when indicating meant sticking your arm out of the window, and the brake pedal was located to the *right* of the throttle!

In modern race cars and supercars such as the F40, the pedals are aligned closely so that your right foot can easily cover both the brake and the throttle pedals. This allows the driver to apply pressure to the brake pedal with the ball of the foot, while simultaneously 'blipping' the throttle by swivelling the side of the sole.

The blip is a short sharp snap of the gas pedal that sends the revs high enough to match the running speed of the shorter gear. Matching the revs cushions the bite of the down-change and prevents a sudden load of engine braking from snagging the driven axle. In the case of the rear-wheel-drive Ferrari, its engine braking was strong enough to stop the wheels from turning and skid across the road. I was certainly keen to avoid spinning backwards; it would have presented Clarkson with an enduring, unbearable punchline.

Well, my right foot went deep into the brake and past the point where it was able to reach the throttle. Perhaps the owner had set the pedals to suit a lighter braking style, but it came as no surprise. With the majority of cars I lapped on *Top Gear*, I found it impossible to heel-and-toe.

Unless the pedals are perfectly aligned *for you*, the technique does more harm than good when you're braking close to the limit because the slightest imbalance in your foot affects the pressure asserted on the pedal. My solution was simply smooth clutch work. I remembered my ice training and treated the left pedal like a second brake.

I delicately released the clutch, and the thunderous engine of the F40 sprang slowly back to life, pulling gradually on the hard rear suspension, helping me to slow for the corner. I boldly shoved her into second and repeated the process. With the weight over the fronts and the nose tucked in, I bled off the foot brake and turned the chunky wheel towards the sharp left.

The hard steering communicated everything the tyres encountered; she was growing on me, and I switched directions for the longer, bumpier ride onto the next stretch of runway.

The suspension and springs that supported the car like a mattress were fairly compliant as I plodded through the corner in the lower rev range. In fact, at 2,500 rpm I could have mistaken it for a Fiat Punto. Then something shuddered

'I delicately released the clutch, and the thunderous engine of the F40 sprang slowly back to life.'

inside its belly as a pair of turbos spooled up behind me. The Ferrari's phenomenal torque tapped me on the shoulder and whispered, 'You should've brought more guys.'

The F40 only had 470 horsepower, so I had driven beefier models in terms of power output. But the turbo-charged 2.9-litre V8 engine in the F40 produced a colossal amount of torque at around 4,500 rpm. Torque is a wonderful feature for tractors that plough fields, with hundreds of gears to harness the gob of pulling power packed within an infinitesimally narrow rev range between, oh, 4,468 and 4,496 rpm.

The torque surging through the car lifted its nose and squashed the rear tyres into the ground, taking the tyre rubber to its limit. I noticed the steering was no longer taking me where I wanted to go. I knew what was coming next, just not how much.

With the wheel cranked to a perilous degree, the savage turbos suddenly erupted. The car snapped sideways as the power overwhelmed the rear tyres. I squeaked involuntarily, the way you do when you bench-press one too many and nearly swallow the bar. I span the wheel as many times as it would go like a submariner closing the hatch to prevent the flood as the F40 embarked on the gnarliest powerslide this side of a Prince concert.

Even Iain May, the toughest cameraman ever to wear North Face, took his eye off his camera monocle to cock an eyebrow and check my trajectory as I streaked past in a blaze of glory. About half a mile later I had the rig back under control and sort of fell in love.

With the F40 the rev needle never left your attention because it was the best way to time the rush of power and live to die another day. It was undoubtedly the best supercar to come out of the '80s, but you really had to grab it by the scruff of the neck and hold on for dear life.

Ferrari built another box-shaped car in 2002, but this was no Airfix model. The elongated wheel arches, thinly veiled F1-style front wing and hench rear end with its kick-up spoiler generated nearly a ton of aerodynamic downforce at the tender speed of 186 mph. Another flick of the sequential gear paddle behind the steering wheel teleported you to a top speed of 218.

They only produced 349 of them, agreeing to build 399 after a lot of begging before finally adding one more … for the Pope.

## 'Handling:
## *Biblical.*'

Designation: F60 – aka Ferrari Enzo.

Engine unit: 6 litre V12.

Power: 650 horsepower, *no turbos required*.

Handling: *Biblical.*

This was the only car Ferrari deemed worthy of adopting the name of its founder, Enzo Ferrari. Like the F40, it bore a spartan interior but nonetheless weighed 200 kgs more than its grandfather.

The steering wheel bonded to my hand like the hilt of Excalibur, feeling both light and deadly accurate thanks to the carbon fibre construction and leather grips at the quarter-to-three positions of the wheel face.

In terms of performance quality it reminded me of the mighty Porsche Carrera GT minus the demonic frenzied howl of its V10 engine. The Ferrari V12 had the mature boom of a cello at low revs, turning more alley cat locked inside a steel drum when you gave it some hammer time. Unlike the F40, the Enzo's flexibility of power throughout the rev range offered phenomenal control for every millimetre of throttle.

Big brakes annihilated my speed efficiently enough to dislodge unwanted nasal hair. I eyeballed the corner across a panorama of red bodywork and Excalibur took me there effortlessly. In the middle of the corner the Enzo developed a reassuring moment of front-tyre scrub, resisting the true direction I was aiming for, but that soon balanced as I opened the tap on the V12.

The crisp steering connected me to a magical four-wheel drift, with one minor design fault reminding me that I hadn't died and gone to heaven: the honking of the rather inappropriately wheel-mounted horn …

Changing Gear

# Steering

'If boys saw at the wheel or jab at the brakes, you just know they'll be hopeless in the sack.'

*Vicky Butler-Henderson*

'Steering technique is the subject of furious debate in the driving community.'

The aim with steering is to be able to place the car precisely where you want it, whenever you want to, and without any hassle.

Believe it or not, steering technique is the subject of furious debate in the driving community. As I get underway with this section, police driving instructors and test examiners are sharpening their pencils, dipping them in poison and preparing to fire them into my eyeballs. 'This is heresy, burn him!' they cry. Read on at your peril.

Your choice of style ultimately boils down to what makes you feel most comfortable. Here are the different options:

## The Shuffle

The technique we learn by rote to pass the test – passing the wheel from one hand to the other at points in its upper hemisphere to turn the car in the desired direction. The hands generally operate in the ten o'clock to two o'clock positions. For many, it's the simplest way to get from A to B, and a method that lasts a lifetime.

For very tight manoeuvres in city centres and supermarket car parks, shuffle steering is a simple and effective means of progress.

The shortfall is that you lose a sense of balance and the ability to gauge how much steering has been applied, which in turn can affect your reaction to an incident. And unless you're really slick, making a turn tends to be a jerky series of direction changes rather than a smooth curve.

I find it pretty daft for anything other than the most basic applications, but it didn't do Simon Cowell any harm. Simon shuffled his way to two record lap times at the helm of *Top Gear*'s Reasonably Priced Car. He was so comfortable

'Scandinavian rally drivers refer to it a touch unflatteringly as 'milking the cow'.

with it that breaking the habit would have done more harm than good. And Simon generally gets his own way.

However, when he tried his hand behind the wheel of a 450-horsepower Noble, we ended up heading backwards into a field at 120 mph – the result of too much steering with a precision instrument which required finesse, unlike the old Suzuki Liana.

## The Push and Pull

This is the time-honoured system of the police, the Institute of Advanced Motorists and many others – a more formulaic version of the Shuffle. Scandinavian rally drivers refer to it a touch unflatteringly as 'milking the cow'.

Going into a left-hander, the left hand rises up the wheel and pulls it down. As it does so, the right hand slides down the other side, until it comes level with its partner-in-crime. If more steering is required, the right hand pushes the wheel up, while the left hand slides up the wheel, ready to pull down again if required.

When Cottenham designed Police Roadcraft in the 1930s, you had to manhandle a wheel big enough for an America's Cup super-yacht, without the benefit of power steering – and the castor angles made them excruciatingly heavy to turn. Pulling and pushing was the only way to make a corner without breaking your wrists.

The system encourages anticipation of corners by readying the hand positions in advance, but in my view it's completely outdated, overly complicated and inefficient for skid control – because it forces steering activity to alternate between the lower and upper hemispheres of the wheel, making it harder for the human brain to register the subtle forces feeding back from the tyres.

Crucially, you also lose a sense of balance by pulling into a corner with one hand rather than two – and, as we'll see, how you enter a corner has the greatest effect on weight transfer and stability.

## Rotational Steering (Also Known as Crossed-hand)

If you asked any Formula 1 driver which method he uses to hold the steering wheel, he would stare at you for a very long time. It would never occur to him, or any other pro racing driver, to control a car in any way other than this: your hands grip the wheel in a fixed position, opposite one another, at a quarter to three on

# 5. Rotational Steering

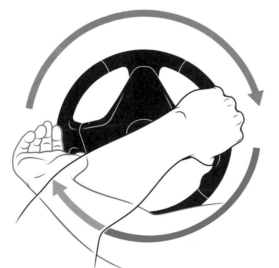

This range of steering is adequate for the majority of corners on the open road

Where further steering is required for especially tight corners, such as hairpins, the lower arm takes a new hold on top of the wheel

> 'Your hands grip the wheel in a fixed position, opposite one another, at a quarter to three.'

the wheel face, where they have best leverage. Your thumbs latch over the top of the wheel spokes for added grip – unless you're Jean Alesi, who used to hold the wheel further up, to match his aggressive driving style.

Rather than changing your grip position to pass the wheel from one hand to the other, you just turn the wheel and allow your arms to cross over. Your hands balance each other, keeping the wheel steady over bumps, potholes and other forces that might act on it.

With both hands on, you have far better control if the car slides or pitches. Most crucially, by keeping your place on the wheel at all times, your brain registers precisely how much steering has been applied. This provides a physical cue when the front tyres are starting to skid.

It also means that unwinding the wheel couldn't be easier – or smoother. As we shall see later, straightening the steering is essential if the rear tyres skid.

To negotiate especially tight corners and hairpin bends, you release the lower hand and carry on turning with the uppermost arm, repositioning the other hand as required. It balances the weight on the steering wheel equally to create a single graceful turn rather than a sequence of clunky shuffles.

A study by the Department for Transport examined how the two techniques performed in terms of matching the steering to a visual target. It concluded that 'drivers who used the crossed-hand technique significantly improved their time-on-target as compared with drivers who used push–pull' and that their performance improved more over time. The study theorized that rotational steering is probably a more natural way to drive, and advantageous when sudden steering corrections are required.

It is no coincidence that this is the technique used by racing drivers worldwide, from F1 to Le Mans, NASCAR and World Rallying. We use it because it works. And as much as I tease my friends in blue, many constabularies are starting to teach the 'new' method. As for the diehards out there, I eagerly await your emails.

When you hold the wheel, slightly spread your fingers so that you can feel the feedback from the road. By enhancing your sensitivity, you can learn to read beyond the vibration and tune into the slightest changes in grip via the weight of the steering.

Steering

**Hot Tips**

> Many people jiggle the steering around for no reason. Less is more.
> Avoid rough, jerky movements.
> Lighten up on the wheel and feel the road.
> Avoid the 'Wide Boy' technique: one hand on top of the wheel and the other hanging out of the window. I'd be lying if I said that I never drive one-handed, because there are times when it makes life easier, such as winding on full lock to navigate the confines of a car park. But for real driving, it takes two hands to tango.

After all that wheel-work you're probably thinking that the steering actually turns the car. As with any good story there's a twist because it doesn't, the tyres do. Meet the real heroes.

'We use it because

it works.'

2.6

# Braking

Understanding the marvels of physics taking place on a molecular level when you hit the road helps you to comprehend the part that you, the driver, play in the process.

If it wasn't for grip you would never leave the driveway, the wheels would spin hopelessly and you would just be sitting there inside an expensive smoke machine. Tyres are gripping all the time, even when you're driving straight. You only become aware that they are working on your behalf when you put a force through them by turning the wheel or pressing a pedal.

As we saw in the first section, the rudimentary tyres of yesteryear have evolved into their own form of suspension, working closely with the mechanical features of the car to balance and control the demands of the road.

These doughnut-shaped bags of air cling to the wheel hubs with bands of steel wire called beads. They can withstand enough pressure to carry the weight of the car owing to their immensely strong, but flexible, construction of textile cords bonded to a rubber matrix of vulcanized elastomers, themselves composed of entwined chains of molecules called polymers. The sulphur that Charles Goodyear added back in 1839 acts like a glue to anchor these molecules in place – and their structure supports the black carbon and sticky silica in the tread blocks that get on with the job of gripping and throwing water out of the way.

As the tyre meets the road surface it binds to it in two ways. The rough edges of the road material indent into the blocks of rubber and lock, while on a molecular level the surfaces on both sides are attracted to each other by adhesion. These bonds form, stretch and then break faster than a *Big Brother* romance, allowing the tyre to distort, develop grip and create an elastic force for cornering, braking and acceleration.

When you turn the steering wheel towards a corner, it rotates a metal column, connected to a pinion, which in turn swivels the wheel hubs on which the front tyres are mounted.

'If it wasn't for grip you would never leave the driveway.'

When the hubs turn, the tyres resist, causing them to stretch, and this creates the elastic force that pings you around a corner. The human eye never sees this, but the patch of tyre, no more than the size of your hand, stretches away from the hub considerably when in contact with the road.

The degree to which this happens is called the 'slip angle' – perhaps confusingly, because the tyre isn't slipping, it's gripping. The 'angle' is the degree to which the rubber distorts away from its hub without giving up and springing back to Mama – or skidding, as it's sometimes called.

The pull or self-aligning torque of all that stretching rubber creates cornering thrust, the lateral force dragging the car in the direction you steer. The more elastic strength the tyre can generate, the more grip you achieve. You can simulate this in the comfort of your own kitchen if you press the end of a rubber eraser onto a table and twist it. The harder you press down, the more you can twist the rubber – up to the point where it just breaks free of the surface regardless of how hard you push.

But more of that later.

When the tyres lose traction, for example through a change in the road surface, they will stretch less, creating less torsion, and we feel the steering 'go light'. That's why smoothness is particularly important on a wet road, because the car is generating lighter forces than usual.

Now we know how the tyres work in conjunction with the basic elements of weight transfer. It's time to step it up a gear and explore the most challenging and rewarding skill that a driver can perfect: braking.

## Braking

There are two kinds of braking: everyday and on the limit. If readers of this book unleash extraordinary new powers of the latter on the road, it is fair to say that insurance claims will skyrocket and my head will end up on a spike outside the Tower of London.

My view on this is that everybody, even the little old lady in the Honda, will brake on the limit at some point, and everyone would benefit from understanding what it feels like and what it means. For now, let's just make sure we can pull up at the drive-in without spilling our milkshake.

'The harder you press down, the more you can twist the rubber – up to the point where it just breaks free.'

## Everyday – Smooth Braking

The goal for everyday driving is to be as smooth and progressive with the pedal as possible, and to moderate your speed in a single graceful exercise. To do this you deploy a widely accepted technique of *feeling* your way into the brake pedal, *firming* up the pressure to remove the bulk of your speed and finally *feathering* off the pressure for a smooth transition.

I still set my standard to that of the chauffeur who once zapped me across the Italian Alps to work on 007's *The Quantum of Solace*. He was so smooth that whenever we pulled to a stop and the springs began to rebound, raising the nose of his Mercedes, he bled the pressure off the brakes in the final few feet to perfectly counter-balance the effect. You could have performed open-heart surgery in the back seat.

I am considerably more accustomed to the bump and grind you get in the back of a minicab, where the guy bangs on and off the brake pedal like it's a tambourine. Observe your passengers. If their torsos are jiving back and forth like the crowd at an Eminem concert then you are guilty of this most heinous crime.

By looking ahead and planning your braking phase, you should be able to squeeze the pedal gently without needing to come on and off it.

'Let's just make sure
we can pull up at
the drive-in without
spilling our milkshake.'

# 6. Tyre Grip Area

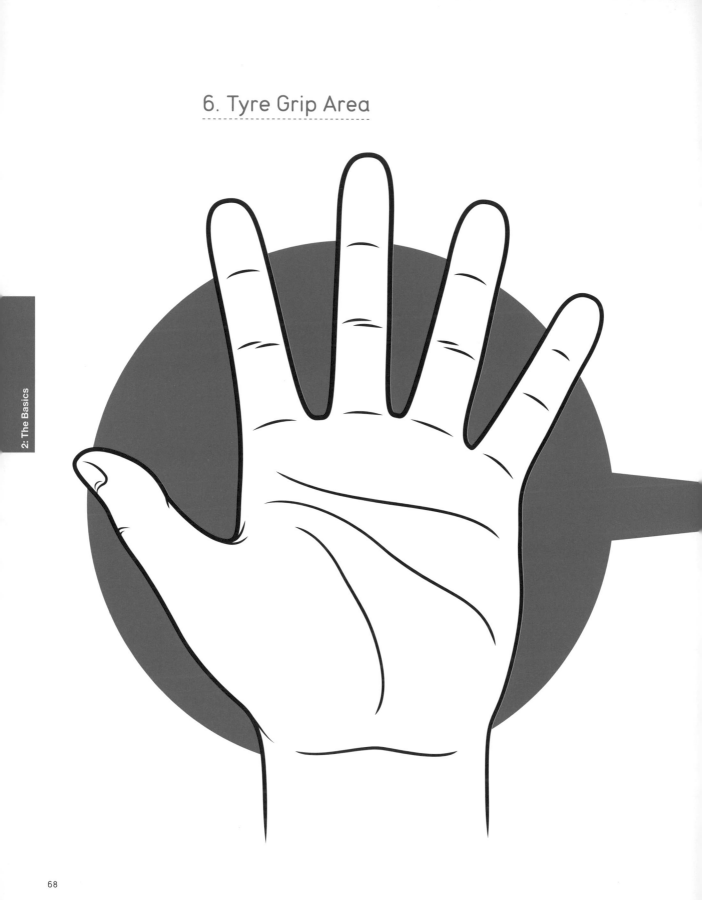

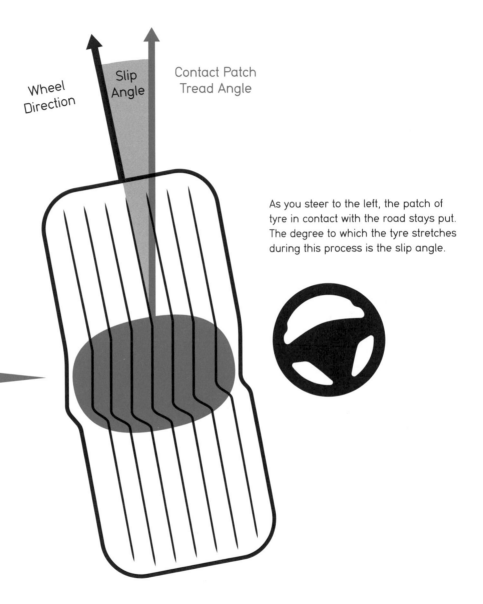

Wheel
Direction

Slip
Angle

Contact Patch
Tread Angle

As you steer to the left, the patch of tyre in contact with the road stays put. The degree to which the tyre stretches during this process is the slip angle.

# How Smooth Driving
# Can Save the Planet ... and
# Save You Money

'It is amazing how many drivers, even at the Formula 1 level, think that the brakes are for slowing the car down.'

*Mario Andretti, F1 world champion, 1978*

The media's conviction that *The Day After Tomorrow* spells global catastrophe means that eco driving is here to stay. I'll risk the curl of the Clarkson lip now and go into tree-hugging mode, because going vegan with your motor can also help you reduce your fuel bill by 20 per cent.

Diesel is currently more fuel-efficient than petrol (though not necessarily cheaper to run, and hybrids will set the tone in the future), and cars with automatic gearboxes use around 10 per cent more fuel than manuals – but the most important part of the fuel-saving equation is you. The harder you press the pedal on the right (*powerrrr*), the more gas you're using. If you're driving over the speed limit, you save time, but you're definitely burning gas and money. Driving at 70 mph uses up to 9 per cent more fuel than at 60 mph, and up to 15 per cent more than at 50 mph.

However, before you start driving around like a sloth and making yourself about as popular as herpes on the open road, here are some tips on how smooth driving can help your wallet as well as your cool quotient.

1.  Accelerate gently and read the road ahead to avoid unnecessary braking, because the brakes are the enemy. Every time you touch them, you're paying fuel tax. Try leaving a gap to the car in front so that you don't need to brake when it does and roll off the gas early for red lights, queuing traffic, pedestrian crossings, etc. The more you preserve momentum, the less fuel you require to accelerate again.

2.  Stay alert so that when you have to slow down or stop, you can decelerate smoothly by climbing off the gas pedal ahead of time and drift to a stop.

3.  Change up gears earlier to avoid revving the nuts off the engine. Changing at around 2,000 rpm in a diesel or 2,500 rpm in a petrol, when appropriate, ramps up your efficiency.

4.  Cruise control is an easy way to maintain a constant speed, and therefore save fuel.

5.  Hills. Where cruise control fails is on varied terrain with hills because the engine strains to hold a set speed uphill, burning a higher ratio of fuel. It is more economical to gas it downhill when the engine is hardly working, instead of coasting down, then carry the extra momentum into the hill. That way you need less power and burn less fuel on the way up the other side.

6.  Ditch the air conditioning. At higher speed it doesn't matter so much, but at low speeds switching off the air can improve efficiency by 510 per cent! In the summer you can always open the window and treat every drop of sweat like a pound coin. You'll smell like a hermit, but a wealthy one.

7.  Pick your route. Optimizing your route and not getting lost is the simplest common sense saver. When we filmed Top Gear for the 780-mile race from Switzerland to Blackpool on one tank of gas, route selection was the key to victory above everything else.

8.  Tyre pressure. The love affair continues. Under-inflation lets the tyre's tread bulge, creating a broader contact with the road surface. The extra friction creates terrible rolling resistance, and your engine has to work harder to compensate, burning loads more fuel in the process. For the average family saloon, just a 6 pounds per square inch drop in pressure leads to a 20 per cent increase in fuel consumption and 30 per cent increase in tyre wear.

Braking

## Bad Habits

1. Coasting. Knocking the car out of gear and letting off the gas to save fuel is pretty harmless when pulling slowly up to a junction, but there are major drawbacks on highways or around town. Firstly, you lose the ability to quickly accelerate out of tricky situations because you are stuck in neutral. Secondly, without engine braking you lose braking performance generally – and on mountain roads the brakes could overheat, and you might drive off a cliff. Money saved for the funeral though.

   Some folk turn their engines completely off whilst moving, which is plain dangerous. If you rotate the ignition key fully off it engages the steering lock, meaning you can't steer, precipitating your accident and much laughter at your expense. Modern cars rely on power-assisted boosters called servos to apply force to the brakes and the steering, and without them no human can push the brake or turn the wheel hard enough to get them to work properly. These servos only work with the engine turned ON!

   Modern fuel injection systems reduce the benefits of coasting anyway. Unlike the old days with a carburettor, engine management systems control fuel and ignition electronically. The car's brain, the ECU, automatically cuts the fuel supply to the injectors when you stop accelerating.

2. Drafting. This involves tailgating of the car or truck ahead to benefit from the slipstream, the invisible hole in the air created by the lead vehicle, in order to save fuel. Unless your name is Cole Trickle and you're a NASCAR racer, drafting really pisses off other motorists and usually ends badly. That's why NASCAR races nearly always involve a massive pile-up.

3. Turning off the electrics – in some parts of the Far East, I've seen people driving around at night without their lights on ... to save the bulbs and reduce fuel consumption. Some people apply this logic to their heated rear windscreen and de-mister. Whilst turning them off saves a tiny fraction of fuel, it is generally considered more important to be able to see where you're going.

'That's why NASCAR races nearly always involve a massive pile-up.'

'You're
heading
towards
the wrong
kind of
rendezvous.'

## Braking in the Real World

The best brakers have an acute sense of vision, which has as much to do with eyesight as it does with forward planning. You look further ahead and wider than the average driver. This guarantees you the time needed to form an accurate braking plan based on your speed and the landscape feeding your eyes.

For switched-on drivers, the physical operation of your foot on the brake pedal is pre-planned on a subconscious level, based on the continuous assessment of the scene to ensure that you can always stop within the distance you can see is clear ahead.

As you approach the corner or obstacle you adjust your braking plan according to any new developments.

## Stopping in an Emergency

When you want to stop in a hurry there are several factors that will define the outcome:

- thinking distance: how quickly you react;
- stopping distance: speed vs grip;
- your car – and how well your brakes work;
- technique.

### Thinking Distance

This is the distance you travel during the time it takes to spot a hazard worth braking for, and then do something about it. Thinking distance is entirely linked to your powers of observation and your speed.

The *Highway Code* suggests *thinking* and *braking* distances for bringing a vehicle to a stop from different speeds. With modern tyres and a trained brain, you can beat the distances it quotes. At 60 mph the average alert citizen's reaction time is 0.6 seconds = 18 metres, or about four car lengths. If you double your speed it naturally doubles your reaction distance, which is why you extend your vision at high speed in order to see things coming from further away.

After a gut-busting meal or when you're tired you edge closer to 1 second or seven car lengths, maybe a lot longer. With your finger up your nose and head craned towards a two-for-one offer in Ann Summers … you're heading towards the wrong kind of rendezvous.

# 7. Thinking and Braking Distance

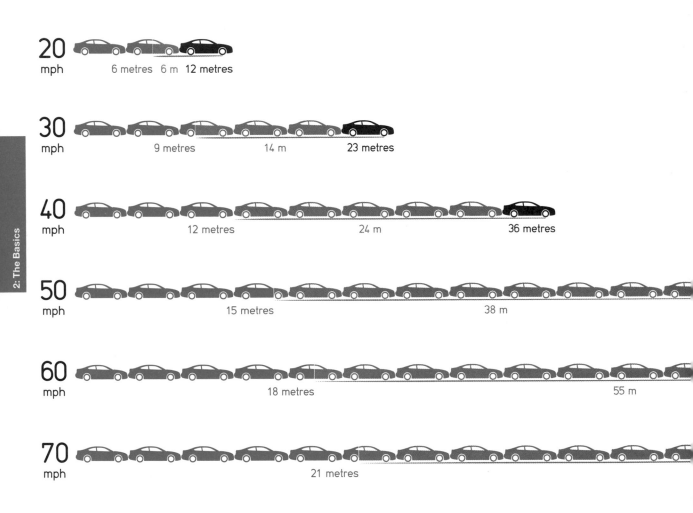

**20** mph — 6 metres · 6 m · **12 metres**

**30** mph — 9 metres · 14 m · **23 metres**

**40** mph — 12 metres · 24 m · **36 metres**

**50** mph — 15 metres · 38 m

**60** mph — 18 metres · 55 m

**70** mph — 21 metres

Note the difference in braking distance between 30 and 60 mph – at double the speed, it takes four times as long to stop.

*Source:* Highway Code

Average
car length

4 metres

 Thinking
Distance

 Braking
Distance

 Combined
Braking Distance

53 metres

73 metres

75 m

96 metres

The trick is to reduce the *thinking* distance closer to zero by anticipating the situation and covering the brake pedal with your foot, so that you're ready the moment you need to use it.

Expect the confused individual, or moron, looking for a parking space in front of you to anchor up without warning and you can't go wrong.

Anticipation replaces a reaction to an event with a true action. As for the unexpected, it pays to be decisive and measured.

**Stopping Distance**

The battle between speed and grip. The important thing to comprehend about deceleration is that the process is not a constant. Our perception of the slowing process is linear because we tend to think in terms of time and we generally shed around 20 mph for every second of braking. A car that doubles its speed will take twice the *time* to stop. And that sounds OK.

However, during that extra time it travels twice as fast and covers *four times the distance*. You might also think that a vehicle travelling at 60 mph would shed a larger proportion of its speed at the onset of braking. The opposite is true.

Over a total stopping distance of say 40 metres, over half the speed is wiped off in the last 10 metres, or two and a half car lengths. 30 metres to get from 60 to 30; just 10 to get from 30 to zero. That's scary when you put it in context with thinking distance.

You're on a motorway where everyone is travelling at 70, then you remember the chocolate bar you hid in the glovebox and go for the grab. Tick. When you look back up there's a sea of brake lights across all three lanes. In the second that passed the traffic ahead slowed to 50. Tock. By the time you react they are doing 30 with a rate of deceleration that is a hell of a lot faster than yours. You can't match them, so unless you have the distance you find yourself at the wrong end of the braking curve, and the last one to collide in the concertina.

This is Newton's fault. A vehicle builds up kinetic energy by a factor of its weight multiplied by the *square* of its speed, and as a result the braking distance increases exponentially. So, if you double the speed, you quadruple the braking distance; and a Fiat Cinquecento moving at 40 mph hits with the impact energy of a Juggernaut doing 10.

'If you double the speed, you quadruple the braking distance.'

'The fastest cars on the road also tend to be the best at stopping.'

This physics lesson matters for several reasons. Anything that postpones the onset of braking poses a similar problem. Locking a tyre at higher speeds when you first brake creates immense heat and reduces the tyre's friction just when you need it most. A lock-up at lower speed is far less punitive, and we'll explore this in the techniques section.

**Your Car**

Your ability to stop will be governed to an extent by your car's braking system and the adhesion of your tyres. Surprisingly, your car's weight has little to do with stopping *in a straight line*, but heavier cars will encounter greater trouble stopping in a corner. Weight is generally a bad thing.

Here's some lemon in the eye for the anti-fast-cars lobby. The fastest cars on the road also tend to be the best at stopping. Here's a few examples of sports cars:

| Make and model | Average of 10 stops from 62 mph |
|---|---|
| Porsche Boxster S 3.4 | 30.68 metres |
| Audi R8 4.2 FSI | 32.75 metres |
| Nissan GT-R | 33.02 metres |
| Lexus IS 250C | 38.20 metres |
| Alfa Romeo Spider 2.4 | 39.49 metres |
| Honda CR-Z 1.5 IMA | 39.73 metres |

And for comparison, here are some 'others':

| Make and model | Average of 10 stops from 62 mph |
|---|---|
| VW Polo 1.2 | 34.16 metres |
| BMW X6 xDrive 35d | 34.31 metres |
| Ford Fiesta 1.25 | 34.66 metres |
| Toyota Prius 1.8 Hybrid | 40.11 metres |
| VW Passat 1.8 TSI | 40.17 metres |
| VW Caravelle 2.0 BiTDI | 40.36 metres |
| Mitsubishi Lancer 2.0 DI-D | 40.51 metres |
| Mitsubishi Grandis 2.0 DI-D | 41.53 metres |
| Nissan Murano 3.5 V6 | 41.81 metres |

| Land Rover Freelander Td4_e | 42.04 metres |
| Chrysler Grand Voyager 2.8 | 43.49 metres |

*(Source: Which Car)*

## 'Beyond that you'll need a parachute.'

It's worth noting that even the *worst* performer, the Chrysler Grand Voyager, stops 40 feet, or three car lengths, shorter than the British *Highway Code* suggests.

Assuming that your car doesn't fall to pieces, your main allies for stopping are your tyres. Their ability to grip is loosely defined by the variable conditions of the road surface, over which you have no control, and by the quality of your tyres, depending on their make, tread and inflation, all of which you do control … Admittedly not at the precise moment when you panic-brake and the adrenaline is fizzing in your fingertips. But if you inspect your rubber once a month and don't buy cheap, then your odds of stopping short will improve dramatically when some wildebeest pulls out in front of you.

Boring but important: under-inflation can extend your braking distance by 10 per cent, more if the car is loaded up with passengers. It can cut cornering power by a third.

In the wet your braking distance is about 40 per cent longer when the tyres' tread depth reaches the legal limit of 1.6 mm, beyond that you'll need a parachute. It's best to change tyres when at 3 mm on summer tyres and 4 mm on snow.

Here are some tyre test figures for the same car stopping from 70 mph to zero riding on different tyre brands. These are straight-line tests only, so if you were to add in any fancy moves then the gap between the winners and losers would grow wider.

**Tread Depth vs Braking Distance**

**Test 1: Dry**

| 1. Michelin Pilot Sport 3 | 48.5 metres |
| 2. Continental ContiPremiumContact 2 | 51.1 metres |
| 3. Sunew YS112 | 52.2 metres |
| 4. Goodyear OptiGrip | 53.4 metres |
| 5. Ovation VI-182 | 53.4 metres |
| 6. ArrowSpeed CP661 | 53.9 metres |

**Test 2: Wet**

| | | |
|---|---|---|
| 1. | Michelin Pilot Sport 3 | 59.5 metres |
| 2. | Goodyear OptiGrip | 62.1 metres |
| 3. | Continental ContiPremium Contact 2 | 64.3 metres |
| 4. | ArrowSpeed CP661 | 68.2 metres |
| 5. | Ovation VI-182 | 76.0 metres |
| 6. | Sunew YS112 | 82.4 metres |

(*Source*: MIRA c/o Continental website)

Yes, the tyres with shorter stopping distances cost more, but I have to be honest: I'd rather shoot myself in the face than use a tyre that takes longer than 70 metres to stop.

**Technique**

First, the basics. There are many braking styles with subtle differences for varying circumstances. We'll cover all of them but let's begin with the moment when your driving instructor had that twinkle in his or her eye and said, 'When I slap my clipboard, I want you to make an emergency stop.'

After weeks of training, finally something exciting was about to happen. The street ahead lay empty bar a few parked cars and an old man checking his post box. The seconds elongated, your heart skipped a beat, and you wondered how hard you should actually …

*Slap!*

You lurched for the brake, possibly even remembering to apply the clutch to avoid the embarrassing shudder from the stalling engine, and came to a rest. A box was ticked, and off you went.

The above technique works fine for braking to a stop in a hurry. But I can almost guarantee that you could have stopped faster because the vast majority of drivers never push the brake pedal hard enough in an emergency.

The reasons for this lie in a conceit of technology called 'ABS' and people like me preaching smooth driving. When it comes to stopping in a hurry, forget smoothness. The objective is to stop safely in the shortest possible distance, and to do that you need to brake as hard as possible in order to make the most of the available grip.

'When I slap my clipboard, I want you to make an emergency stop.'

## Braking with ABS

Sixty-five per cent of all cars have ABS, and most countries require new models to have it as standard. ABS stands for 'anti-lock braking system', itself a misnomer because the system permits the tyres to lock partially during heavy braking. 'Locking' is when the brakes ask for so much slowing that a tyre stops turning altogether and drags along the road surface.

Road cars assign most of their total braking force to the front tyres in order to benefit from their rising grip level as weight shifts forwards during braking. A fully locked tyre provides no steering at all, and this is the point that ABS was designed to address. ABS works by sensing that one of the wheels has momentarily stopped turning, or is about to, and it reduces the braking force to that individual wheel, allowing it to rotate again and retain enough grip to steer or continue slowing the car.

In simple terms, all you have to do with ABS is press the pedal as hard and fast as you bloody can and keep the pressure on. Ironically, when you do push hard enough, the pedal vibrates, snaps, crackles and pops underfoot as if you had just trodden on a Rottweiler's tail, which can be disconcerting. So a lot of people take their foot off it and have an accident.

That snapping just indicates that the computer is doing its job by fluctuating the brake pressures up to fifteen times per second. The pulsing will be accompanied by mini lock-ups and squeaks from the tyres as they scrabble between the stages of gripping, stopping and rotating again.

It's a weird sensation, so it's not a bad idea to try it out in the safety of an empty car park. Remember to check that nobody's following you …

In summary, ABS filters the effects of panic by preventing major wheel lock-ups that might otherwise reduce your stopping power and allows you to 'stomp and steer'. Stomp on the brakes as hard as possible, and steer around the terror. It is critical that you keep your foot pressed hard on the pedal so that the ABS can do its job, even when it comes to steering. The car will turn more lazily than usual so you'll need to apply extra force to the wheel to make it obey.

For me that's where the honeymoon with this technology ends because having ABS onboard doesn't mean you can stop shorter than without it. In fact we were safer as a species before its invention.

In the 1970s vehicle manufacturers were producing galactic-sized cars like

'The pedal vibrates, snaps, crackles and pops underfoot.'

'ABS filters the effects of panic by preventing major wheel lock-ups.'

the Ford Capri, the Rover SD1 and American muscle machines like the Corvette and Mustang. These big beauties lumbered around roads like bulls in china shops and squealed through corners at the behest of men with dubious 'taches, bell-bottom trousers and permed mullets. It didn't escape the attention of software engineers that these mullets were getting bent out of shape whenever their owners were required to take evasive action on slippery roads. Skinny front tyres would lock up under braking, and the driver lost all steering control as the fronts ploughed along the tarmac, unless the leather loafer relinquished pressure on the centre pedal to unlock them again.

Back at work with a fresh set of paisley-patterned underwear, mullet man would regale his brush with death to his colleagues. A healthy focus group would dissect the incident with much tooth sucking on whether the brakes had been applied too heavily at the first touch for the slippery conditions, and how one should always avoid severe braking in the corner itself. Those stories kept people informed and alive.

Meanwhile, the cone-heads designed software that could control the brake pressure without macho intervention, so that in the event of a driver panicking and pressing the brakes too hard the tyres would only lock a little bit and he would retain some steering. At first there was a debatable safety improvement, but any benefit quickly evaporated. People felt safer so they switched off, followed closer and started braking later.

The average crashing-in-a-straight-line-with-the-fronts-locked experience was replaced by a faster accident further around the corner, with a higher and more dangerous incidence of rolling over. But ABS is here to stay, alas, with more cotton wool in the pipeline.

**Common Mistakes**

>The tyres have fundamental limitations. If you exceed these with a combination of speed and heavy braking, the ABS won't save you.

>ABS-fitted vehicles are not designed to run without it. When ABS develops a fault the system usually sends too much braking to the rear, which can spin the car. Another fault is false recognition of a skid and the pedal goes solid without slowing you down. Been there, got the T-shirt. If you see an ABS warning light on the dashboard it genuinely needs love from your mechanic.

# Braking on the Limit

As the description suggests, this means developing the maximum braking force from the tyres up until the point where they stop turning. By virtue of the fact that this style avoids locking the tyre, it is the fastest way to stop in a vehicle, with or without ABS.

A skilled driver with good observation skills and sensitivity underfoot to manipulate the pedal can apply an infinite range of brake pressure to match the conditions in order to stop the car in the shortest possible distance.

## The Limit

Instructions from your foot apply pressure to the braking system, which creates reverse torque at the wheel hubs, causing the tyres to slow down just before the car does. When things are going well, the tyres will be turning about 15 per cent more slowly than your road speed before they begin to lock.

The tyres *streeetch*, and their elastic force pulls the speed off the car. As brake pressure increases there comes a point where the tyres begin to slip *before* the wheels actually stop turning and lock up. That point is the braking limit, the threshold beyond which the tyre starts skidding.

Your brain detects these minute changes in physical forces through a mix of instinct based on experience of similar conditions, the varying pressure you get from your body pushing into the belts and your sense of speed. Honing that ability requires superb familiarity with your car, feel for the conditions and practice in a safe environment.

The world's finest racing drivers have an innate sensitivity for the available grip feeding through their backsides and the ability to tread the pedal with surgical precision, prompting the adulation 'he was the last of the late brakers', often a reflection in the past tense, since the bravest brakers also tend not to live long. Sometimes it pays to be the guy who brakes first …

## Technique

It always pays to optimize the circumstances for braking. Wherever possible you aim to brake in as much of a straight line as possible so that the tyres can focus on one job only.

'The threshold beyond which the tyre starts skidding.'

'The nose dives as weight shifts quickly onto the front tyres.'

Your front tyres alone perform over 60 per cent of braking, and to help them do this you want to transfer some weight onto them. Here's the trick, and it flies in the face of my philosophy about resting a glass of water on the dashboard.

In dry conditions, you initially stab the brake pedal to shift weight forwards onto the fronts and then squeeze until you reach optimal pressure, modulating as required.

*Stab*: You dig your foot about an inch into the brake pedal, and the nose dives as weight shifts quickly onto the front tyres. The more weight bearing down on the fronts, the harder you can then squeeze the pedal.

Braking very gently (like the *feel* then *firm* model, page 67) doesn't send enough weight to the front tyres, and they will never develop their full braking potential regardless how hard you brake later.

*Squeeze*: The first touch is immediately followed by a more gradual but firm building of pressure, hopefully based on the good foundations laid by the initial stab. You increase pressure to the point where you can feel the tyre almost start locking. In your average road car the foot pressure is around 40 pounds, or the weight of two watermelons.

*Modulate*: Limit braking is based on constant, instinctive assessments of the available grip. When it's going well you don't have to adjust the pressure too much once you reach the limit, it's just fine-tuning as you feel how much the tyre is biting

## 8. Stab and Squeeze

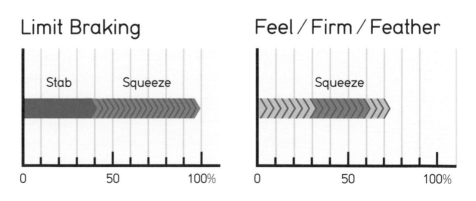

### Limit Braking

Stab   Squeeze

0        50        100%

### Feel / Firm / Feather

Squeeze

0        50        100%

'This initial
stab does
not mean
slamming
the brakes
like an ape.'

from one moment to the next. But on bumpy circuits or country lanes with big surface changes, things can get quite lively.

This style of performance braking is equally valid in cars fitted with ABS. In a state of emergency you can apply the panic model described above, but on track whenever I push for a record-breaking time, be it on *Top Gear* or anywhere else, I generally try to avoid triggering the computer and drive to the threshold of the tyre, the point *before* locking. The Bugatti Veyron Record was a classic example of how this technique enabled me to unlock an extra 10 per cent of performance.

Into the sweeping first corner at Dunsfold I would line up on my 'Stig Line', which was tighter than that used by the F1 mob, and allowed me to brake more in a straight line as the car went over a crest and turn in with less effort. With 1200 bhp underfoot, my approach speed was high, and the strain on the tyres considerable. If the Bug crested that rise and the ABS kicked in, I lost enough steering and braking control to push me wide of the mark by 40 feet and on to a totally different arc. Enough to convince a very reluctant cameraman, the ever-adventurous Iain May, to position himself further away from the danger zone.

## Common Mistakes

> **Those inexperienced with limit braking will master the stab, and reach a mental block after about 70 per cent on the braking scale. Christian Slater was a prime example when he was competing to be Top Gear's fastest 'Star in a Reasonably Priced Car'. His brain recognized that further braking force would exceed anything he had experienced previously and refused to utilize the grip created from the generally good weight transfer he was creating. There's only so many times an instructor can shout 'Braaake!' before turning into a crow.**

> **This initial stab does not mean slamming the brakes like an ape. The reason this technique separates the men from the boys is because it requires such sensitivity. To achieve this remember to position your heel on the deck with your knee bent so that it's your foot doing the work, rather than your entire leg delivering enough force to produce diamonds from coal. Overdoing the stab at high speed and locking a tyre carries a penalty equal to the potential gain, because a high-speed lock-up has an exponentially detrimental effect on your deceleration curve. Some big words there.**

Remember that the braking curve in relation to speed takes time, or distance, for the speed to fall sharply. The friction of a stopped tyre when the vehicle is travelling at high speed creates an enormous amount of heat, and the molten rubber causes extra slippage. This kind of overload needs to be rectified early on by quickly releasing pressure on the brake and then reapplying. This technique is known as Pulse Braking.

## Rock, Paper, Scissors

I took a lesson in brake modulation from a fire-breathing V8 Supercar in Bathurst, Australia. The thundering V8s boast over 600 bhp and achieve the highest road course speeds of any Touring Car series anywhere in the world, NASCAR included. They also run on tyres so skinny as to make a lawnmower seem over-endowed, not that you would notice beneath their flared wheel arches and aggressive contours.

Every year the V8s assemble at the foot of a great mountain, Mount Panorama, the passage across which is fraught with more danger than any Tolkien chronicle.

The track climbs vertically from the pits before dropping over a crest so sharp that the wheels spin in fifth gear. You plunge down a way until your tail pipe clanks the tarmac and you veer uphill again to face a wall of tarmac bordered by solid concrete. You stab and squeeze the brake pedal, and the opposing force of gravity stops you dead in your tracks. The waist belt clinches you like a boa constrictor. The car shifts restlessly as the weight of the machine thrusts forward and the tyres dig deep into the hill. You float into a banked right-hander with an apex kerb high enough to put a van on its roof, shoot out of the corner towards a wall and breathe again.

Squeeze up to the steel guardrail on the right to approach a sharp, blind left-hander. Only a fool would continue accelerating at this point. You floor it and change up a gear. You pass the last chance to brake before the corner, still flat out, squint, and point the car towards the wall on the left before finally applying the brakes, just a soft touch as the car turns, and then fully once you can straighten the wheel on the way out.

Braking is king when it comes to rock, paper, scissors. If you need steering, you can't brake hard, because the braking force will hog everything the tyres have to offer.

Beyond the wall the road opens to reveal the orange hue of the mountain as the circuit cuts sharp left and rises. Beyond this 'cutting' the wheels spin over hidden bumps, throwing you from one wall to the next, snaking and sliding as the camber of the road swivels and pitches, the speed ever rising.

An unhelpful thought from Bathurst winner Rick Kelly comes to mind: 'It's just uncomfortable. You only have to go off line once and the show's over.'

Pluck fourth gear, the rear shakes and wobbles out over the crest towards a left-hander and its metal 'grate', a deep compression so severe that you have to turn away from it early to prevent the power steering from seizing. Still the throttle is mashed.

The car loads into the positive camber, a tiny lift, the tyres are maxed, sucking you towards the wall until you jam the steering to the left and wait. Silence. The nose creeps to within a wing mirror's distance of the wall and lazily peels away. You collect the throttle again and speed over another blind crest.

For me, getting to the top of the mountain is the easy part. It's all downhill from here.

As you aim for the skyline at about 120 mph, the only indication of a corner is the wall that meets the track on the right-hand side. You aim towards it, press the brakes, plunge downhill, and everything goes into denial.

Barely have you dealt with the crisis on the right when the flik-flak, left-right wall weave appears in the windscreen. Gravity will punish the slightest transgression as it exaggerates your momentum, and your eardrums will blossom to the tones of the 'squeaker', an electronic device fitted inside the helmet that informs you in no uncertain terms when the tyres have locked. As if you didn't know already from the fleshy rumble underfoot and by virtue of barely making the turn.

Each movement of the brake requires the delicate, immediate response of your foot on the pedal and not the squeeze of a slice of lemon more to ride the limit …

Assuming you make it through, you descend into another slow double whammy left-right called the 'Dipper', listening for the squeak and feathering back the pressure by a slice or two, before emerging and finally remembering what the gas pedal feels like. One last sharp hairpin and on to 'Conrod Straight' for a well-earned rest while the V8 winds you up to 185 mph.

## 'Hit the brakes like your life depends on it.'

The speed isn't such an impressive number until you arrive at the end and have to reduce it. Conveniently, the grass border on the left turns into tarmac just prior to the ridiculously fast, bumpy right-hander that drops you down into a relatively slow leftright chicane.

At the last moment you whip the rig across to the steel Armco on the left to benefit from the easier line this affords for sweeping into the right, then hit the brakes like your life depends on it.

Having spent most of my racing career in high-downforce cars that maintained a constant high level of grip throughout the corner, I expected similar support from the V8, albeit on its skinny-ass tyres. As I probed the limits of adhesion during practice, I postponed my braking point until the car was part way through the fast right and encountering the bumps at the crest. This was the prelude to my first, and hopefully last, 185 mph lock-up.

At the first touch of the pedal, both front tyres seemed to explode. The heat of dragging, locked rubber at 185 mph was phenomenal, and I was trailing more smoke than the Red Arrows. The lock and burn, combined with all the inertia of a supersonic oil tanker, was too severe for squeezing lemons. I had to fully release the brakes, reclaim a moment of steering and have another go at braking. And a few more gos after that … this was full disaster recovery mode.

The gravel beds around the chicane were starting to welcome me like an errant golf ball departing the fairway, and my tyres, now freshly coined million-degree 50-pence pieces, were not cutting the mustard at all.

The wall on the right side looked uninviting, but the gravel looked thin on the far left, so I used my Xbox training to the full by giving up on the brake and straight-lining the whole deal at about 130. It was bumpier than on TV, but I made it.

I brought the car back to the pits, and the smouldering tyres were removed and inspected by my old mate and crew chief Joe Bremner. His thatch was even thinner on top after a few extra seasons coping with the likes of me. He inspected the tyres with their fist-sized holes and gurgled like Yogi Bear, 'Havin' fun out there, are we? Fresh set for Mr Collins.'

Joe brought me a data sheet with an overlay of my speeds and braking inputs versus Rick Kelly's, who was a bit of legend down under. Old Rick had beaten me at my own game.

Braking

He treated the bumpy crest of the curve like a slippery surface and just lifted off the throttle to let his engine braking slowly transfer some weight to the front end. After the turn, as the car settled into the slope, he braked softly for a microsecond to let the tyres soak up the load and then dropped anchor. The subtle loading made all the difference, and I never had a problem there again.

Bathurst demonstrates the full range of braking characteristics from the good to the bad and the ugly. The principles enshrined are thus:

- Longitudinal forces from braking and accelerating are always the kings of rock, paper and scissors at the expense of steering, so you try to brake in a straight line before the corner to avoid compromising your ability to turn.
- In high-grip situations you attain best braking using the stab and squeeze model.
- In low-grip situations (downhill, cresting, slippery surfaces) you dial back the stab and gently apply the brake.
- A locked tyre at high speed should always be avoided and requires urgent redress.
- A locked tyre at low speed is less of a problem and can usually be addressed by modulating foot pressure by a slice of lemon or two.

At Silverstone driving school we used to compete to see who could stop shortest in an emergency from 40 mph on a dry surface. After a few tries we were all level because everyone dialled in to the available grip by using limit braking. Prior to that there was a big divergence.

The guys who reacted instantly when the chief instructor yelled, 'ALIENS!' locked up and screeched to a messy halt.

The clever ones who spent a second trying to feel the limit by easing into the pedal, and avoided locking up, actually took longer to stop. Their advantage in braking *performance* was slighter at low speed, where a locked tyre loses only 15 per cent of its stopping power, and not enough to compensate for their initial delay in applying pressure.

I think I've made it clear that you want to avoid locking up, but when you need to stop in an emergency it is critical that you act quickly. Just remember that when the tyres are locked you have absolutely no steering (see also Pulse Braking in Winter Driving, page 229).

## Trail Braking

Trail braking in its pure form is a performance driving technique for posting lap times. It allows you to brake later by extending the final phase of braking into the initial part of the corner itself. Limit braking wipes most of the speed off in a straight line, then you bleed off the pressure as you start turning the steering wheel. You have to reduce brake pressure to compensate for the tyres as they juggle two jobs at once, otherwise you lose the ability to steer, or brake, or both!

For everyday driving, the benefit of overlapping a hint of braking as you turn into a corner is that the weight stays put and you get a smoother flow into the corner. It feels natural as long as you don't overdo it.

'He braked softly for a microsecond to let the tyres soak up the load and then dropped anchor.'

# Left-foot Braking

Certain racing cars with extreme set-ups require you to left-foot brake, such as NASCAR, where the off-centre axle has to be kept under constant acceleration to stop it driving in the wrong direction. You continue to accelerate with your right foot while braking with your left foot to keep it stable. This specialized kind of oval racing is the only environment where I left-foot brake. Everywhere else, I always stick to the right foot.

On the race track some drivers use left-foot braking and some don't, with no discernible performance advantage either way. At Le Mans a car full of left-foot brakers would lose. The combined braking and accelerating burns a lot more fuel and chews up brake pads, so they would have to make extra fuel stops and replace the pads more often.

Three-time British touring car champion Matt Neal races a front-wheel-drive car for a living and says, 'It's gimmicky, you hear people overdoing it and the brake temps go insane, but really the benefits are neither here nor there. I'd never use it on the road.'

Even in rallying, the role of left-foot braking has changed since the turbo era, when drivers used it to keep the revs up and work around problems in the suspension. These days it's more used for fine-tuning the weight around the apex.

Left-foot braking on the road is as useful as an ashtray on a motorcycle, and don't let anybody tell you different. If you want to train your left foot usefully, keep smooth clutching. Transferring it to the brake will only mean a clumsy push followed by a gum full of steering wheel. It takes a lot of practice to prove otherwise.

# Cornering

## We've covered stopping, steering and going – which, in that order, is effectively how you take a corner. It's time for big boy's pants.

The biggest misconception about racing drivers is that our job involves piling through corners as fast as humanly possible. It doesn't. I'm not sure many of my passengers would have agreed when I took them for a ride as The Stig, but cornering is about compromising. Some people find that harder to accept than others.

'*Hammerrr!*'

Not the mating call of the lesser-spotted Stigasaurus, rather the piston-rattling caw of a primate better known as Jeremy Clarksonzilla. Jezza makes every car he climbs aboard look small, and they positively shiver when he turns the key.

Despite his sins as a car surgeon, Jeremy has quite a natural feel for the amount of grip a car has through a corner and regularly consumes it from start to finish. Flying in formation with him requires patience, lots of patience, and admitting to yourself that he can drive around the corner a little bit faster than you.

'I beat Steve Soper once, y'know,' he remarked as we climbed aboard a pair of evenly matched sports cars.

Unaware that Jeremy had defeated a world-class touring car champion, I steeled myself as he described the manner in which he dispatched not just Soper, but all manner of racing pros during a time attack around Silverstone's Grand Prix circuit.

'Soper was in tears,' he continued. 'He simply couldn't believe that some overweight journalist could possibly have beaten him. He drove his nuts off for the rest of the afternoon trying to clip my time, but he couldn't.'

'How did you manage it?' I asked, kind of knowing the answer.

'I cheated, of course.'

So off we went for a choreographed race and some tandem drifting around our favourite corners at the *Top Gear* track.

'It's time for big boy's pants.'

When you run super close to another vehicle, you learn to read its body language and to anticipate where it's going so that you avoid getting tangled up. From behind it's easy because you can gauge the attitude of the car in front by how much the front wheels are turning in the bend. If the fronts seem fairly straight inside the wheel arches it means the car in front is oversteering as the rear tyres lose traction, but if the front wheels are visibly turning a lot then it means they are resisting and beginning to understeer.

Even when I was ahead of Jeremy, I noticed his front tyres twisting outside of the bodywork and could practically hear him swearing above the tyre squeal. We pulled to a halt.

'You're too f***ing slow into Chicago,' he advised. (*Chicago*: low/medium speed, increasing radius corner – see p103.)

'No I'm ...'

'*Yes,* you *are*. And it's making this car understeer like a bloody pig.'

I studied the outside of his front tyres, which admittedly were more grained than a photo of Jordan without touch-up. We swapped cars, and Jeremy's signature was clearly stamped all over the 1,000-degree rubber-cum-molasses. Much to his dismay, I proceeded to enter the corners even more slowly to allow the molten tyres to recover and effect a perfectly balletic flying exit. I tried explaining the racing credo of 'slow in, fast out', but the resulting conversation would make a sailor blush. If you want to hear my side of the story, please read on.

'Braking, turning and accelerating.'

## Viewing the Corner

In its simplest form, there are three overlapping phases of cornering: braking, turning and accelerating.

To plan these phases you must make a visual assessment of the approaching bend to gauge the sharpness and direction of the curve, then plan the appropriate speed and line for dispatching it.

You continuously update your view of the corner, road surface and situation as you approach the braking zone. You squeeze the brakes, release pressure as you turn in, all the time looking through the corner to chase the vanishing point.

The vanishing point is the furthest point of the road ahead that you can see and is a good rule of thumb for matching your speed to the curvature. When your viewpoint is extending through a corner at the same rate as your speed, it means the corner is opening with you and matching your speed. If the vanishing point stops moving it means that the corner is tightening up and you're going too fast.

On the track we say that the next corner begins before the last one finishes. In other words, we keep one eye permanently on the horizon, so we can plan the next turn well in advance and ensure that we are driving into clear space. Anticipation is another way we 'slow down time'.

## Rhythm

Taking a corner well depends on a number of factors, but these are all governed by a single principle, which is rhythm. Once you get a handle on the right way to position yourself for a corner, it becomes a way of life.

Bad positioning will make the car inherently unstable because it will be fighting you all the time, and your erstwhile passengers will seek less dangerous pastimes elsewhere.

Timing the moves, swinging the controls and seeing the situation develop ahead of time closely resembles some of our finest moments on the dance-floor. And because there will be less commotion with the machine, driving it requires less energy, and you can focus further ahead.

Racing drivers use the rhythm of a circuit to develop a system that guides them from one corner to the next. We call that system the racing line, and although every driver has subtle preferences according to his feel for the beat, it is a universal language for describing the way to maximize a machine's stability through a curve.

2: The Basics

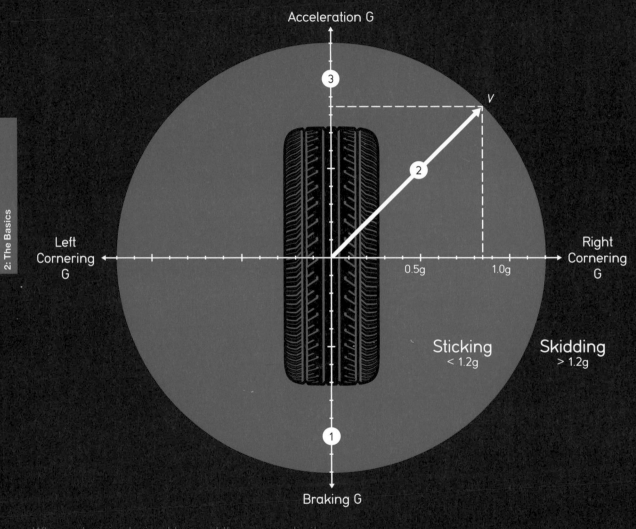

Acceleration G

3

V

2

Left
Cornering
G

0.5g          1.0g

Right
Cornering
G

Sticking
< 1.2g

Skidding
> 1.2g

1

Braking G

When a tyre is strained beyond the orange limit,
it starts skidding and you'll need to skip
to Section 4 to deal with the mess.

The tyre can generate a maximum force of 1.2G under braking or
during cornering – but it cannot achieve 1.2G of peak braking and
1.2G of peak cornering at the same time.

When a tyre contends with lateral cornering forces as well as
longitudinal braking or acceleration forces, it develops less grip
for each task than when handling them independently. Line 2

describes the combined forces of a vehicle accelerating while
turning right. The resulting vector V this creates has less grip on
the scale as indicated by the dotted lines.
Although we view the tyre's performance as a circle, the reality is
that the longitudinal forces of braking and accelerating are the
dominant players. If you overcook either of them during a corner,
you start falling off the road.

## The Physics of Cornering: The Tyre vs Isaac Newton

Sir Isaac Newton's Third Law of Motion asserted that no object could develop a force greater than that being applied to it. But by stretching in two directions (lengthwise *as well as* laterally) when introduced to a corner, the modern tyre develops forces the *combined* value of which can exceed the loads being applied to it. Clever. However, while celebrating its capacity to multi-task, one shouldn't forget that it can never do two jobs as well as it can do one. We therefore separate the cornering process into three phases in order to maximise their potential:

1. Best braking takes place in a straight line, because weight transfers to the front tyres, which aids braking and initial turning power.
2. Best cornering takes place with no braking or throttle. You reduce braking as you start steering. The body of the car will lean over; the weight transfers to the outside tyres, creating maximum cornering power.
3. Cornering power reduces as acceleration begins – and best acceleration happens in a straight line.

Pursuing this sequence is a whole lot more reliable, and comfortable, than dancing on the pedals.

Racing drivers are known for being prima donnas with custard for brains and a heavy right foot. But in 1958 one of the brethren, an F1 driver called Piero Taruffi, became momentarily possessed by some kind of Einsteinian spirit. His eyes rolled inside their sockets like the dials of a fruit machine, and he spat out an equation for predicting the maximum cornering speed of a car through any given corner – $F=mv^2/r$ – then he skipped back to the swimming pool and demanded more factor 20.

'Your car's tyres have four potential enemies.'

Your car's tyres have four potential enemies, excluding your erratic enthusiasm, during the cornering process: the nature of the road surface, the vehicle's weight, your *speed* and the tightness of the bend.

In true game-show-host style, I will not reveal which of these vital elements is missing from brother Taruffi's equation until later on. For now, just consider that your tyres have to create an equal or greater amount of grip than the centrifugal force – $F$ – of cornering.

### Weight: m

The weight of the car rounding an arc creates a centrifugal force, just like spinning a conker around the end of a string. As any conker champion will tell you, it doesn't pay to rely on big nuts for conkering *or* cornering because the *heavier* the conker; the greater the force trying to shear it away from the string and off into next door's garden.

When you swing through a corner the centrifugal force wants to throw the car off the road in the same way, but it meets resistance from your tyres, which cling stubbornly to the road surface. If you were to let go of the steering wheel the car would instantly go straight, because the only things forcing it to turn are the front tyres. The heavier the car, the more passengers you carry, the more work the tyres have to do.

### Speed: $v^2$

Alarmingly, the effect of your speed on your cornering force is exponential. In the cornering equation, your weight is multiplied by the *square* of your speed!

### Bend: r

In a perfectly planed curve, the apex is exactly halfway through the corner. The example opposite shows a geometrically perfect 'radius' (driving line), which with its maximum radius length offers the greatest cornering potential as far as equations are concerned.

In the example opposite, a driver could take this corner at a higher constant speed of 55.2456784 mph using line M by driving like Jezza. However, his tyres would have spent all of their potential grip in the process, leaving nothing left with which to accelerate onto the straight that follows. The time advantage you gain by travelling faster down the straights significantly outweighs any short-term gains from screeching through the bends. So although it's been fascinating to swallow a geometry book, you'll be glad to know that taking a corner is a lot more artful than driving by numbers.

# 10. Taking Corners

## Perfect Geometric Driving Line (J Line)

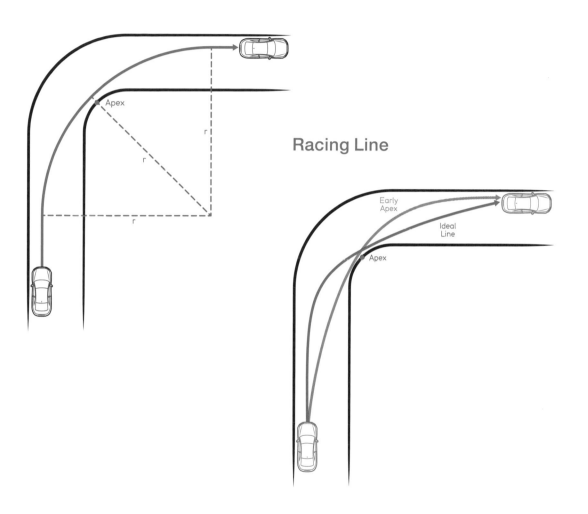

## Racing Line

## The Racing Line

The racing line is not geometrically perfect. It can best be described as a variable radius, because it sacrifices corner entry in favour of expanding the space available for the exit. You spend a little more time setting up for the corner by turning in a hint later, clip the apex slightly further around the corner and reap the benefits as you depart.

'The tighter the turn, the harder the tyres have to work.'

'This is a dangerous and lazy habit.'

## 'Slow In, Fast Out'

This means taking control of the biggest part of the equation, speed, by braking early so that you have enough grip in the middle of the corner to make a clean getaway. The tighter the turn, the harder the tyres have to work until they reach their 'limit', so you brake earlier and harder to give them the stability they need at the apex for when you start to accelerate.

## Cutting Corners

When you look at a corner you might think that there's nothing to it in terms of choosing the direction you follow. But by making subtle adjustments, you can position the car so that it follows a gentler path.

Racing drivers cut corners to shorten the distance their machines have to travel and increase the radius of their turn. They use the full width of the track because there's nothing coming the other way and thereby have the maximum possible amount of grip at their disposal. On the road with two-way traffic this is a dangerous and lazy habit, and not what I'm suggesting at all.

Using the available space between the roadside and the white line, you can shape the curvature to your benefit. By turning in from a wider position, accurately cutting in towards the centre of the corner and gradually releasing the steering as you leave, you can potentially drive around it faster, or in safety terms will have more grip in hand to tackle irregularities in the road surface. A small uplift in accuracy provides a big benefit to the machine.

When I raced at Charlotte Motor Speedway in a NASCAR support race, the track conditions would change by the hour depending on the temperature. During the daytime I found that the fastest way around the kidney-shaped oval was to enter the two flat-out turns by turning in quite late, missing the apex by a few feet and straight-lining the exit. However at night, when the temperature dropped, the car became unstable and was 'walking' towards the wall on my right.

'Get your ass down on that white line,' came a voice over the radio. It was my first night outing on an oval so I obeyed, ran all the way down to the white border and listened to the motor perk up on the way out. Longer radius. Duh.

The voice belonged to the NASCAR legend that was Dick Trickle, winner of basically every race around a circle and infamous for smoking during the extended caution periods while the officials scraped the wreckage off the floor.

## Benefits of 'Late Apexing'

Delaying your turn-in gives you a truer perspective of the corner. You have to make a tighter arc at the beginning, which forces you to reduce speed early, and gives the car (and you) room to breathe on the exit, and a straighter line for acceleration.

**Hot Tip**

> The added bonus of the racing line is the enhanced viewpoint for seeing through the bend. You have a clearer picture of approaching traffic, for gauging the severity of the curve and planning ahead.
> To keep ahead of the game, you always keep a little margin in hand, especially on unfamiliar roads. Keeping your chin up and anticipating the road all the way should keep you out of the ditch.

## Premature Ejection

If you crash out of a corner, in most cases it'll be because you accelerated and 'apexed' too early. People often lament that their car 'wouldn't make the bend' or 'ran out of road'.

Turning into a corner early is a common mistake; it feels great at first because it doesn't require as much turning force and the car feels stable because you have unwittingly created a gentle radius. That good feeling lures you into your second mistake: to accelerate prematurely. If your speed increases, the radius of your arc has to get bigger too. Your life has been reduced to an equation.

Sadly, as the exit approaches you'll be required to do the exact opposite – to perform a second tight radius turn in order to avoid the oncoming hedge, wall, tree or fireball … Unless your speed reduces miraculously, you will be taking in some real estate.

'That good feeling lures you into your second mistake.'

# 11. Tyres vs Isaac Newton

# The Right Way

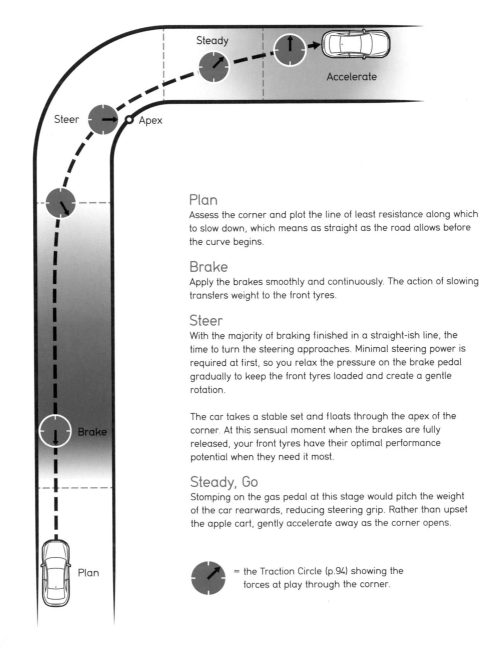

### Plan
Assess the corner and plot the line of least resistance along which to slow down, which means as straight as the road allows before the curve begins.

### Brake
Apply the brakes smoothly and continuously. The action of slowing transfers weight to the front tyres.

### Steer
With the majority of braking finished in a straight-ish line, the time to turn the steering approaches. Minimal steering power is required at first, so you relax the pressure on the brake pedal gradually to keep the front tyres loaded and create a gentle rotation.

The car takes a stable set and floats through the apex of the corner. At this sensual moment when the brakes are fully released, your front tyres have their optimal performance potential when they need it most.

### Steady, Go
Stomping on the gas pedal at this stage would pitch the weight of the car rearwards, reducing steering grip. Rather than upset the apple cart, gently accelerate away as the corner opens.

= the Traction Circle (p.94) showing the forces at play through the corner.

# The Wrong Way

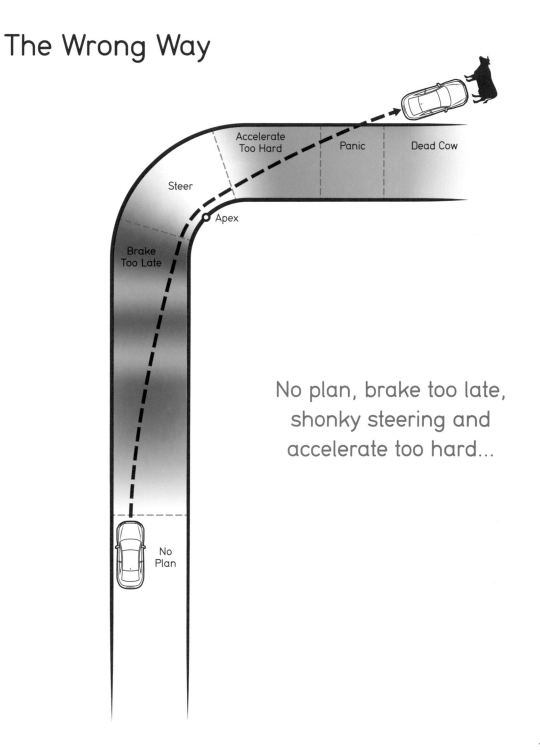

Accelerate
Too Hard

Panic

Dead Cow

Steer

Apex

Brake
Too Late

No
Plan

No plan, brake too late,
shonky steering and
accelerate too hard...

## The Real World

Over the years I have noticed that corners, with the exception of the ones on Playstation, don't have dotted lines on them showing you 'the line'. And you'll never need them to. Once you dial into the notion of accurately working an apex and pushing your gaze further towards the exit of the turn, it becomes second nature.

Below are some garden-variety types of corner that should help you to identify what you're dealing with.

## Types of Corner

An *increasing radius corner* is the easiest to handle because it naturally opens up on the exit.

But its evil twin brother, the *decreasing radius corner*, tightens up when you least expect it on the way of the corner and wants to invite you to a party in the woods all alone. Train your eye to notice when the corner is closing you down.

The *double apex* at first sight might look like a long radius arc. The easy mistake is to presume the corner is opening and accelerate after the first clipping point and then wish you hadn't. On closer inspection the corner has two clipping points and the last one always has priority.

*Hairpins*. On track it's the slow corners like these that often cost people the most time, because this is when the car is most reactive to braking and acceleration in lower gears. Both can quickly overload the tyres, and a little sympathy goes a long way, especially in the Alps. The common mistake is to rush into the corner too quickly or start accelerating too soon. By obeying the racing line, you take a fraction longer to slow the car and have a straighter, easier ride out.

*Connecting corners*. When one corner is immediately followed by another one. This is where it starts getting interesting. Rural roads are nearly always connected, meaning that the exit of one flows right into the next. Rather like the double apex corner, if you're too greedy or not paying attention during the first part then you suffer in part two.

By keeping some margin in hand through the middle of the corner you automatically set yourself up for anything that follows, be it the next turn, clump of traffic or that moose we keep reading about. Anybody taking the first part of the corner anywhere near 100 per cent of the tyres' capability could be in for a nasty surprise further down the road.

'But its evil twin brother, the decreasing radius corner, tightens up when you least expect.'

# 12. Corner Types

Connecting / Linked
Corner

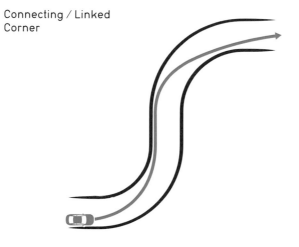

Double Apex

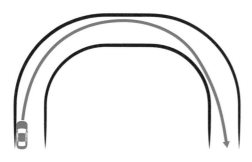

Hairpin Corner

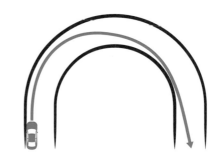

Decreasing Radius Corner

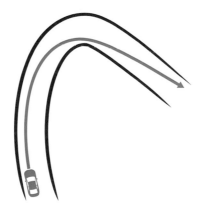

Increasing Radius Corner

## The Road Surface (the Missing Link from Taruffi's Equation)

No corner is ever the same twice, and no equation can predict the *ever-changing* condition of the road surface. It's up to you to become the connoisseur, and thankfully this doesn't involve slipping your tongue into bitumen.

The primary factors that determine the grip of the road surface are: type, temperature, weather, incline, camber and foreign bodies.

### Type

The basic rule with tarmac is that the rougher the surface, the better the grip, because it gives the tyres something to bite on. Conversely, the smoother or more worn it becomes, the less grip it has. Visually, when you notice a sheen on the surface, especially towards the end of the summer, you can expect reduced grip. The problem is compounded when it rains.

Anti-skid surfaces come in a variety of colours and designs: red, sand, chevrons. They provide extra grip in hot spots, typically braking areas. They are expensive and not always maintained, so as they wear away they become bumpy, polished and less supportive.

Concrete is the noisy stuff that drives you mad. It has decent grip in the dry but beware of freezing water in colder temperatures and aquaplane in heavy rain (see p212). It is slippery when wet.

Bumps and potholes in the road shift the weight bearing down on your tyres. Your suspension does its best to iron this out, but bumps nevertheless reduce road holding and make cornering less predictable. As long as you're delicate with the wheel as you cross them, then there's no drama.

Some drivers swerve around potholes as if they contain anthrax, and a friend of mine wrote his car off doing this. Common sense prevails.

Manhole covers and heavily painted lines can be slippery in the rain. In the US they love a raised cover, and the extra jolt to jelly-like suspension can put you in freefall for a second or two if you're not careful.

### Temperature

Anything below 5 degrees affects the way your tyres generate grip. The colder they are, the harder they become and less reliable at gluing themselves to the particles on the road.

'The rougher the surface, the better the grip.'

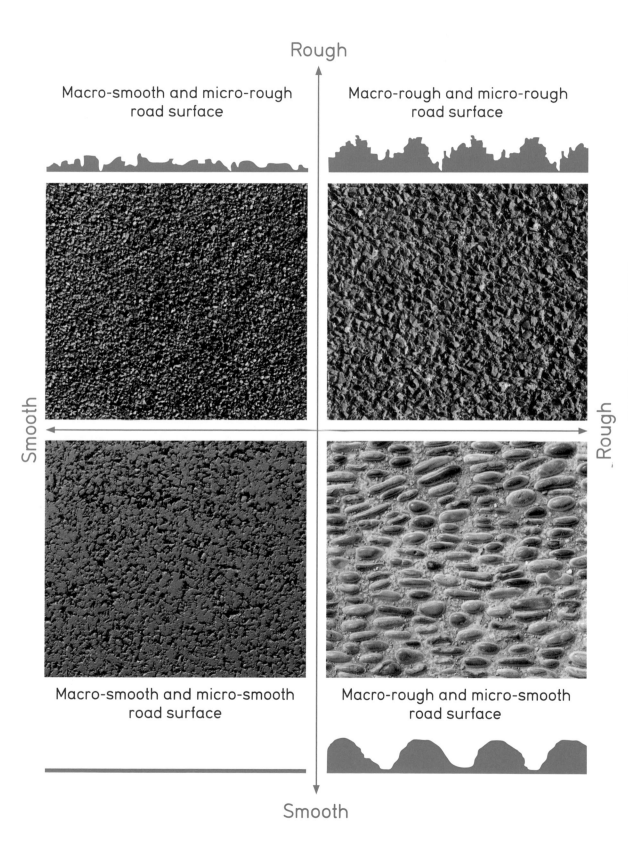

Rough

Macro-smooth and micro-rough
road surface

Macro-rough and micro-rough
road surface

Smooth

Rough

Macro-smooth and micro-smooth
road surface

Macro-rough and micro-smooth
road surface

Smooth

## Grip Levels

## Effect of road surface variations on tyre grip

|  | Grip Level % |  |
|---|---|---|
| Dry surfaces | 75–100 | |
| Damp surfaces | | |
| Macro- and micro-rough surfaces | 58 | |
| Wet surfaces | | |
| Macro- and micro-rough surfaces | 50 | |
| Macro- and micro-smooth surfaces | 16 | |
| Snow | 12 | |
| Ice | 4–8 | |

'The extra
jolt to
jelly-like
suspension
can put you
in freefall.'

**Weather**

Rain cuts down braking and accelerating grip by a third, but reduces cornering potential by *half* with a good tyre. If you're driving on cheap ting-tong rubber you could lose 75 per cent of your grip. I'm not making it up!

Snow and ice coat the tarmac with an entirely new surface with further reduced grip. The right tyre compounds really walk the walk when it comes to bite.

**Incline**

What goes up …

When you drive up a hill, the angle at which the tyres meet the surface has the effect of pushing them into the road much harder than normal, providing more grip.

… must come down.

This wonderful boost in grip only lasts until the moment that the gradient reduces and the car 'goes light'. If you crest the brow of a hill at speed, all manner of weird sensations travel through the car as the forces of gravity affecting it flip into reverse.

---

**Hot Tip**

> **When cresting, keep the steering as straight as possible, no sudden movements.**

---

When you travel downhill, everything works against you with the exception of acceleration. Your gutless good-for-nothing car will surge forth like a Lamborghini. Before you know it you're experimenting with physics.

Gravity, the merciless overlord, accentuates the forces of inertia trying to push the car wide of the mark, and you need to throw a parachute to get the thing to stop. That's why everybody crashes on the way down hills. It's another reason to like engine braking because not only does it assists your brakes, the noise of the engine reminds you that you're speeding up.

### Camber

The camber of the road is the level to which it slopes left and right on your horizontal plane.

Positive camber, the helpful kind that squashes your rump into the chair, absorbs some of the centrifugal force of cornering and uses it to press the tyres significantly harder into the deck, producing more grip. Negative, or off-camber, does exactly the opposite: steals your cornering ability and spills drinks from the cup-holder. It pays to spot the difference early since failing to notice the latter can really bite you in the bum, especially when the road is bumpy.

**Hot Tip**

> Most roads are crowned in the centre to allow for drainage, which means that your average British road offers positive camber helping you into left-handers, and negative camber working against you in right-handers.
> Satan has a hand in shaping certain B-roads. He cleverly hides off-camber corners behind hills to lure you into his low-grip trap and he loads a sequence of innocent-looking bends with concealed bumps to throw the suspension skywards and spit you off the road.

# 'Satan has a hand in shaping certain B-roads.'

# 13. Road Camber

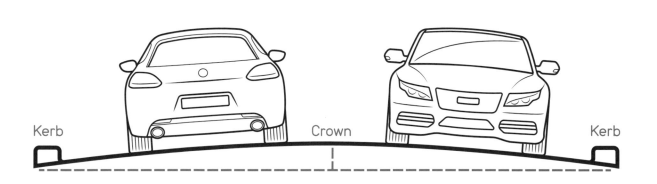

Kerb                                    Crown                                    Kerb

Rubber and dust accumulate on the outside bends to form what are known as 'marbles' – and they are just as slippery underfoot.

**Foreign Bodies**

Oil, mud, wet leaves, gravel, dust and sand can reduce the quality of the surface close to that of ice. Observation techniques are vital to see them coming.

**Big Bailaderos**

The Dark Lord left his mark in Tenerife on the cliff road from Los Bailaderos. It tracks the twisting coastline like a demented Scalextric circuit, relentlessly rising and falling around the crumbling mountain. Car-sized boulders continuously fall off the mountain and explode into the road, so it was finally closed to the public a few years ago. The carcass of carriageway that remains is littered with all manner of dents and hasty repairs, giving it a sort of pummelled surface-of-the-moon render. But the views were 'to die for', so they opened the road for us to film the intro for *Fast & Furious 6*.

*Fast 6* was like the *Jurassic Park* of car movies, and the primordial beasts at our disposal could shake the landscape with the roar of nearly 100,000 horse power.

About 200 cars met their maker during filming, mostly at the hands of the battle tank, which turned cars into confetti. During testing at the ever-grey Chobham proving ground in Surrey, we observed the effect of a glancing blow from the tank tracks on a Vauxhall Corsa. The only recognizable component we could pick from the Tank's teeth was a masticated steering column. Note to self: you touch the tank, you die.

Our skeleton stunt crew of Brits came under the charge of Greg Powell, son of the actor, stuntman and boxer Nosher, whose legendary right hook must have passed on to Greg's right foot, because we never saw the man but for the plume of smoke from his cigar whenever he tore off in a motor.

Joining our gang was the sun-kissed crew from California, who greeted our weather as enthusiastically as a tax bill. Their rap sheet read like a Hollywood roll of honour, from the original *Dukes of Hazzard* to almost everything else since. Everyone felt a lot more comfortable when we shifted from rain-soaked Cold War airfields to the scorching hot coastline of Tenerife.

We measured the route and worked out that you could make two cars fit side-by-side all the way around – just. Looks-wise, the black Dodge Challenger SRT I was driving had one up on the Nissan GT-R running alongside it, and with

'Then something grey loomed into my peripheral, like a scene from a *Jaws* movie.'

470 bhp under my right foot it packed plenty of muscle. Mark Higgins, my oft-time compadre for tandem missions, was wetting his lips with a mixture of excitement and dismay about the Nissan. 'Too much grip.'

With a helicopter chattering overhead recording every ounce of adrenaline for the camera, we set off around the mountain at a speed that was guaranteed to put the Challenger's comfortable suspension to the test.

At the midway point we emerged from an underpass before plunging downhill into a long left-hander slightly off-camber and with a tightening radius. So far the Challenger had been wagging its tail delightedly at my inputs, and the opportunity to punch a spectacular high-speed drift for the camera beckoned.

On the run downhill I slipped past Mark, and with less weight on the molten rear tyres it was easier to flick the old gal sideways. I pitched into an arc that matched the corner as it began to develop, maxed the throttle, and everything felt great as the nose slipped past the cliffside barrier. Then something grey loomed into my peripheral, like a scene from a *Jaws* movie, as a patch of tarmac rose up from the road by nearly a foot.

The Challenger made a real meal of this, and its weight lurched everywhere but onto the tyres. I had to contend with the tightening radius of the bend and worsening camber as I slid outside towards the angry mountain. I just about had it under control, when the outer bead of my rear right tyre popped down into a drainage gulley and pulled the tail wider – and into a freshly fallen … *boulder*.

Mark had the bird's eye view that afforded him a sense of humour.

'Coorrrrrrr, nearly 'ad that,' he chortled, before consoling with: 'Looked mega.' My thoughts precisely. It was only a flesh wound, but the car was out of the picture. And I think it belonged to the producer.

That ordeal might sound like an unlikely extreme, but it demonstrates how the pendulum effect over bumps can combine with bad camber to dictate your destiny. Even at much lower speeds, innocuous-looking features like drains and verges can quickly pull you into trouble, which is why accuracy with the steering is vital.

**Summary**

The road surface is ever-changing, which is one of the things I love most about driving. As much as I admire its majesty, I always observe the revolving patchwork with a cynical glare.

# 03

# The Open
# Road

# Avoiding Accidents

Now that you've spent some quality time with the beast and taken it round a few corners to warm up, let's take it out on the open road.

The one thing we haven't talked about yet, of course, is other cars and the dangers that come with them. It's time to work and play well with others.

## Mind the Gap

Before you get far you're bound to contend with an element of squeezing as you leave the driveway and head into the urban sprawl. Getting to know the width of your car and the design nuances by which you can judge your positioning will save some visits to the paint shop further down the line.

My instructor, Dave Clarke, was a diamond in the rough, and he taught me something that up to that point had had no meaning in my life: patience. Dave's Marlboro-hushed voice coached me in how to set off in a gear without ever touching the throttle, a simple lesson in sensitivity that I've never forgotten. And he egged me on when it was time to 'Give it some rice, boy.'

His advice on reverse parking was equally acute. He would get me to line up alongside the car in front of the space I wanted, reverse back until my head was level with the rear wheel of the other car and then turn into the space. He had me look over my shoulder and use the rear wiper post like a rifle scope to aim for the centre of the empty space, then straighten the wheel, switch to the wing mirror and line up with the kerb as I drove in. A hole-in-one every time.

Fixed features inside the car such as the A and B pillars to the front and sides of the driver's eyeline are a burden in the sense that they create blind spots, but are useful when it comes to formation flying as you observe the movement of other vehicles relative to yourself, and for gauging distances to objects outside of your bubble.

'It's time to work and play well with others.'

In NASCAR, where you have over forty racers fighting wheel-to-wheel for a short stretch of tarmac, the drivers regularly splatter their machines across the track whenever they misjudge their length or width. Every inch of space counts when you're gliding past a concrete wall at 180 mph in a machine that handles and generally feels like a high-speed tumble drier.

Brushing the wall is deemed acceptable up to the point that they classify as a 'sticker rub', a streak of skin-deep scratches that would reduce you to tears if it were your personal ride, but a sign of accuracy in speed world.

Working through the pack of swarming racers is different gravy. On an oval circuit, everybody is slithering around on tyres that are stretching physical boundaries, and a little kiss can turn into a catastrophe. You have to run exceptionally close to one another to benefit from the aerodynamic slipstream – so close in fact that your stomach reverberates from the throb of the engine in the car alongside you, and the windscreen is filled with the bouncing tail of the one in front, pressure-spraying your world with debris and exhaust fumes.

To prepare for this type of excitement I used to enlist my main man Vinny, who would stand patiently at different points around the car in the pit lane, at a top speed of zero mph. It gave me the opportunity to stare directly at his proximity to the car at different points and acclimatize to that distance, then look ahead as if I were driving, and back to Vinny again.

A few of my competitors would snigger, but it was worth it. A dozen or so laps into one race at Rockingham Motor Speedway I entered turn two at 160 mph, and the whole track was blocked by crashed cars. There was a tiny gap between one yellow car and the wall, and everyone ahead of me who tried to make it through was stonking into the concrete. I aimed my front left wheel arch at the tail of the stopped car, rather than focusing on the wall, held on to that view all the way and cleared it.

Whenever I get in a new car I do the same thing. I never asked Clarkson to help because the temptation to run him over would have been overwhelming. If there's nobody around, you can do the same thing with a big cardboard box and practise driving up to it, or line it up alongside to test your width.

The trick with passing through the middle of those evil metal bollards springing up in city centres is to line yourself up centrally using your peripheral view and make several sharp focuses on each bollard before driving through.

## 'Speed, pure and simple.'

Try to spend less time fixated by the obstructions you want to miss and more time focused on the window of space that lies between, then trust your body to handle it. Jonny Wilkinson does exactly the same thing before he magically converts his kick through the posts.

A common fault people develop is to continuously work the wheel for no reason and weave in and out of gaps between parked cars, simply because they failed to fix a course and stick to it. Aiming for a point in the distance makes it much easier to follow a smooth groove, and when you do find a challenging pinch, just kill the speed and allow yourself the time to handle it properly.

## Death by Slow Motion

As you drive into busy urban areas, it's time to start thinking about how to avoid taking out all those cyclists and pedestrians who are going to start running out in front of you. Who are these people? The very young and very old are most likely to be hit and least likely to survive – but just as dangerous are the rising numbers of zombies patrolling the pavement wearing iTuned earmuffs to drown any chance of hearing your approach. And that's before we even get to the drunks tripping over their kebabs in the evenings and at weekends …

We'll look at some of the key triggers for accidents shortly, but I want to start by talking about speed, pure and simple. Doing 45 mph in a 30 stretch increases your chance of an accident by … twenty times! That's more risk than doing the whole of the M4 at 100. Exceeding the speed limit in these areas by just a few mph can mean the difference between life and death. It's all physics and biology.

Experts in the latter are Hollywood stuntmen like Batman's double, Bobby Holland Hanton, who gets run over for a living. 'Car knockdowns', he calls them.

'I'm just glad I'm a bloke,' he explains whilst strapping a knee-pad over the top of his gel-cushioned shorts. 'The stunt women are worse off because they usually end up doubling some glamorous starlet in high heels and a mini-skirt, so they can't pad up.'

Bobby is built like a brick shithouse anyway, but by the time he's finished padding up he looks more like a medieval knight than your average pedestrian. His upper body is contained within another layer of neoprene, and all his pointy bits, like elbows and ankles, are encased in impact-resistant plastic. Once Bobby's final layer of clothing goes over the top he is ready for action.

*When Bobby's not diving over them, he's diving through them (Ford B-MAX commercial).*

This week Bobby is playing the part of Joe Public who drops his mobile phone whilst crossing the street and gets run over when he doubles back in front of a taxi. Bobby eyes up the cab's bonnet and sucks his teeth.

'Yeah, gonna be tricky this one because I'll probably collect the windscreen. What I really want is to get flicked over the top.'

His main concern, however, is the taxi's speed.

'We never, ever do more than 20 miles an hour. Any more than that and you're guaranteed A&E for sure.'

The ideal speed for being hit by a car, he explains, is more like 15–18. Bobby is a trained gymnast, is warmed up and knows the car is coming at him. As the vehicle rolls in Bobby starts crossing the street on cue, turns and just as the car reaches his legs slams himself into the bonnet by imperceptibly tucking his legs up at the last moment. He cartwheels over the roof and lands hard on the tarmac. And doesn't move.

A real paramedic rushes in like an Olympic sprinter.

'Get off the set you idiot, he's just *playing* dead!'

Bobby is fine.

The good news is that pedestrian fatalities like this, which make up nearly a quarter of all road deaths, are the easiest to prevent. As we already know from the section on braking, a car travelling at 30 can stop almost twice as fast as one doing 40. It literally adds seconds to a short leg across town, but it might save a life.

## Not Now, I'm Having an Accident

'I've got better now I don't have to concentrate so much on driving properly.'

*Freshly licensed driver*

So, pedestrians aside, what are the things that we should be looking out for on the open road? Before we do that, let's dispel a myth: they say that most accident *claims* occur within five minutes of home, which is hardly surprising when most journeys start and finish there. Anecdotally, there's an element of truth that concentration might reduce as you near home. Oops, I drove into my house again.

In reality, an insurer judges your risk profile – your likelihood of crashing – by your postcode because it is a convenient method of gauging guilt by association: their spreadsheet looks at a national claim database broken down by postcode and cross-referenced by credit rating. People with bad credit tend to claim more, so if you're unfortunate enough to live in an area where people tap their insurance in order to fund their new plasma screen then, wallop, up goes your premium.

The latest figures from the Department for Transport record a remarkable downward trend in casualties over the past decades, with less than 200,000 injured and 2,000 killed last year. The fall is largely due to vehicle safety design, although insurers point out that the number of accidents is actually *rising*.

A driver's risk profile is shaped like a horseshoe depending on your age. Young drivers account for a quarter of fatal accidents, as well as those leading to life-changing injury. Your likelihood of injury plunges as you get older, owing to the better decision-making skills that come with experience, until your risk spikes again in your sixties as your vision and reflexes dim, and perhaps a few bad habits come home to roost. Passengers make up a hefty proportion of casualties, and 30 per cent of those killed weren't wearing seat belts.

'Oops,
I drove
into my
house
again.'

Although young drivers pose the biggest risk on the roads, however, they also adapt quickly, and their crash rate plunges during their first two years of driving. The vital knowledge that these youngsters acquire is a clue as to what it really means to be a good driver. Their experience of near misses and general observations develop into a broader, fuller view of the task.

That skill is grandly titled 'hazard perception'. It means the ability to analyse the scene and prioritize the aspects or risks that might affect you and sort them by their importance. It means taking a busy road or a jammed street loaded with shoppers and being able to see the wood for the trees. A honed visual strategy and a simple system of car control makes the job a lot easier. Time to learn from a master …

## Chasing Ghosts

North London, 10.22 a.m. – in hot pursuit. For once I'm the passenger, listening to a man in complete control of his vehicle, and the rolling reality in front of it …

Officer Silkglove: '*Vehicle is failing to stop, it's a black BMW, outside weather conditions, it's 5 degrees above zero …* [it feels colder when Silkglove drops the windows so we can hear the road] *… overcast with some light rain, no wind, traffic is moderate, risk at the moment is low given the road surface is dry, HOTEL KILO SIX ZERO LIMA OSCAR JULIET is engaging the suspect. Ident, Officer Silkglove, I am a pursuit commander in a vehicle suitable for a pursuit to take place in an advanced covert car.* [It's an Audi A4 – pimped, but not visibly so.] *I'm a level one-trained driver, and seeking assistance of the DSU* [dog support unit vehicle]. *In the distance the road bends round off to the left-hand side, row of tan brick housing set well back and pavement is clear, rain is spotting, headlights on for adverse conditions … Mirrors, looks like he's going left, left, scanning right, mindful I'm lacking side profile equipment so traffic may not react, gear for speed now is 2 at 19* [mph], *now at decreased speed it increases his options, easier for him to change direction …*'

I shift in my seat and quickly recoil to move away from Silkglove's wing mirror as he rattles off information like an air traffic controller. His running commentary outlines the relevant details of the traffic picture *before* they affect him, forcing him to maintain an active visual search. Verbalizing every decision makes them accountable, if necessary, in a court of law.

# The Who, Where
# and What of Accidents

70 per cent of serious casualties are male,
although on a crash-per-mile driven basis the
gender gap closes.

The busiest traffic results in the highest incidence of crashing, so the rush hours offer notable peaks, especially the later one at 5 p.m. When your boss hands you a bigger-than-expected paycheque, be careful driving home, because when the economy picks up so does traffic density and bent metal. We don't build roads any more.

More crashes occur as the week edges towards Friday and concentration levels drop. Your odds of piling in rise as darkness falls, regardless of day, in particular between midnight and 3 a.m. Teenagers have another spam spike from 5 a.m. because their body clocks work more like a werewolf's.

The most dangerous time of the week, however, is that part of Friday night that blurs into Saturday morning, at 3.18 a.m. to be precise. If you're driving at that time you have your best chance of crashing into something, or being run over when you drop your kebab. The obvious reason why the weekend is so dangerous is that so many people are drunk.

Pay particular attention to schools and pedestrian crossings, especially those littered with parked or stationary cars that block the line of sight between traffic and pedestrians and lead to most of the trouble. That's why wardens go apeshit if you park on the zigzags next to zebra crossings. Driving a door's width away from parked vehicles makes you less likely to hit them when they open, and affords a far better view of these blind hotspots.

Black cars are currently the most popular colour of choice for having an accident, and this year it will most likely be a Seat – unless the driver paints it dayglo yellow.

## 'Silkglove smoothly closes in on his target and snaps the trap shut.'

*'Cyclist ahead, he looks steady, and no wind to upset his balance, and past, mirrors, limit point is matched, speed at 84, steering set, straight before bend left, thumb up into fourth gear, limit still running, mindful of that greasy surface …'*

The sirens wail, and traffic peels away to our left as Silkglove smoothly closes in on his target and snaps the trap shut.

*'He's on his brakes, he's committed to the turn, one coming up behind me is signalling left, nothing inbound, so I can quarter him by moving across into his off side* [Silkglove restricts the suspect from turning right], *now I can fall behind, mirrors, off the brakes, back on the drive, no vision through the apex, applying a constant drive, to a junction left, mirrors, he is braking, in second, gone left left, one inbound, so I'm now signalling, nearside mirrors and brake, left left, slippery, two-wide, caution for gravel, concealed entrance 80 yards, very large vehicles use this route, leaving plenty of room for them, gently on the drive, in second at 30 mph, firming up the drive to a double bend, first left sharp deviation so mirrors full off the drive, 3,000 revs in second, limit point is now clear, opening towards the construction site, suspect is slowing, he's just twigged it's a dead end, moving in close now to reduce his options, he is braking, driver's door is opening. HOTEL KILO SIX ZERO LIMA OSCAR JULIET, suspect is on foot and moving towards the west side of the ACME plant on Leggit Lane. 10.55.'*

A youngish man sprints across the open ground while trying in vain to maintain the benefit of his grey hoodie. Silkglove, still calm as a weatherman, explains that it would be bad form to step out of the car before the dog team arrives. Besides spoiling the scent for the world's finest hunting dogs, you never send them home on an empty stomach.

During the debrief in the canteen at Hendon, it dawned on me that these police were new guard. Their approach to pursuits bore no resemblance to the 'GLF' attitude of the '90s that saw police drivers in a state of tunnel vision, buzzing red lights and doing virtually everything you saw in *The Sweeney* to keep up with the suspect. Yes, we drove quite fast, but speed was largely irrelevant, and Silkglove never lost control of the situation or endangered anyone.

When I asked the rest of the Hendon driving team about their thoughts on, dare I say it, some of the outdated police methods like push–pull steering, I wasn't prepared for their response. Most of them, though not all, said they would 'drop it tomorrow'. Suffice to say that a lively debate ensued.

## 'He was Yoda with a badge.'

Driving with a commentary like that was the ultimate, black-belted demonstration of awareness and anticipation. Beneath Silkglove's swan-gliding-over-water patter, the internal cogs of his supreme system of awareness were spinning like Catherine wheels as he acquired, prioritized and addressed key information. If he could have planned my life for me up to that point, I would never have stepped in a dog turd or eaten a dodgy pizza. He was Yoda with a badge. His ability to read every situation before we arrived was phenomenal, and I can't remember a smoother journey. He passed the 'glass of water test' and then some. Mind you, this was no ordinary driver. Silkglove was a thirty-year veteran, and nobody was slipping straight into those loafers fresh out of a multiple-choice questionnaire, least of all me.

You can always find someone else to blame if you end up having a shunt, but all crashes are avoidable. Every near miss or hot flush when something takes you by surprise is a signal that you missed something. It pays to catalogue bad experiences and dwell on them, so that you can recognize the warning signs much earlier in the future.

I begin every journey by preparing for the worst and conduct myself accordingly. Hardening a few prejudices is really just honing your survival instincts. As sure as eggs are eggs, the man in the battle-scarred white van won't check his mirrors as you squeeze past – though, contrary to what Jeremy Clarkson seems to believe, not all Audi drivers are tossers. I know this because *I* drive one. (Oh… *now* I get it …)

I take it personally if someone else's bad driving interferes with my perfect execution because I should have seen it coming and read a vehicle's body language to see what it might do next. For example, a car lurking slightly off-centre in its lane means the driver can't gauge the width of his car or is thinking of turning but hasn't yet lit the indicator. Side-to-side motion is easy for the eye to detect, and if a car wanders all over the place, the driver is probably either drunk or plain awful. Harder to detect, and more dangerous, is movement forward and back. The image of a car slowing ahead just grows or shrinks slightly. Viewed from a distance of around ten car lengths, a change in proximity of one or two lengths is barely noticeable, a minor design flaw in the Mark 1 eyeball, of which more later. When someone slams on the brakes in front of you, the sensible gap you maintained up until that point should enable you to stop gradually in order to give the poor bugger behind a chance to recognize what is happening, and make it less likely that he will give your rear end a good stuffing.

Many drivers are oblivious to what takes place behind them and miss out on a rich palette of disaster trailing in their wake. On one occasion in Pittsburgh I stopped for a junction at the bottom of a hill with a truck coming up behind. It wasn't slowing, so I checked the light was still red, looked behind and saw the big trailer was jack-knifed and inbound. I drove up onto the kerb to give it space and avoided being flattened.

Clairvoyance came in handy when I worked in Johannesburg on the *Top Gear Live* show where we had a convoy of red Audis taking us to the venue. They drove too fast and too close for my liking, a military convoy but without the war or the training. After my driver conceded that his hometown was actually Cape Town, I rented a car for the remainder of my stay. Two days later I drove past the Audi packet, with the fearless leader firmly embedded into the sharp end of a flat-bed trailer and the two sidekicks rammed up each other's exhausts like some sort of insect incest.

### Summary

There are drivers who cause accidents, those who share other people's and those who avoid them. Good drivers learn to adapt to an imperfect world by accommodating and anticipating other people's mistakes until it becomes a habit. As Aristotle said, 'We are what we repeatedly do. Excellence, then, is not an act, but a habit.' If you can learn from Officer Silkglove, you will become the master of your fate – unlike these unfortunate 'ultimate insurance fails':

'Excellence, then, is not an act, but a habit.'

'*Coming home I drove into the wrong house and collided with a tree I don't have.*'

'*I started to slow down, but the traffic was more stationary than I thought.*'

'*I saw a slow-moving, sad-faced old gentleman as he bounced off the roof of my car.*'

'*I was backing my car out of the driveway in the usual manner, when it was struck by the other car in the same place it had been struck several times before.*'

'*The pedestrian ran for the pavement, but I got him.*'

# Channel Your
# Inner Jedi Master

## 1. Observe

Use your vision to create a 360-degree rolling map of the environment: the dog on the lead, the car speeding towards a side road, tiny feet visible behind a parked car, a sharp curve ahead …

Listen to the sound of the engine, the chirp of a tyre, the protest of a gear change, and the sound of children breaking up from school and spilling onto the pavement.

With your hands, feel the weight of the steering, how much it's turning and responding, looking for any tell-tale vibration from a loose wheel or under-inflated tyre.

Hear what your backside is telling you: this precision instrument has guided me through more situations that I can remember. The more elegantly you balance the car and feel it hug the road, the more eloquently your rump will squeak, I mean speak, to you.

Trust and develop your gut feeling.

## 2. Interpret

Filter the information coming in by ignoring the irrelevant and prioritizing the key hazards and road features along your path. The monkey smoking a pipe wearing pink pyjamas in the back of that Mercedes as you approach a traffic light, however fascinating, is less relevant than the lights turning red …

Use your imagination to predict the paths and intentions of everyone and everything in sight. By projecting potential scenarios onto the scene, and creatively considering what might be around the corner, you won't be surprised by the guy picking his nose on the wrong side of the road.

## 3. Act

Does the scenario you encounter actually require you to do something? If so, formulate an appropriate plan of action. Nothing too fancy. Calmly deploy a reasonable response while maintaining oversight of the bigger picture as it evolves with you. And continue to cycle the information stages every step of the way.

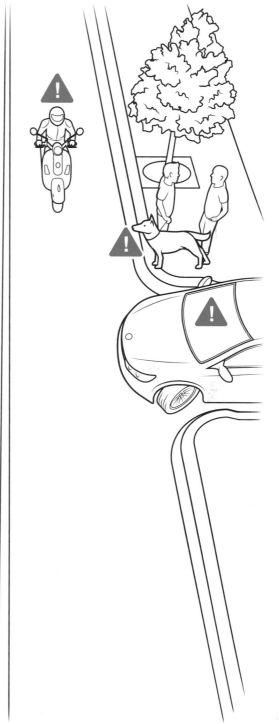

# Junctions

You've secretly been waiting for this section all along. Forget the thrill of conquering a corner or taking on a snowdrift, let's talk about rights of passage.

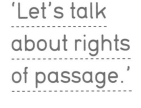

'Let's talk about rights of passage.'

For starters, the majority of car-on-car collisions occur at junctions and for one single reason: failure to look properly, while a combination of converging speeds and optical illusions conspire to unseat you. Junctions lurk everywhere in all shapes and disguises, from the bog-standard Mr T junction to their more effervescent cousins in the form of roundabouts and the insane crossing points across major trunk roads. Vanquish them with your all-seeing eye …

As you run through town you should become accustomed to looking along the length of the car to the fore and aft using regular scanning and observation. The T-junction throws up issues in the lateral plane, and with it comes new blind spots, while the oblique angles to opposing traffic make it harder to judge their approach speeds.

But that's nothing compared to leaving a junction during rush hour and making for the far side of the road. As you inch out of your itsy-bitsy tributary, you've got to establish eye contact with somebody who might be stupid enough to let you out, because everyone crossing your path will pretend that you don't exist.

Sweet old ladies, fresh from rescuing stray cats, whiten their knuckles and stare ahead with grim determination if you dare to pop out of your hole and try to join their ill-tempered crawl. They have right of way, and never shall they yield.

The art of cold-shouldering will serve you well when it's your turn to punish potential joiners. But first you have to make it out alive, and to do this you have to perfect the halfway house manoeuvre: that is, creeping forward with the tacit approval of incoming traffic until, surely for the love of God, somebody will play ball with you.

The key to defeating the cold shoulder is to point your melon in the direction of other drivers so that they realize you mean business. Humans find it hard to resist looking at another face, regardless how ugly, and, once engaged, you quickly close the deal with an open-palmed salute and a Colgate smile. Then pull out.

Assume nothing. Make sure you have a reasonably sized gap and delicately ease out while engaging with your fellow protagonists. On reaching the halfway mark, your odds of getting to the far side greatly improve as people realize you have the minerals to join their team.

## Bogey at Seven O'clock

In lighter traffic you have to be even more careful because speeds and expectations are higher. This is when the 'look left, look right, look left, whoah, is that Cameron Diaz behind the wheel of that jeep, pull out and crunch into the unnoticed car from the right' catches drivers out.

The Diaz moment is what psychologists refer to as an 'elongated fixation', which is as naughty as it sounds. Something in the scene draws your attention for longer than it should, you lose track of the time that has passed since you scanned each hemisphere, and it leaves you vulnerable.

Besides thinking faster and looking more often to keep your information live, there are certain skills that improve your odds. When vision is restricted you can often use reflections in shop windows to see other cars approaching, or look through the windows of parked cars to see what's behind. For tricky exits onto more open roads you can wind the window down and listen for road noise. That noise can even give you an impression of the vehicle's speed.

Ditto, when you're on the main road it helps to keep an eye out for side roads using telltales such as telegraph poles and street lights that suggest a side entrance, or scanning through open hedgerows for approaching vehicles. Expect people to come out blind from recessed entrances and position away towards the road centre for a better view. Again, reflections help, as do shadows from vehicles hidden behind walls.

Junctions

# 16. Hazard Perception

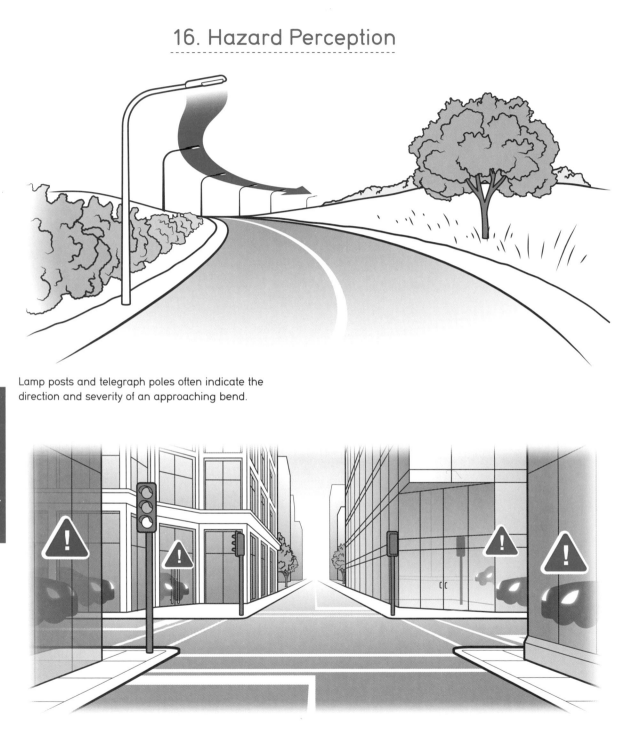

Lamp posts and telegraph poles often indicate the
direction and severity of an approaching bend.

Reflections, shadows and sounds provide reliable clues
for detecting the movement of other cars.

## Junction Etiquette

As you approach a junction, whether you're leaving or joining the road, you check your mirror and position yourself towards the side of the road that tells everyone around you the direction in which you're turning: right side to turn right and vice versa. That way, nobody will be enticed to squeeze up your inside or try to overtake (see 'Overtaking', page 135).

Here's the biggest piece of advice for pulling up at a junction and preparing to cross traffic: keep the steering wheel straight with your foot on the brakes until you pull out. Why?

Getting rear-ended at a junction is as common as flatulence at a vegan BBQ. If your wheels are turned when you get punted from behind, it will launch you head-on into opposing traffic for an additional, much nastier, shunt. If there's a car in front, leave enough gap to it so that its rear wheels are visible on the tarmac. There are various reasons I like this drill, so take your pick.

Whether you're just driving locally or around the streets of Johannesburg, the car-jacking capital of the world, maintaining a gap in front of you means keeping your options open so that you can move if you have to. At night it pays to creep slowly up to traffic lights so you spend less time stationary: a moving target is less attractive.

'Karma works both ways.'

If the car in front breaks down or selects reverse by mistake, you can get around it.

In busy urban areas leaving a gap helps pedestrians to cross. You were once a pedestrian, so you should sympathize with this terrible affliction, and by clearing them away from the junction it will afford you a better view when you come to pull out. Karma works both ways.

## Roundabouts

How would you explain a roundabout to a Martian? Easy, you might say, simply mirror, signal and give way to traffic already on the roundabout, then choose a lane that matches the hemisphere from which you plan to depart.

'What about trucks?' says the Martian.

Oh those. Trucks tend to run the outside lane regardless of the situation because it gives them an easier turning arc and is a notable reason for 'conflict' over perceived rights of way when it comes to the exit. They should indicate their

Winding up to 200 mph during the Le Mans 24 Hours in 2011 aboard the RML Honda HPD Prototype.

## 'Vous n'avez pas la priorité.'

intention, but don't count on it. The beauty is that, if you get cut off or make a hash of things, just go for another lap like Chevy Chase in *European Vacation*.

'The French?'

Until recently the garlic brigade gave priority to vehicles *entering* a roundabout under the arcane *priorité à droite* rule, where traffic gives way to the right. Given that the French drive on the right side of the road, you would have expected them to give way to the left, but they don't, giving rise to the farcical situation of drivers already on a roundabout yielding to inbound dive-bombers.

That was recently overturned, unofficially, and cars entering French roundabouts now *cèdent le passage*, the same as the Brits, most of the time. The sign *Vous n'avez pas la priorité* means it's English rules, but if there are no signs or one of these bad boys ⚠ ◈ then you can expect a wide-eyed Frog to come speeding towards you, waving a baguette and flashing his lights to warn you that he is claiming right of way – not to invite you to pull out, as in England.

'C'est la guerre!'

Our American brothers have vast swathes of big country to drive through, and everybody spends considerably longer driving than in Europe. This is reflected in the accident toll, which is nearly three times higher than the UK. Half of these wrecks happen at intersections along with the majority of pedestrian fatalities.

If you try crossing one make sure to tighten your shoelaces. It's a long haul to cover ten lanes of traffic that never quite stops moving. In the States they have a magic law that allows you to turn right on a red light if there's no incoming traffic, but it's a gauntlet if you're on foot.

The quaint British roundabout is coming to the rescue and rolling out nationwide. After they were introduced in Maine, fatalities were cut by 90 per cent. The very complexity of roundabouts and the way they force you to interact with other drivers, to make eye contact with a fellow human being even, is what makes them work.

## Rural Roads

As you leave town, the speed rises, and the road starts twisting up hill and down dale. Single carriageways like this and the rest of the 'rural' road network are where 80 per cent of *driver* deaths occur.

Mention 'dangerous road' and I picture Indiana Jones dangling from the door of a runaway truck on some Amazonian mountain, rather than the passage from Knutsford on the A537. Scottish roads are amongst the most dangerous in Europe, as well as the most beautiful.

It is here that we see the highest number of 'single-vehicle accidents' caused by folks losing it on sharp corners all by themselves, or by misjudging an overtake. The heady cocktail of turnings, crossroads, roundabouts and two-way traffic fuels too many opportunities to cross the path of another vehicle.

These roads cross the heart of the countryside and entail all the wildlife that goes with it. Trees kill about 130 people a year in the UK alone. You really don't want to hit one. Lamp posts, telegraph poles and other permanent objects like bridges will beat you in a game of slaps every time. A friend of mine, a stuntman, drove into a tree head-on at 12 mph to see what it felt like. He told me he regretted doing it. Apparently it hurt more than doing a car hit at 45.

One in five young drivers will crash during their first year, mostly on these so-called minor roads. Cornering is handled elsewhere, or skidding for those who never read the label. For now let's focus on overtaking.

# 'As you leave town,
the speed rises.'

3.3

# Overtaking

## Before Gary Powell had finished his question about the new Bond movie I'd already said 'yes' twice. Gary was a 007 veteran.

In *The World Is Not Enough*, he perfected flipping the Q speedboat on the Thames by jumping a smaller vessel – wait for it – on to dry land.

'At that speed, water's harder than concrete, basically …'

He also became inseparable from 'his' T-55 tank in *Goldeneye*, powersliding it around the streets of Moscow, through walls, and anything else that got in the way. And you should see him drive a car.

Gary was the stunt coordinator for *Quantum of Solace*, which picked up where *Casino Royale* left off. The script had a dark side to it. Bond's girl had been murdered at the end of *Casino*, and *Quantum* was about revenge. Gary was assembling a team of experts for what was being billed as the biggest opening sequence in Bond film history, with a visceral car chase followed by a bloody rooftop pursuit. The locations, vehicles and stunt crew were handpicked to guarantee action, and the driving needed to put audiences on the edge of their seats. Which is where I came in.

The first stop was the Riva resort overlooking Lake Garda, itself overshadowed by the imposing and beautiful Dolomite Mountains. The stunt team took a guided tour of the Gardesana Road, which rose from Riva and wound its way around the mountainside, punching straight through it in places to form the most spectacular tunnels and galleries that overlooked the restless pool of water below. We entered the mountain and crossed a gingerbread bridge that was wide enough for a horse and cart. It spanned a yawning abyss over a stream that trickled its way down to the lake. The road opened out into a cavern with a low bulging ceiling that could work metal like a pummel stone. Gary's assistant pointed this out as a potential overtaking spot …

My first call every morning was at 5.45 with the costume and make-up department for forty-five minutes of hair bashing and metamorphosing. I climbed

Doubling James Bond during the filming of *Quantum of Solace* in 2008 – and treating the Aston Martin DBS with less respect than it deserved.

into a Tom Ford suit that was customized for Daniel Craig and donned the Omega Seamaster. I remember thinking I had a lot to live up to. Awaiting us down on set were no fewer than twelve Aston Martin DBS cars for Bond, worth £160K apiece, as well as six Alfas and a fleet of 'ND' (nondescript) background cars.

Time for one last espresso: it was time to burn rubber.

Gary conducted the 'stunties' with the tip of his radio antenna. 'Ben, jump in the Aston. We're doing the high-speed stuff first, so make sure you're 'appy wiv it.' With that, the DBS became my office. A 200 mph workstation.

The DBS was one of the most sophisticated machines on the market, perhaps the best front-engine sports car ever built. Its graceful curves kept its brute performance covert; beneath the mature exterior was a recalcitrant wild child. It boasted 6 litres of devilish horsepower, totalling over 500 bhp. The V12 engine responded to every millimetre of movement in the throttle, like an F1 car. It howled on full song but quietened to a whispering burble at low revs. The ceramic brakes clamped like vices, but with such sensitivity that you could modulate them at the limit of grip from its fat tyres.

There was scarcely any visible difference between the DB9 and the DBS, yet the slightly lowered, delicately enhanced suspension turned the girl next door into a supermodel. Beneath her hemline, the heightened technology of the braking and traction control systems was streets ahead. Where most anti-skid systems prevented the tyre from getting anywhere near to locking during braking, the Aston's onboard computer took it to the limit several times a second, and you sensed its work underfoot.

I selected the largely unmodified 'Car 5', running standard tyres for maximum grip and outright speed. I climbed aboard and plugged in the crystal key to spark the engine into life. The words *power*, *beauty*, *soul* were thus illuminated on the dashboard.

I pulled onto the main road and joined the convoy en route to the first set-up of the day. To check the traction was disabled I slammed the accelerator and steered right, laying two fat stripes of rubber across the pristine tarmac as I headed towards the Limone tunnel. The Italian *polizia* in their pretty blue and red striped uniforms tugged at their crotches and cheered. The reverberating drumbeat of the DBS zapping through the wide-columned tunnel was majestic.

'The words *power, beauty, soul* were thus illuminated on the dashboard.'

We gathered in a lay-by overlooking a coiling stretch of road that plunged downwards, following the curvature of the mountain. Each Alfa contained a driver and a passenger, and they would be leaning out of their windows to fire automatic weapons in my direction. Jagged rocks bordered the nearside while a thin line of Italian mortar stood between the road and a vertical fall into the bottomless lake on the right. There was no room to deviate either way, no quarter given for error.

At a normal driving speed, the curves were sharp enough for the rocky bluffs to block the view of the road ahead. We would be racing at full pelt through a convoy of trucks, box vans and NDs spread around every turn while timing our run for a near miss with traffic coming the other way. That meant leaving each move deliberately late, the last thing you would ever do in the real world.

Without line of sight, it was challenging to gauge the timing and movement of other vehicles in order to dodge between them and slide into a gap when you needed to.

A big skip truck would gallop uphill at 50 mph minimum. I would lead the convoy of three Alfas downhill and aim to pass the first box van after the apex of the second bend, then sneak into a gap between the traffic as the truck swiped by.

In order for the near miss to look real, it had to *be* real. There was no CGI faking the stunts in a Bond movie.

Gary brought us in close. 'Ben, whatever you do, you need to get back into the right-hand lane before the truck comes through – or else you're wearing it.'

As with any overtaking move, timing was critical. You practise the same thing every day walking past people on the street. They just weigh less.

Rounding the second corner too late would mean facing the skip dead ahead with the box truck blocking my escape to the right. Arriving early rendered the shot useless, and during the timing runs I found my foot creeping onto the accelerator whenever I disappeared behind the coves and lost vision. I had to hold back and count time, then the sequence clicked.

Rowley, a seasoned veteran, was behind the wheel of the skip truck, which gave me the confidence to go head to head with it, because he would do the same thing every time. But pity the Alfas. They had to find their own space between the traffic. And with them on my tail I couldn't just pull the ripcord and

'In order for the near miss to look real, it had to *be* real.'

'I zapped the throttle and swerved.'

jam on the brakes if I mistimed the run without compromising their space. We were in this together.

I lined up next to a boulder with a face in it, my start marker, with the Alfas behind.

'Action, Action, ACTION!'

I feathered the Aston away to keep the Alfa group in tow, tight as a trailer.

We moved down the lakeside at a reasonable speed, and I counted the beats with Gary running a commentary from his cliffside balcony. I lined up behind the first car, jinked left and overtook it, ducked back in behind a van, passed it on the left and stayed on the wrong side of the road for the agonizing length of time it took to round the blind bluff and start passing the box truck.

I cleared its front as the skip truck appeared large as life in my windscreen. The top arm snagged the overhanging rocks above the road, shaking the rig and spewing shards of rocks and dust as it bowled towards me.

I zapped the throttle and swerved to the right to get out of its way. It passed my driver's side. With no door to deflect it, the dust from its wheels blew straight into the Aston. I surged down the hill until I was out of shot and then exhaled.

We made a few more runs like that and increased the speed. Each pass teased my nerve as I got as close to the truck as possible before swerving. When my retinas became the size of soap dishes, that was my cue to break off. Staying jacked was the best way to stay focused and instinctive, which was vital for self-preservation. Jackie Chan put it this way: 'The worst thing isn't doing a stunt or not doing a stunt, but half doing a stunt.'

Rowley managed to keep his foot hard on the throttle until he passed the Alfas. He was on the mark every time.

'Nice one, Rowley,' Gary said over the radio. 'Ben, you don't want to get any closer than that from where I'm watching, I tell ya.'

The constant highs and lows were mentally draining, and we maintained a sense of constant alert. With so many vehicles it was a case of keeping everyone in the zone.

We went over our timings and walked the route over and again. One of the Alfas had spewed oil precisely where I was dodging the truck, so we cleaned it up as best we could and cracked on. The surface change would delay my rate of turn by two seconds, so I factored this in for the next run. I braked a tad earlier, and the

Aston slewed predictably across the wet surface in front of the truck, the rear end nipping out of the way as we crossed. It was the kind of high-octane driving I had always wanted to do.

Late in the day we were resetting the cars, and I was making a three-point turn under the watchful eye of the first assistant director, Terry Madden. He was effectively the producer's quarterback. You could be filming a movie about nocturnal animals and his wizened face would still be tanned from the previous shoot. As I nosed up to the cliff edge he sprang into action with a twinkle in his eye,

'That's far enough you, just wait there.'

The return up the mountain looked clear to me, and he clocked my expression.

'There's been more fatalities during resets than all the stunts in this business put together.'

It was easy to forget that the return journey, despite being at half pace, bore the closest resemblance to the haphazardness of real life, where there are no practice runs or people with radios to tell you when to abort the run.

Overtaking is probably the riskiest and most complicated manoeuvre we undertake on the road. Perhaps that's why your driving instructor never taught you how to do it.

As a racing driver, there's nothing worse than listening to armchair heroes bang on about the lack of overtaking in a motor race. The last thing any driver wants to do is sit behind a slower car and miss the opportunity to squirt champagne in their eye. However, overtaking is one area where you may not live to regret a mistake because once you commit to a move it can be difficult to unravel yourself when things go pear-shaped.

For me the first consideration regarding a potential overtake is: can I be bothered? If the traffic level is high, then it's pointless risking life and limb just for the opportunity to read a new number plate.

If the answer to the first question is yes, then I need to come up with a plan that passes muster with the part of me that doesn't want to become an organ donor. That plan requires having the clear space and enough speed to pull off the move: simple enough, but it's the detail in arriving at that conclusion that requires your attention. These preliminary checks involve looking near, far and wide for obvious reasons *not* to overtake.

'The riskiest and most complicated manoeuvre we undertake on the road.'

'Those vehicles will open and close like logs floating down a river.'

## Space

You can usually get a better view of what lies ahead by favouring the centre of the road next to the white line. However, if the road curves away then you can see further by moving to the inside line and looking past the passenger side of the car ahead. If you're following something big always check both sides anyway to clock what you're getting yourself into.

## Body Language

Check if the target car looks erratic, lost … or is slowing and might be about to turn off at a junction, which is the number one cause of overtaking accidents.

These crashes often involve younger drivers failing to anticipate when someone Is about to make a turn, and older drivers making dodgy turns without signalling. There will be plenty of time to argue the latter point in the back of the ambulance or at the pearly gates if this was your final sin. Or you could read the situation better.

If you discover a train of cars ahead of you, the gaps between those vehicles will open and close like logs floating down a river. Overtaking one car may be futile in these conditions anyway, but if you go for it you need to be doubly accurate with your observations to ensure that the inviting space you're relying on will be there when you arrive. It really antagonizes other drivers when you force your way into a tiny gap, so don't expect them to offer you a steak dinner when they pull up alongside you at the next traffic light.

The primary method that racers use to predict traffic flow is by constantly judging their 'delta' speed – the divergence in speed between vehicles. If the car in front of you has a high delta of say 40 mph closure on the traffic ahead, it probably means he is about to overtake, close the gap or have an almighty accident.

## Approaching Cars: the Second Most Likely Cause of Accidents

If a car seems to be far enough away that it won't affect you, keep tracking its progress because speed is difficult to measure when you're facing an approaching target down the barrel. Establish its speed in the context of background features that help to measure distance or do a double take to help your brain process the space it covered in that time.

If there's a corner in the distance, assess its severity to predict the exit speeds of cars that *might* potentially emerge from it during your move. Rehearse this imaginary relationship continuously throughout the overtake because at some point the ghost car will become a real one, and it should come as no surprise.

---

**Hot Tip**

> **When you're waiting for an approaching car to clear, the point where it will converge with the target vehicle is predetermined. By measuring their rate of closure you can anticipate this point and build your acceleration in advance of your move.**

---

Cast your eyes to the furthest point you can see ahead to ensure you have a comfortable gap in which to make your pass before the next corner, obstacle or approaching traffic. The common mistake people make is to misjudge the amount of time they have to spend on the wrong side of the road. It's better to imagine the single vehicle you want to overtake as a row of parked cars because the effect is the same.

With a target travelling at 50 mph and you passing at 55, it will take 50 metres to get past it. That's ten parked cars. At 65 you can clear the same vehicle in a little over three car lengths – the smaller the difference in speeds, the longer the move takes.

## General Observations

Trust nothing that you can't see is clear: blind bends, brows over hills and undulations that can hide a car.

Beware any junctions or hidden entrances along your proposed trajectory, because cars can and will emerge from them without expecting to see you on *their side* of the road. These encounters make number five on the list of greatest hits.

Check for legal restrictions that forbid overtaking such as solid or double lines and other signs which, though not legally binding, might prove useful in the near future: railway crossings, traffic lights, single-lane tunnels, minefields and junctions(!).

'At some point the ghost car will become a real one.'

# 16. Overtaking Line

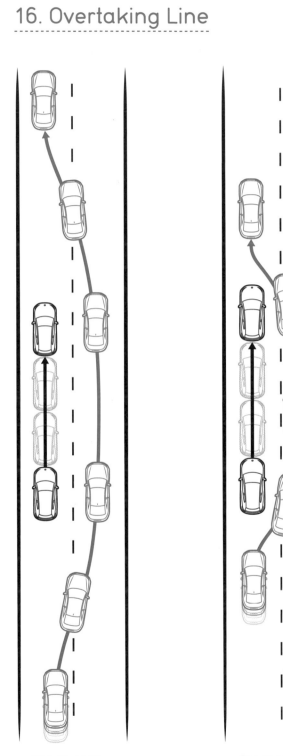

The Right Way                    The Wrong Way

Make sure the road conditions are appropriate: flooding or snow on the far side of the road might cause a problem. And finally, trust your gut feeling. If it doesn't feel right it probably isn't.

## Speed, Momentum and Positioning

On closing behind a slower-moving vehicle, you analyse the situation from a distance to see if the move is on. The earlier you slow down the better because it gives you time to think while preserving your approach speed. Momentum is absolutely key to making a clean pass because it minimizes the amount of time you spend on the wrong side of the road with your foot to the carpet.

If you pull up to the target's bumper you will have to slow right down to its speed and subsequently overtake by gunning it from a standing start, albeit a mobile one, greatly reducing your acceleration power.

In situations where you need to be patient, it's best to hang back about three car lengths and match the target's speed from there. There's no point positioning yourself on its exhaust pipe because this limits your field of view and prevents you from rolling into the pass. This is especially true when following something big like a truck, when all you can see is 'Wide Load' through a cloud of diesel.

'Hang back about three car lengths and match the target's speed.'

# 17. Reasons not to Overtake

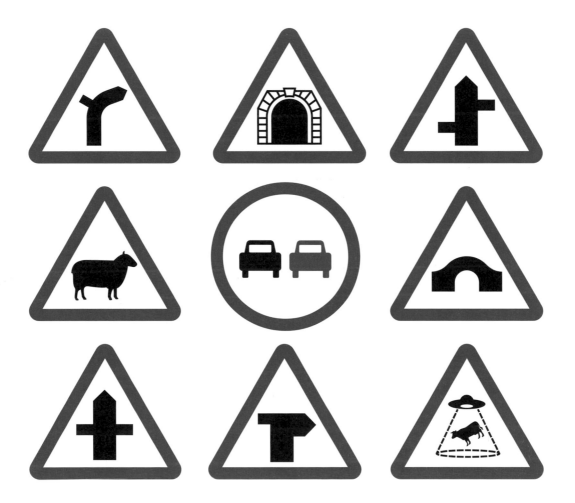

## Final Checks

Select your best gear for power, ideally one that won't run out of guts halfway through the move and require a rushed, easily bungled gear change. Are you still sure that your car could rip the skin off a rice pudding at this speed and get the job done within the identified space? Check.

Mirrors: are you about to be overtaken? No.

Sanity check: if you need to, you can ease onto the other side of the road to expand your viewpoint to double check that the space ahead is clear before you commit to overlapping the target, or duck back to your side if you change your mind. Clear.

Go!

Be smooth, be decisive, flick your indicator and make your move.

Roll in: accelerate into the move to build momentum and boost you past the other car, and if you need to abort for any reason you still can before you overlap it.

Commit: the move is on, and you drive past the other car. Your focus is the furthest point ahead in search of an oncoming vehicle as well as the gap you're aiming for. Keep the target in your peripheral vision, give it plenty of room and track your rate of progress until you're sure you're fully clear of it, then ease back to your side of the road.

---

**Common Mistakes**

> *Side-swiping* the car you're overtaking or clipping its nose is a common mistake. Linked to a bad judgement call followed by an over-reaction to an approaching car or corner, common sense leaves the room and people just cut across, hoping for the best. *Whack.*

> If you clip the nose of another car on re-entry, the combination of your steering input with the impact on your rear wheel will likely cause your rotation. Be accurate from start to finish.

---

*Losing control* during the overtake. Most roads are crowned in the middle, and as you swing across it, the effect can cause the suspension to go light and destabilize. Combining that with rough steering or harsh acceleration can lead to a dangerous loss of control. This is naturally exacerbated by wet weather or a curve.

---

**Hot Tips**

> Stay smooth and steady – rolling into the move should alleviate the excesses of a lead foot on the loud pedal or being hung out to dry on the wrong side of the road. With a front-wheel-drive-car there can be considerable torque steer under heavy acceleration, particularly in powerful hatches, which literally pulls the wheel from your grasp and sends the car off course. Equally, with a rear-wheel-drive, heavy acceleration can break traction when you really don't want it to.

> *Panic.* I mean, don't panic. Keep calm and floor it.
> If you find yourself getting well and truly hung out to dry, on the wrong side of the road with another car coming at you, then you need to make a judgement call. If you're most of the way past, and still passing, then floor it to get the job done. Otherwise you need to abort your run by braking sensibly and returning to your side.

> Cover the horn as you overtake. If the target hasn't seen you and creeps over, let him feel your presence.

---

The problem with braking can be that the person you're overtaking is actually a human being and has been watching your antics closely all along. On seeing the approaching tractor that you missed, he or she might apply the anchors at the same time as you do, leaving you no room to return. I wish you the best of luck.

Assuming that you all survive, a sharp burst of adrenaline will raise your endorphins for twenty minutes or more, but don't be fooled into developing a superhero complex. This was a big mistake, so be sure to log the experience and visualize where you went wrong.

**Hot Tips**

> Practise using vision, space and momentum to overtake on dual carriageways or highways without the worries of oncoming traffic. Gauge your machine's performance at different speeds in different gears and develop your feel for timing.

> Boring but important: hatch marks, the diagonal stripes between two white lines, mean you can't cross them when their white border lines are solid unless it's an emergency. However, you can legally overtake when the lines are broken, and most drivers are unaware of this.

> Dotted white lines on your side obviously permit overtaking – when the broken centre lines grow longer and the gaps between them shorter, it indicates a hazard up ahead.

*'Panic.* I mean,

don't panic.'

# Dual Carriageways

## For some, this is the moment they have feared since day one.

But with a little forward planning and gamesmanship you can enter the gateways to the world with confidence.

On the whole, dual carriageways and multi-lane highways are just like motorways, but without any of the restrictions. In one moment it can be a big, three-lane carriageway that looks and sounds like a motorway, and the next moment it can run into a roundabout, or a traffic light, or a central reservation with a horse on it – some even have public footpaths running over them.

For me the A38 has it all. There are chicanes cutting through forests, crossroads on the tops of blind crests and exposed bridges with enough wind sheer to launch an armada of sailing ships.

To my knowledge it is the only dual carriageway that invites you to stop at a 'dusk till dawn' service station where leaving is a choice between life or death. After fuelling up and consuming a sordid Ginsters pie, your stomach churns afresh when you realize that returning to the A38 involves crossing a high-speed filter lane before you even reach the carriageway bit.

You creep up to the starting position on the slipway and hold her steady on the incline, your side profile open to a full broadside if your left foot whimpers on the clutch, and prepare to gun it. Nobody belting along at 80 even knows you're there with your beady little eyes scanning the traffic for an open window as nervously as the rabbit doing his business in the woods alongside the big brown bear. Finally, you take courage and let slip the cogs of war.

Running southbound, the A38 swoops downhill then bottoms out before arching right and back up. The Armco crash barrier gradually fades out to the left of your peripheral view, and at night there's a tendency to follow it. It's a trap!

If you've started to fall for it the realization comes too late as you discover yourself straddling a grass divider and hoping for a gravity-defying return to the black stuff. Hidden in the depression to the left is a tight junction, and yet another cursed petrol station. I recently drove past it, and for the second time in as many years I saw a car parked beside the petrol pump, on its roof.

The signpost is king when it comes to getting the jump on potential hotspots. When visible, carriageways are lined with reflective studs that should point you in the right direction: white studs mark the middle of the road or the lane dividers, red studs mark the outer edge, amber the inner, with green for lay-bys and slip roads.

'Just like motorways, but without any of the restrictions ...'

------------------------------------

# Motorways

In 1973 the Arab oil cartel OAPEC stopped supplying oil to the United States, and President Nixon was faced with an energy crisis that slapped every American across the face and threatened to bring the economy to its knees.

'The safer you feel, the dumber you drive.'

Amongst other measures, Nixon enacted an emergency 55 mph speed limit for one year to improve fuel efficiency. As with all recessions and petrol-price hikes, people drove less and had fewer accidents. Safety campaigners misused the information to make the double nickel law last another *twenty-two years*.

In 1995 Congress bent to public opinion and repealed the speed limit to a cacophony of apocalyptic predictions from the safety lobby: 'History will never forgive Congress for this assault on the sanctity of human life.' But, gee whizz – the speeds went up and the highways became *safer*. The increase in the speed limit saved 200 million man hours and $23 billion each year.

Why? Because the safer you feel, the dumber you drive.

In America each state varies, but the majority now operate a 70/75 mph limit on highways, with one glorious stretch of 85 in Texas. Back in England we have as much control over our laws as we do over the sands blowing in from the Sahara. Combined with toxic gases arriving from Northern Europe, our air quality has landed us in trouble with the European Union and led our government to reduce speed limits in 'affected areas' to 60 mph. Common sense and safety are no match for good old-fashioned politics.

But I digress … because the point regarding motorways is that they are *by far* the safest places to travel. Less than 6 per cent of fatalities occur here. The greatest danger you face on highways is dying of boredom. The UK's Highways Agency, a self-appointed lawmaker, has a lot to answer for. Its mind-bending phrase to explain the phenomenon of permanent roadworks is 'traffic calming'. It *isn't* calming. Deep-sea divers experience lower blood pressure than anybody

'I sleep better thinking there's a former F-16 pilot at the helm.'

entering the coned forests of a three-lane highway and slowing to 50 for a workerless workzone.

Perhaps it's no surprise, then, that teaching motorway driving ranks lower with driving instructors than spending an afternoon with an incontinent student after a ferocious tandoori. It isn't even covered by the driving test. Consequently, newly badged drivers are terrified of the safest roads in the country and avoid them as much as possible. They shouldn't, because motorway driving is phenomenally easy. And despite the high speed and volume of traffic hammering up and down the motorway, it is by far the safest way to get from A to B.

I use the word 'safe' with the guarded scepticism I hold for anybody preaching the safety of airline travel. When Dustin Hoffman refused to board the plane in *Rain Man,* I fully sympathized with his risk assessment because I don't like the thought of my person being reduced to a crater either. I don't like the fact that certain airline companies view the process as so routine that their pilots are denied a little extra fuel in the tank 'just in case' they need it. And I sleep better thinking there's a former F-16 pilot at the helm, rather than some Xbox bunny with loads of sim-time.

The beauty of driving, of course, is that *you* have control. And it's perfectly sensible to respect the nature of high-speed traffic because when things do go tits up, it happens fast and there's precious little time to *react*. That's why I never rely on reaction time. Neither should you.

## Rules

I follow some basic rules to keep myself clear of trouble on motorways and find the game of high-speed chess curiously satisfying. About half of motorway inhabitants play this game, and you can communicate with them on a quasi-Masonic handshake level. The other half are physically present but mentally abstaining. These people typically languish in the middle lane. Sometimes I join their group as well, usually in average speed zones, where my focus is obliterated by the need to strain at the needle lest it passes 53 mph.

## Warm up

Stretch your eye muscles and prepare to look *much* further forward towards the horizon. Your mental radar needs to become a 360-degree scanner, which means

Motorways

153

'Motorways are gloriously suited to their purpose.'

actively revolving your observation from side to side, forward and back using your mirrors. Constantly.

You need to think several moves ahead, and concentration must be continuous to monitor the ever-changing flow of traffic.

## The Pitch

Motorways are gloriously suited to their purpose, with wide lanes and one-way flow. The slower traffic is meant to stay in lane one with overtaking taking place in lanes two and three.

British adherence to these rules has lost some of its lustre in recent years. The grandmasters of lane discipline are currently to be found in Germany, where middle-lane hoggers are summarily shot at the roadside.

## Hard Shoulder

Nearly one in every ten cars that stops in the hard shoulder is involved in a collision. Only stop here if you're in dire straits, not for picnics. The hard shoulder is a kill zone. You are stationary, while everything around you is moving at high speed. Park as far to the left as possible, turn the front tyres to the left, get everyone out of the left side of the car and move away from it.

## Joining

By observing certain physical features you can effectively predict changes in traffic flow. The on and off ramps are prime examples of where you can expect 'displacement' from traffic joining or slowing to depart the highway. The resulting compression of vehicles in lane one causes a knock-on effect that you can see coming a mile away.

Displacement is the buzz-word that covers every scenario where a vehicle is *likely* to change speed or course. Your ability to predict how displacement might affect your progress will deeply impress Master Yoda.

Conversely, when *you* join the motorway, you want to create as little effect on the surrounding traffic as possible. Your blind spot is accentuated by your angle of approach to the slip road; a problem that is easily, though seldom, overcome by leaning forward and rotating your noggin like an owl so that you can look at what you're driving into. Combine this with mirror, signal and move into

# 18. Joining Motorways

Don't steal people's oxygen. Hold back to create a clear gap to the front and side, and work the traffic to your advantage from a position of strength.

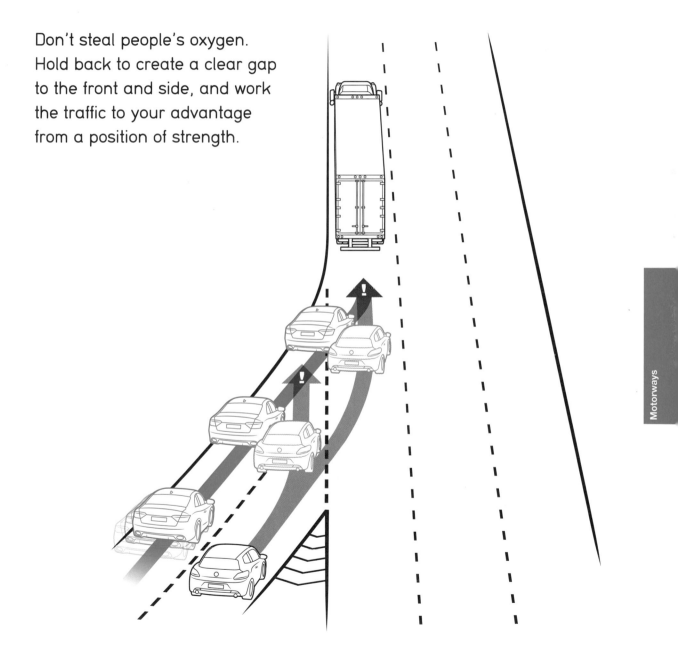

# 19. Displacement

In this scenario both drivers will probably blame each other, but each is at fault.

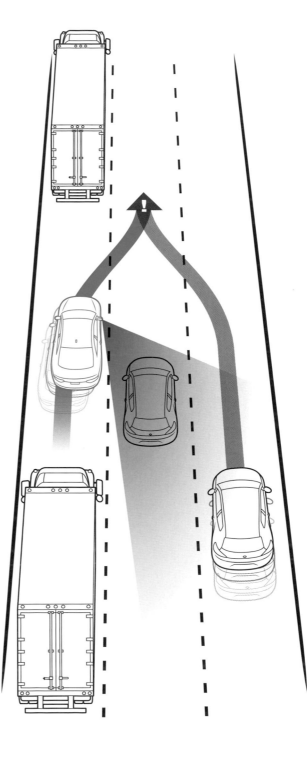

lane one with all the confidence of John Wayne striding into a saloon full
of Indians.

---

**Common Mistakes** > **Anybody behind you is welcome to tailgate, but they should wait their turn. Just keep enough room to the front and ideally to the sides to avoid being squeezed by anybody. It's all about creating clear space.**

---

## Leaving

The problem with satnav is that it crushes forward planning and makes thinking a crime. Motorways are still littered with quaint signage indicating the range to potential destinations, and assuming you're not too enthralled with your screen to notice it means that you can plan an exit ahead of time.

At Le Mans we spend 85 per cent of the time with the pedal to the metal, and the average speed is above 140 mph. My brain becomes so accustomed to it that when I've finished a three-hour stint behind the wheel, I can close my eyes twenty minutes later and still see the dotted white line flashing past my retinas.

As you enter the pits, a sharp corner around a sand pit physically enforces the speed limit of 40 mph. It feels so slow that the world seems to stop turning, and there are more tears than sand in that pit from drivers who overcooked it on the way in and cost themselves the race. You have to flick a mental switch and remember that the world just got a lot closer, smaller and slower.

'The trick is to anticipate change.'

*Boring but Important*

As you exit:
- do mirror and shoulder checks;
- check the speedo;
- prepare for two-way traffic;
- prepare for sharper corners;
- beware slippery spillage deposited where the slip road meets the junction or roundabout.

## The Game

The motorway game is just like musical chairs, with long periods when nothing happens followed by sudden bursts of activity. If you can still remember, the winning strategy with musical chairs was to hold back a little and let the herd

Motorways

## 'The motorway game is just like musical chairs.'

in front bunch up. You kept your eyes on the prized empty chairs, and listened. Then, when the music stopped and everybody slammed on the brakes you quietly slipped into the empty space, assuming that you weren't rear-ended by the kid with braces who kept slugs in a jar.

Motorway speeds are higher than other roads, but the traffic flows at *relatively slow* speeds to one another. The speed differential, the delta, between lanes might be less than 5 mph, but when the music stops, or if someone cuts in front of you, then relative speeds can change quickly.

Rather than reacting to slowing traffic, the trick is to anticipate change well before it happens and create an opportunity with enough space to handle it. Using this fluid map of your surroundings means you can pick your moments to pass other vehicles without being cut off, while staying out of the way of those overtaking you.

Mind out for hazards like speed cameras or the shattered remains of a crashed car that prompt lesser drivers to deploy a negative-G emergency brake and gurn at the scene. Debris such as detached bodywork or a shredded truck tyre also tends to spook the herd. Lane closures and other roadworks will compress traffic, causing it to slow.

---

**Hot Tip**

> **Everything should be happening more slowly for you at high speed. Turn the steering more slowly, take longer to do things and allow more time for people to register your intentions.**

---

## Space, Time and Relativity

The space in front of you acts like a buffer zone that gives you the room to manoeuvre and the safety to stop in a hurry. The space required to perform the latter governs the amount of buffer you need to maintain. By forward planning you also burn a lot less fuel, and money, jumping on and off the throttle.

Most officials measure this safety zone using time, but I really prefer distances, because the brain recognizes these instantly, and time cannot be trusted.

When you brake from any speed, you shed roughly 20 mph every second in dry conditions. Your perception of slowing in relation to time is that the process is constant, but, as we saw in 'Stopping Distance' (page 76), this doesn't hold true on the ground.

The way in which speed reduces across a distance varies *drastically*, and it takes much longer to shed higher speeds than slower ones. The result on a motorway when the music stops is that the early adopters of the middle pedal end up decelerating at a considerably faster rate than the ones who didn't see it coming. The late brakers cannot possibly slow down in time, and they all get smashed up, hence the term 'concertina'.

For that reason it's a good idea to keep an eye on your tail too, especially if a big heavy truck has taken a shine to your rear bumper. Generally tailgaters have one of two intentions: to overtake you because you're in the way, or to sit there idly because their brain is in neutral. Switching to an inside lane should resolve the first problem. If it doesn't solve the second then you can gently roll off the gas to encourage your new best friend to find another attraction.

## Following Distance

As a general rule my following distance is at least the length of an articulated truck, increasing to two trucks for motorways and three if the weather turns extra British. An artic is about 52 feet long, so this equates to a distance of 104 feet on the motorway, which is a little shy of the separation between the painted chevrons you sometimes see.

By positioning slightly to the side of the vehicle in front, you can see well beyond it as well as through its windscreen for a meaningful glimpse of what you're heading into. It also gives you space within which to back away from slowing traffic, or gradually build acceleration to overtake, which saves fuel.

From this enhanced vantage point you can see the world ahead in all its glory and predict the future. Anticipation of an event reduces your reaction time to an incident considerably. Assuming that you see it coming, the delay in your foot reaching the brake pedal is just over half a second – or 60 feet at 70 mph. That length of thinking distance is fine when you're monitoring the flow.

If your observation is less than constant, a few missed seconds suddenly translates to 250 feet driving blind. It then takes a minimum of one full second for the brain to calculate your rate of closure to the incident and *then* react. You've travelled the length of a football pitch, and by now everybody in front is decelerating faster than you can. Good luck.

# 20. Following Distance

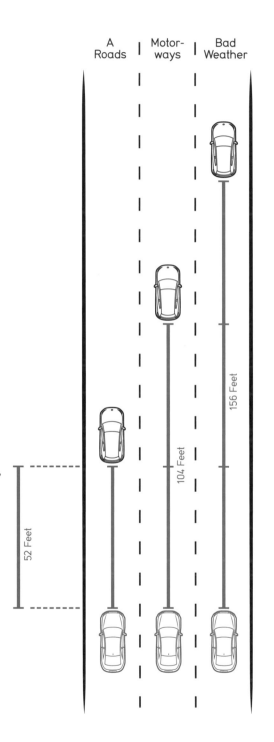

A Roads | Motor-ways | Bad Weather

52 Feet

104 Feet

156 Feet

**Hot Tips**

> Be fast and fleeting with glances at the radio or gorgeous passengers or suffer my fate from 'King of the Road' you will, young Jedi.

> Tailgating the car in front denies you any situational awareness; you're just a sheep.

## Communication

The vernacular that drivers use to communicate with each other is based on the sharing of information. Forget the hand signals, white van men: the focus is making your intentions clear and being seen. Don't loiter in people's blind spots and use indicators with plenty of warning before switching lanes.

'Predict the future.'

If someone isn't paying attention and strays towards your lane as you run alongside, give them a short blast of the horn. Anything longer might be mistaken for a request to partake in a duel at the next service station.

Besides the obvious signs you might receive when people actually indicate, this is a game of innuendo. Study the other players for potential signs of movement as they close up on each other in front and as they approach you from behind. Relative speeds and traffic compression provide the best clues as to when vehicles might switch lanes.

Body language like a turn of the head or a wobble of steering might suggest an impending lane change, or it could just be the second coming of that steak and ale pie. When a vehicle strays from centre lane it suggests the driver isn't switched on and might also intimate a lane change. People often turn the wheel and indicate at the same time, which rather defeats the purpose, but you get used to it.

## Blind Spots

I love it when Europeans describe the business of NASCAR and oval racing as 'shoving your foot down and turning left'. It reminds me that the secrets of driving at continuously high speeds are known only to a few.

When you stand on the straight part of a 2-mile superspeedway, it looks like a very long corridor that runs into a wall. You start driving along it with every intention of running into the apparition of banked tarmac at the end with your foot completely nailed to the floor. Sadly, there's more than enough time to debate this strategy several times during your journey …

# 21. Motorway Blind Spots

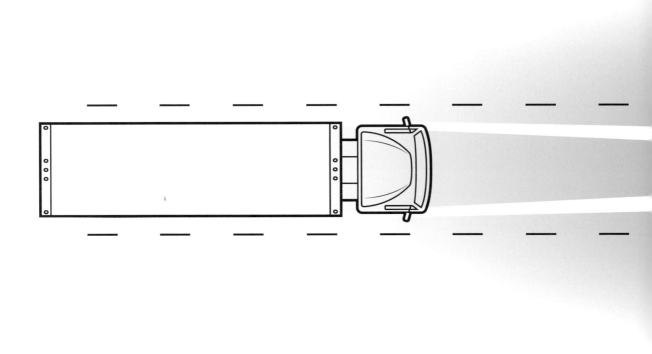

Eliminating the blind spot is as simple as looking over your shoulder – but don't be the joker in the bottom car loitering out of sight, waiting to be side-swiped.

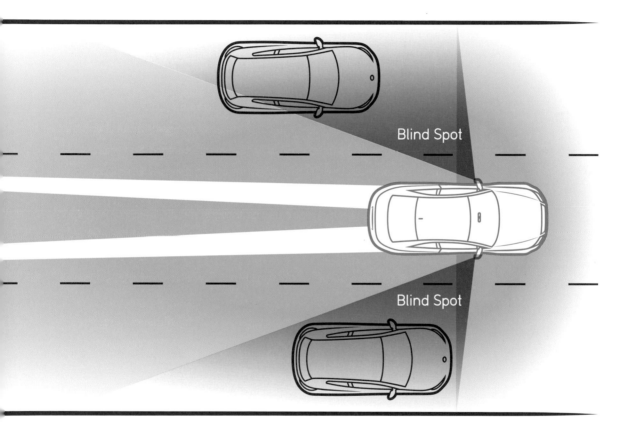

Blind Spot

Blind Spot

'When you stand on the straight part of a 2-mile super-speedway, it looks like a very long corridor that runs into a wall.

You expect the wall to open into the longest and most forgiving corner you've ever seen, but it really doesn't. There's an abrupt camber change as you enter, and bumps of the 'Jes-sus, why the f*** didn't somebody tell me about those?' variety that would loosen the bowel of the stiffest stool pincher.

The extra G created by the banking squeezes your delicate juices firmly into the chair, and if you didn't swallow enough air before going in, your next draw of breath results in a feeble whimper. The steering goes so heavy you think it might snap, and as per tradition for a first oval adventure, your knuckles will whiten around the wheel in an attempt to force it to stop frightening you. This creates a tighter arc around the turn than necessary, followed by a savage response over the Jesus bumps and a far-from-pleasant 'lightening' at the rear as you exit.

Misery loves company, and there's plenty to be had when the green flag drops to start the race. Forty cars join the party, packed so tightly around you that there's no space for wing mirrors, so you only have a head mirror. Your saucer eyes spend almost as much time there as they do facing the cars filling your windscreen.

As the swarm veers into the turn, it carves through the air, leaving a messy vacuum in its wake. An invisible god called turbulence reaches deep into the pack and slaps you all around. With inches to spare to the car in front, one on your ass and lanes of shuffling traffic huddled close to either side, there's precious room to spare when your car squirms and kicks in the jetwash.

The most sensitive part of your operation is the one bit of the car that you can't see: the rear quarter. Unlike on the open road, your melon is so tightly tethered with safety harnesses that you can't physically look over your shoulder.

With your vision naturally prioritizing the tangle in front and directly behind, it's easy to forget the blind spot and creep over into a lane of traffic travelling at a different speed to yours. At high speed the platform has to remain stable, and contact with the rear quarter usually results in a spin followed by a thump.

To cover this vital base oval racers have a dedicated spotter high up in the grandstands who chain-smokes while watching your progress through some binoculars. He provides continuous dialogue via radio about everything taking place in the blind spot, offers moral guidance and chivvies you along with a narrative of what is approaching beyond the range of your head mirror.

Spotters are expensive creatures that require constant rehydration at the bar, so in real life you can save yourself a lot of money by looking over your shoulder before you go for broke.

## The Players

Like any sport, the players bring out the best and worst in each other. Your own self-interest should remain your prime objective, but unless you deploy some courtesy and cater to the needs of others you will either cause pile-ups or find yourself being French-kissed by a hairy paramedic. If you find yourself jumping on the brakes a lot and making last-ditch manoeuvres, I'm afraid this means you.

The biggest players on the pitch are the heavy goods vehicles that float up and down the transport arteries like icebergs. They have their own game, similar to draughts, which involves slipstreaming one another and occasionally making the slowest overtaking manoeuvres known to man. It's like turtle sex, and the whole motorway comes to a standstill until it's over.

The majority of trucks are well driven, although a percentage of foreign trucks entering the UK lack brakes on their trailers. Foreign trucks are left-hand drive, creating an even bigger blind spot, and the driver is probably bleary-eyed from the lack of sleep and excessive consumption of boiled herring. Regardless of origin, you don't want to bet your life that a 34-ton articulated truck can stop if you cut in front of it and climb on the brakes. It can't, not even by half.

Owing to their size, trucks have enormous aerodynamic drag, and this vortex can shove your vehicle around. The effect is pronounced on windy days, and if you don't pay attention the effect can be magnetic, meaning your paths collide.

*Boring but Important*

- Keep checking your mirrors. The police take a dim view of following a driver for ten minutes with the blues and twos wailing.
- Own the blind spot.
- Note the air temperature – expect ice below 3 degrees.
- Scan actively – a fertile imagination for potential scenarios will boost your attention span and buy you time to anticipate, rather than react to, events.

'Heavy goods vehicles that float up and down the transport arteries like icebergs.'

## Mergers and Acquisitions

Lane hopping in busy traffic, spurred by the powerful instinct to get ahead of the pack by finding the lane of least resistance, is strong ju-ju. But it's a fruitless pastime that makes you more likely to crash.

However, a closed lane that requires traffic to merge is a different game altogether – one that really separates the philanthropist from the predator. Typically, the warning sign of impending lane closures ahead prompts a sort of dash for the last splash at the watering hole.

You either form an orderly queue with the rest of the righteous or motor on regardless until the last moment and then force your way in. Vigilantes spring to life to defend the sanctity of 'their lane' by straddling the white line to block your entry, or reaching for the Glock 9 mm.

Research has shown that lane-merging is no more a moral struggle than a shoal of fish negotiating a reef. Merging 'late', when the lane ends, shortens the distance spent in reduced space and avoids the back-up from a premature queue. By adopting the 'live and let live' policy, this should make traffic converge as seamlessly as a zip. On average, late merging is faster for everyone. Don't shoot the messenger.

## Game-changing Weather

Weather is dealt with in the 'skidding' section, but it would be remiss to ignore the significant part that weather plays on motorway driving before you pull off for a well-earned coffee break.

### Sun

Low sun in particular zaps you right in the eyes, particularly when combined with grime on the windscreen. I'll never forget a teammate of mine launching out of the pits for a qualifying session at the Lausitzring speedway, hammering down the pit straight at 170 mph and driving straight into the wall. When he told the team manager that he was blinded by the sun, we didn't know whether to laugh or cry.

Drop the sun visor and bang the shades on. If the sun is behind you and reflecting off the mirrors, then adjust their angle.

'If you decide to overtake something like a truck, set the wipers to warp speed.'

### Fog, Spray and Smoke

When your visual range is restricted to less than 100 metres, your ability to predict the future suffers. Distance markers in the hard shoulder are spaced 100 metres apart, which is a good visual aid. Below that distance, you should run headlights, and fog lights *only if* there's fog – otherwise they just blind other drivers and are illegal.

When people can't see they always slow down, so be prepared for this if you spot glare from the sun beating off a wet surface, enter a flash storm, a bank of fog or a wall of smoke … since people still love to light a bonfire close to the road.

### Rain

When it turns moist, the motorway punishes fumbling fingers. With reduced vision and grip underfoot, you need to avoid coarse steering, jumpy braking or harsh acceleration, which are more likely to upset the apple cart.

So long as your car is maintained, it will actually brake quite well in wet conditions. What it can't cope with so well are lateral movements. Swerving will cost nearly half of your grip.

At 70 mph the braking distance in the wet for a *good* modern tyre is roughly 25 per cent longer than in the dry, but you should still extend your following distance by the length of an artic. Why?

You can't see as much, and other motorists are more prone to making mistakes in bad weather. Steamy windows make it hard to shoulder-check the blind spots, mirrors become obscured with drizzle, and knackered wipers smearing the front screen all combine to make it ever so easy to reach out and touch someone.

Giving more space to the car in front reduces the impact of its spray and provides better strategic oversight of everyone's relative speeds and positions. If you decide to overtake something like a truck, set the wipers to 'warp speed' before driving into a bending wall of spray. Pick a straight line of a gutsy gear and get it over with.

Another reason for needing more space is to allow you to scan the road surface for standing water that could cause the car to aquaplane. If enough water forces its way underneath your tyres, it lifts them off the road, and you lose control over them. Aquaplane occurs almost exclusively at high speed, and if your

## 'Jack Frost is paying you a visit!'

observation skills are good, then you can spot these shimmering shadows before they greet your wheel arches. For more detail on aquaplane please see page 212.

**Snow**

Snow is less aggressive than ice but seriously reduces grip on standard summer tyres. The snow often builds up quickest in the fast lane as people migrate to the perceived safety of the slower lanes.

Before the snow gets compacted, it fills up with slippery powder. So if you pile into an uncleared lane to overtake it won't be pretty.

Beware the sludgy ridges that form between lanes, which make life interesting when you try to cross them. If the ridge is small enough, and your speed is low enough, you can turn across it gradually to switch lanes.

The challenges arise as a result of the way in which the sludge interacts with each wheel as it makes contact. It builds at the head of the front tyre, acting like a brake, transferring weight to the front and off the rears, and then when the rears encounter the sludge, well … you already know, they lose grip and probably slide.

To counteract this issue you can take more than one bite on the cherry by steering gently into the sludge, straightening the wheel as the car decelerates on the thick stuff, then very gradually inching your way across with micro movements on the wheel.

**Black Ice**

These conditions are thankfully rare on high-speed carriageways, where regular gritting puts them out of business. But if the temperature drops rapidly, as it can at night, water can freeze and become 'black ice'. Ice tends to be silent underfoot so the road noise will suddenly go absent, but if you're even questioning it just get out of the throttle and let wind resistance take your speed off. Be gentle with the steering and avoid braking until the car lands.

To check for ice, assuming there's nobody close behind, you can dab the brakes in a straight line to test for traction. If there's a hint of trouble or the ABS light flickers, then Jack Frost is paying you a visit!

Braking distances extend by up to ten times in frozen conditions, and the surface grip varies from one metre to the next, so you need to extend your focus at least three times further forward to anticipate events.

# In the Zone

## 'Good morning, Mr Stig,' purred the dulcet tones of Gavin Whitehead, the Scottish producer of *Top Gear*.

'We're gonna V-max a bunch of supercars with you and Hammond out in the desert in Abu Dhabi, so we need to organize a recce and map out the runs. Have you got any special requirements?'

'Water, tons of it.'

Gav scratched some notes, 'H – 2 – O. You're a cheap date. One thing we've flagged is the cat's eyes out there are really big. The concern is that if you strike one at 200 mph it might cause a puncture. What's your view?'

'At £6,000 a tyre I think we should be OK, but we should make a rule not to drive over them. I'm more interested to see if the roadside verge drops away and check for things like trees, bridges and roadworks in case we get a blowout.'

The end of the line went heavy.

'Yeah, that's pretty high on the agenda this time.'

Just three years prior, Hammond had nearly lost his life at the helm of a jet car propelling him down a runway at 330 mph when the front tyre blew out. A big investigation followed, but the lasting impression was that hindsight was a poor substitute for 20/20 forward planning. We left no stone unturned for *Top Gear of Arabia*.

Stepping onto the tarmac at Abu Dhabi international airport, I thought the rubber soles would melt off my shoes. Hammond was rocking a seriously bushy hairdo and absorbing some piss-take about a scene of him riding a horse across the dunes. The producers squeezed some real gems into the risk assessment: 'Ears flat back means "I bite". Watch out for big, heavy hooves, stamping on your feet.'

Our first stop was a palatial building owned by one of the sheikhs with close ties to the royal family. It turned out that this building was just a garage for his car collection. I counted about eighty to-die-for models, including three Bugatti Veyrons: one red, one blue and one in chrome. We were borrowing 'the red one'.

Gav invited me to give it a once-over, and I walked around it like a sommelier judging a fine wine by the shape of its glass. Veyrons usually have a two-tone colour scheme, but this beauty was dipped in blood red from head to toe, accentuating its hench shoulders, steely eyes and bulbous rear end.

'I'll take it,' and with that I was handed the keys to a £1 million car without even signing a form.

Down at the docks a precious cargo was being unloaded from its container and driven onto dry land by a man wearing white rubber gloves. The owner, Rowan Atkinson, would have preferred a full-body condom to anybody driving his beloved McLaren F1. He spent twenty minutes pacing me through its working parts in the UK and was excruciatingly particular that I 'b-b-be very careful with the clutch', the severity of the words bringing out a Mr Bean-like stammer in an otherwise perfect monologue.

We took the two titans to our designated three-lane highway, closed off by our very own escort of armed police. The 1-mile drag strip was bordered with palm trees and ornamental grass in an otherwise barren infinity of sand dunes and blue sky.

We lined up the red Bug alongside the deep-purple Mac and admired the shimmering view of two radically different examples of engineering perfection: modern vs a relic from the 1990s.

Hammond took the Bug, which was fully automated and had every gadget known to man for planting 1,000 bhp safely to the road through its four-wheel-drive system. Traction control prevented any slippage from 0 to 60 mph, in 2.5 seconds, and hydraulics whirred tirelessly to tune the car's considerable aerodynamic stability on your journey to 252 mph. Anti-lock brakes brought you back to earth, as did an air brake that deflected enough air with its wing to put over half the earth's gravity through your coccyx. That alone was more deceleration than most cars achieve with standard brakes. And it even had a launch control system for … pulling away from traffic lights in a hurry.

'Basic, but
bombproof.'

I took the Mac. It had three pedals and came with rear-wheel drive only. It did 0–60 mph in just under 4 seconds and topped out at 240. Basic, but bombproof.

The camera team were ready and had developed a disturbing penchant for stripping off whenever the sun broke cover, gaffer-taping their shorts into a sort

McLaren F1 Supercar, built in 1992. Only the brave should enter these doors, and then wearing Kevlar Y-fronts.

# 'All my hair stood on end.'

of nappy-thong thing to spread the tan. You could probably be shot for lesser offences in Arabia, but they felt the risk was worth it.

Gav told us to stand by over the radio before signalling the local chief of police: 'Please ask your men to hide themselves behind the trees and stand by to shoot.'

An unfortunate choice of words perhaps.

The race would be initiated by countdown. The amateur waits for the lights to change to green before accelerating, adding hundredths of seconds to the departure time. A pro eyes the red and pulls the trigger as soon as the first photons start to dwindle.

'Three …' The Bugatti belched a monotonous drone as Hammond floored the throttle and the launch control held his revs precisely on the red line.

'Two …' I held the McLaren's banshee V12 at bay with 5,000-ish revs.

'One …' The clutch nudged the biting point.

'G—' I let slip half an inch of the Mac's hair-trigger clutch; she nosed up and belted forwards. The rears bit perfectly, and the engine note stayed crisp until I reached a healthy enough speed to let the clutch out fully, causing the rears to chirp in the final moment of first gear with a satisfying *cha-cha-cha*. Rowan had insisted we only make one hot pull away – it was all I needed.

As something red faded from my window, all my hair stood on end. Unencumbered by technology or the weight that goes with it, the McLaren dusted the Bugatti to 60 and beyond. It finally succumbed to the irrepressible volume of power from the Bugatti's W16 engine, the equivalent of two V8s strapped together.

Though the Bugatti and the old McLaren F1 both head rapidly north of 200 mph, the experience inside the cockpits at those speeds couldn't be more different. In the Bugatti you are thinking about where you might like to have dinner that evening, while in the McLaren you are basically shitting yourself.

Its demented engine tone and otherworldly floating sensation from the chassis tell you that if you screw this up, your face will be flat-packed into the dashboard tighter than a wallet at a Scottish auction. The Bugatti has every stability control device known to man, and tyres sticky enough to turn tarmac into molasses. *Yet more have crashed in their short history than the old McLaren.* I'm not suggesting we turn back the clock, but I prefer the McLaren because it really talks to you. Technology cuts off the connection between man and machine, numbs the senses and dulls the mind. And I don't trust it.

Twenty years ago your car's air con came with a handle, and you only got satnav in the Millennium Falcon. By 2020, there will be well over a billion machines talking to each other and making decisions using artificial intelligence.

Google seems determined to take the fun out of things by producing a car which pretty much drives itself … Meanwhile, real car manufacturers are dabbling with partial automation to warn you of the presence of other road users using radar and a suite of onboard safety systems. They indicate Klingons hiding in blindspots off your starboard bow by flashing orange lights inside the wing mirrors, with 'lane change assist' causing the wheel to vibrate and resist your steering input if you mistakenly turn towards one. In the models I've tested, the lights flash all the time, so you learn to ignore your mirrors. Forward-facing radar can trigger the brakes if you doze off and run too close to the back of someone, and the satnav will command you when to actually do something yourself.

Like the *Falcon*, however, I regularly find myself transported to the wrong side of an asteroid belt with greater frequency than I care to admit. The almighty Cloud is as reliable as a South American currency, which makes the prospect of seeing flocks of driverless cars filing around the countryside in the hands of Cybernet seem unlikely from an insurance perspective, let alone a practical one.

Gizmos like ABS have not made us safer. Why? The misconception is that ABS enables you to brake later, which it doesn't. This leads drivers to follow one another too closely or brake too deep into corners. And skidding off the road at higher speeds into immovable objects such as trees or barrel-rolling in the roadside verge is worse for your health than a locking wheel.

For now, at least, I can't help feeling that we should be the masters of technology, not the other way around. If you could have given Mozart a synthesizer, he wouldn't have let it play him.

So now that you're a hardened Garry Kasparov on the open road, your inner chi is braced for impact and you've signed the waiver, it's time to channel your full potential, switch off the autopilot and unleash your greatest asset: your mind. The next few chapters aim to demystify the mental and visual assets that racing drivers use to chase perfection, to get into the zone – and bring it to a road near you.

'Gizmos like ABS have not made us safer.'

# Free Your Mind

The Mark 1 brain continues to outperform supercomputers in a range of complex tasks from instant facial recognition to observing and dissecting complex patterns.

It can multi-task physical operations while prioritizing safe and threatening scenarios, form a plan based on that information and act. All while consuming less energy than a light bulb.

We take this miracle and pack it so full of rubbish that it fails the task of driving. The main drain on the mental system is human emotion. I'm not talking about people who cry when their cat sneezes; it goes deeper than that. There are key emotional triggers that interfere with the cognitive process and they need to be eliminated to cleanse the mind, Buddha-like.

Nearly a quarter of all drivers involved in fatal crashes, more in straight fender-benders, had been upset by an incident or a quarrel during the six hours leading up to the incident.

Stress and the emotional baggage it brings with it come in many guises, and it's sometimes hard to see it coming. It could be a row at home or just hearing Chris Moyles' voice on the radio, but anything that makes you twitch like a psycho or feel negative will affect your decision-making process. Negative thoughts make you feel like the world's against you, so why bother? You abrogate responsibility for your actions, and mistakes follow. It makes it easier to personalize conflicts that don't exist and lose the context of a situation. With adrenaline, you have the happy kind of excited as well as the angry kind. Both can cloud your judgement but none more so than the red mist.

## Emotional Baggage

For those perfect souls for whom nothing could penetrate your ice-cold demeanour, here are a few examples that might still rattle your cage without you realizing.

'Cleanse the mind, Buddha-like.'

'Stay cool
because
you'll live
longer.'

**Time Pressure**

The perception of being 'out of time' can turn you into a time bomb. We've all been to Ikea once in our lives, a black hole of vapid timelessness until you come out the other side with your pride in tatters as you try, and fail, to condense the rich pickings of the last four hours into the back of your wagon. You settle divorce proceedings on the back of an object you could never hope to erect and try to make up for lost time on the way home.

Enslaved to the clock, you become totally uncompromising, shutting down your willingness to adapt to the road conditions or anyone sharing them. In short, you've become a cabbie.

Time pressure also finds traction during a race. As the final laps tick away, drivers start to worry about that extra place on the podium, and that pressure feeds irrational behaviour. The solution? I wish I had one. We are always in a hurry these days; just try to suck it up and smile.

**Perceived Wrongdoing/Rage**

The guy in front deliberately failed to signal at a roundabout so that he could hold you up on the way to work. And it's a BMW, which means he's one of those arrogant bastards who is probably on the phone. You're just reaching for the rocket launcher when you realize he was a granny and she was lost.

Stay cool because you'll live longer.

## Commuted

Stress is the mind killer, the sense of being overwhelmed by circumstances that you are powerless to overcome. Apparently long-distance commuting exerts so much stress it's a miracle we survive the journey. One study concluded that a third of commuters travelling three hours daily in Germany were 'from a medical point of view, clearly in need of treatment'. Their condition was cited as 'terrible' and included a blend of dizziness, sleep deprivation and bodily pains that could only be brought on otherwise by watching *The Jeremy Kyle Show*.

Other studies show that driving stress raises blood pressure and increases the likelihood of heart disease. The only consolation is that users of public transport are more likely to contract infectious diseases or be assaulted for their choice of music.

# 22. Distractions

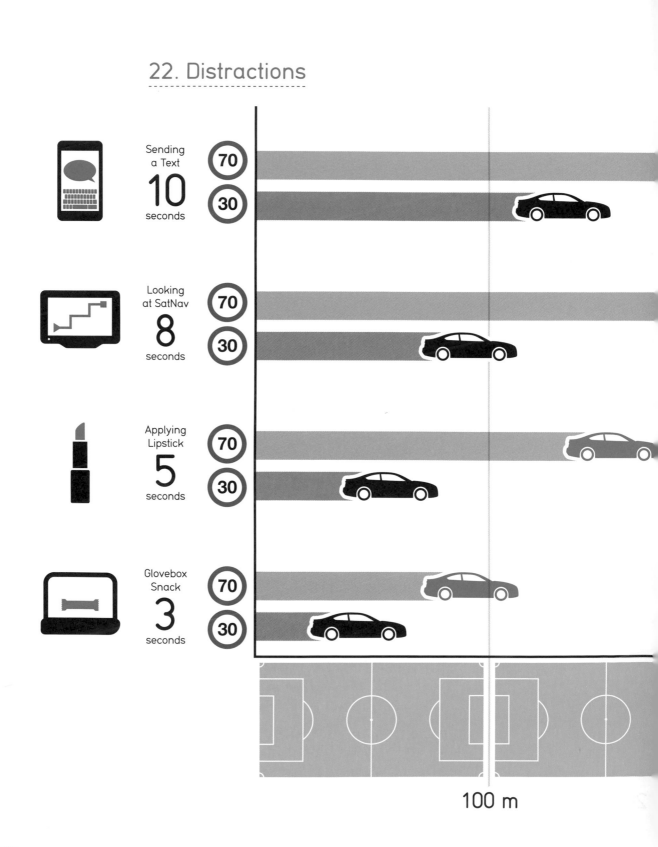

Sending a Text — 70 / 30 — **10** seconds

Looking at SatNav — 70 / 30 — **8** seconds

Applying Lipstick — 70 / 30 — **5** seconds

Glovebox Snack — 70 / 30 — **3** seconds

100 m

3: The Open Road

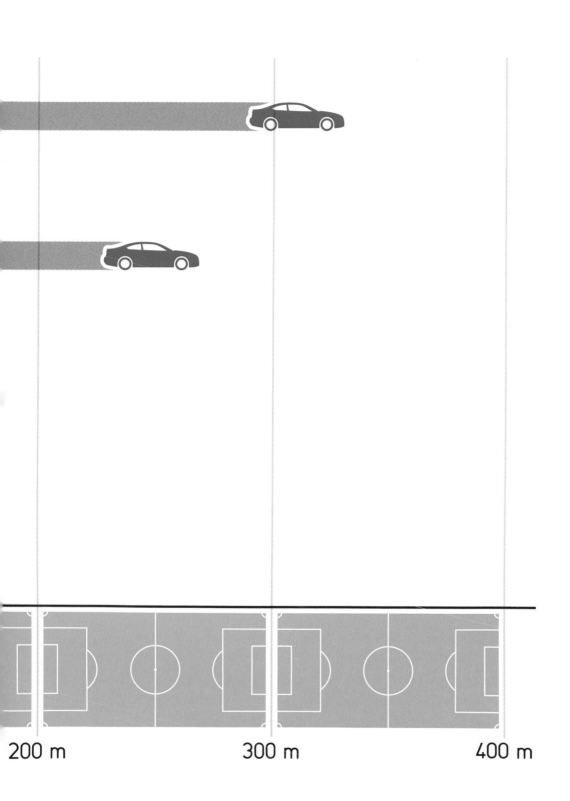

200 m          300 m          400 m

The trick is to remember those Antarctic penguins. You feel sorry for the poor buggers stuck on the edge of the colony, freezing their flippers off – but they know their turn in the wind is about to end. They're only a flipper away from being able to shuffle into the middle for tea and sardines. The end of the traffic jam is usually a lot closer than you think, so crank the tunes, plan a holiday and relax.

## Distraction

It's no wonder that people driving while jawing away on a mobile phone are a nightmare. Kimi Räikönnen said it best when his team kept distracting him on the radio during a Grand Prix: *'Just leave me alone!* I know what I'm doing.' It's fair to say that the clearer the mind, the clearer the road.

The all-pervading screen has infected every aspect of our lives – and phoning or, worse, texting while driving makes you twenty-three times more likely to have an accident *and* make a spelling mistake. It saps the grey matter so much that a study in Utah reckoned it was safer to drive drunk (that is most definitely not a recommendation, by the way).

Satnav is little better, and that blinding screen in the centre of the dashboard with the hypnotic powers of Paul McKenna is turning motorists into zombies. 'Turn left,' and moments later one woman had driven her £96,000 Mercedes SL500 straight into a river.

Remember when Luke descended at breakneck speed into the canyon of the mighty Death Star amidst a frenzy of fire? The rebel base was in the crosshairs, and Luke only had one bomb with which to defeat the Empire, so he switched on his targeting computer. Obi Wan knew that the pressure was on and that the damned screen was ruining Luke's night vision. He convinced Luke to trust his instinct and turn the computer off. The rest is history.

## Dead Weight

We sometimes forget that the most burdensome – and distracting – weight in the car is the passenger. Up to the age of twenty-five, every time you add one, you *double* the likelihood of having an accident. And peer pressure is a continuing nightmare. If I had a pound for every time I've heard someone say *'Go on!'* that Ferrari Italia would be sitting in my front drive. As well as goading you to drive faster, young passengers in particular press too many buttons and affect

*'Just leave me alone! I know what I'm doing.'*

your ability to focus. And in small hatchbacks, standard issue as a first car, the combined weight of your passengers has an exponentially negative effect on the vehicle's ability to handle a corner, or to stop…

As for children, God love them, but they are the worst. There you are, working the wheel, urgently wiping urine and chocolate off your shoulders while a bag of wet wipes silently slips underneath the brake pedal, and all they can do is complain that *Peppa Pig*'s not on, or worse, make happy noise.

**Hot Tips**

> Square away children, audio and satnav before you move. If anybody has a problem with that they can take alternative travel of the two-legged variety. If passengers distract you, tell them to be quiet and pay for your fuel.
> Careful with the mascara during rush hour. That goes for men, too.

## Drink 'n' Drugs

You can't be in control of yourself or the machine if you're drunk, drugged or sick – no matter what you tell yourself. Saturday is the most deadly day of the week for one reason: that's when everyone drinks the most.

## Environment

Weather, traffic, noise, discomfort … these are all triggers that build muscular tension, which impairs the natural flow of blood through your arms and legs and stiffens your responses and buttocks. The resulting lactic acid creeps up on you and ultimately degrades your mental state too.

Blasting around Phillip Island, Australia, in a V8 supercar at high speeds (and in temperatures of around 30 degrees), I noticed after an hour or so that the car wasn't slowing well into a hairpin. There was nothing noticeably wrong with the brakes; the problem only revealed itself after I took the chequered flag.

I knew my seating position would be uncomfortable because I had to make allowances for my vertically challenged teammate Nathan Pretty (aka Randy Corners). I failed to notice that it had entirely cut off the blood supply to my right leg.

The instant I crossed the line, my body exacted its revenge. My right leg went into spasm. It was so dead I had to make it back to the pits using my left foot and hobbled around the paddock like a lopsided cowboy for the rest of the day.

'The most burdensome – and distracting – weight in the car is the passenger.'

Free Your Mind

17

# Vision

'If you are in a good state, psychologically speaking, your sensitivity of vision is so much greater, so much more accurate, it makes everything else much more natural and easy.'

*Ayrton Senna, triple Formula 1 world champion*

Earlier on, we highlighted how important it is to look around you and spot potential hazards, but let's go a little deeper into the techniques that distinguish the great from the merely good. Cleansed of all cerebral impropriety, it's time for your head socket to plug in to God's greatest gift.

**The Mark 1 Eyeball**

The most advanced piece of tech riding onboard with you, 24/7, is the human eyeball. Fitted with night vision, it can detect movement at distances in excess of 2 miles. Your eye can switch focus from a close object smaller than a pinhead to a panoramic view in just 0.04 seconds.

Being hard-wired to your brain, the most advanced of processors, the eyeball can not only read incoming signals but actually predict them. Vision and control are the driver's two most important functions. You can't manage what you can't see. And wherever your eyes lead, your hands generally follow.

United States Air Force hero Chuck Yeager was arguably the greatest pilot of his era. In his words, the key to his success was survival. He had the ability to think one step ahead because he looked *much* further into the distance than his contemporaries.

Analysing the scene from further away means that it takes longer to materialize, time and speed effectively slow down, giving you the strategic advantage to control events. On the road it pays to think like Yeager and stay one step ahead by reviewing the foreground, the middle distance and the horizon.

# 'Look up, look wide.'

### Peripheral Vision

*'When you look up, look wide, and even when you think you are looking wide, look wider still.'*

Baden Powell

Baden Powell was talking about observing the natural world, and his teachings are wholly relevant to driving. The modern world encourages us to be near-focused on everything from TVs to computers. Our field of vision is constricted, and so our shoulders tense up, because it's unnatural. Going wide will be life-changing.

Samurai warriors learned to use the wider-focus technique in combat with multiple opponents. Rather than maintaining a hard focus on one individual, they relaxed their vision, allowing the edges to blur and extending their field of view. Peripheral vision is strongest at detecting movement, so by shifting their awareness around the scene rather than moving their eyes, the warriors were able to monitor multiple attacks.

Extreme sports offer fine examples of soft focus, arguably none more so than ice hockey. The extreme accuracy required to hit the puck into the net is matched by the predatory aggression of the competitors. Wayne Gretzky, aka 'The Great One', chalked up his legendary ability of seeing everything and everyone simultaneously to: 'fear. When you're 170 pounds playing with 210-pound guys, you learn to find out where EVERYBODY is on the ice at all times. If not, you'll find yourself forechecked into the mezzanine.'

To master this technique you don't need black pyjamas or a hockey stick. Stick your thumb out in front of you and look at it closely – your thumb is now in sharp focus at the expense of the wider scene. Now ignore your thumb, and look straight ahead to absorb the 200-degree field of vision without fixing on anything in particular. Move that thumb around and track it using your consciousness *without moving your eyes*. Now you're looking like a ninja and you can process ten times as much information.

It is simply not possible, nor recommended, to locate every threat or hazard on the road using a fixed stare. When you do need to move your head or your eyes to analyse situations, the aim is to flick across to make observations and return to the core peripheral view.

Vision

> A great way to improve your peripheral vision is juggling, and if you do it in public you might even get paid. Tracking each ball's path is impossible, so you pick a comfortable focus with occasional flickering glances at the wayward passes. If you find that easy, try doing it on an exercise ball.

## The Visual Strategy of a Racing Driver

*'We studied the eye movements of a racing driver during high-speed practice to see whether he took in visual information in a different way from a normal driver on a winding road. We found that, when cornering, he spent most of the time looking close to, but not exactly at, the tangent points on the inside edges of the bends … It is the head that performs most of the required movements, while the eyes stay within about 5° of the head axis most of the time'*

(*Source:* School of Biological Sciences, University of Sussex)

For cornering, peripheral vision creates a much more fluid landscape than you can achieve using a series of hard focus points. The enhanced spatial awareness massively boosts your perception of speed and distance.

In biological terms, the Mark 1 eyeball has two types of receptors on the lookout for incoming light rays: 'cones', and 'rods'. Peripheral vision relies on scattered 'rod' cells that provide a loosely focused, but broad impression of the world outside, great at detecting movement and providing night vision. That's right, soft focus is how you drive at night.

Night vision rods are housed around the outside of the eye, which is why stars look brighter at night when you view them slightly off-centre. They are highly sensitive to bright light, so it benefits them to shield them from anything that dazzles them. The centre of the retina is instead packed tight with cones, which provide hawkish, focused visual acuity: the type of vision we use for reading signs, or sending a text message.

Inexperienced drivers with less eye discipline use this type of vision to corner by moving their gaze rigidly from one point to the next along the kerb or the roadside. Alternatively they focus on the area directly in front of them or the tailpipe of the next car, reacting passively to situations as they develop, rather than

'Soft focus is how you drive at night.'

actively anticipating and controlling them. Put simply, they are missing the bigger picture. This is quite a natural way of adapting to being in a big wide car for the first time, and developing the hand-eye coordination to avoid running into stuff. But it puts a major dent in your radar.

Fighter pilots refer to this practice as target fixation. On numerous occasions, pilots have chased their bombs into weapons factories or mistakenly taken Iceman's advice too far by literally following their wingman into the ground during formation flying.

Growing into the wider view takes practice, and it is worth noting that when the shit hits the fan even experienced drivers will often revert to the series of fixed points.

The problem with big eye movements to pull focus, or to use the technical term 'saccades', is that the eye can see only once it stops moving, so it takes a few tenths of a second for it to land and refocus. That may not sound like much, but it adds up and gets compounded by speed, because you travel a considerable distance in that time.

Racing drivers do something else interesting. They flicker. I don't mean inverted peace signs to tell the other guy he's in second place. They flick their eyes rapidly at a scene, without drawing focus, and return to the main view. It's not accurate enough to read a sign, but it suffices to check for something alarming in the rear-view mirror, or just to re-establish the general landscape.

## Hell is Other People

When you drive in circles for a living, it's hardly surprising that what goes around comes around. It's been proven that if you put a man in uniform and hand him a stick – as in the classic 1971 'Stanford Prison Experiment' – he will push and poke people around with it. Not so many years ago I was handed the keys to a really big stick and sent to race it in the FIA World Sportscar Championship as well as at the Le Mans 24 Hours.

My car had 800 horsepower, the hunter-killer look of a stealth fighter ... and weighed less than a Mini Cooper. As if these Le Mans Prototypes, or 'LMP1' cars, didn't look fast enough sprinting down a French boulevard at 225 mph, the race organizers honoured the spirit of endurance racing by allowing different, slower, classes of car to compete for the same piece of tarmac.

The GT class, or cannon fodder, was made up of things like Ferraris, Porsches and Lambos that routinely shuddered every time an LMP1 scythed past and blew their doors off. I could slide out of a corner in my beast, see one of these lowly creatures approaching the next curve and still have time to dive-bomb past it at the last moment before veering off and leaving it behind like a static dot in the mirror. These close shaves would occur up to twelve times a lap, and you couldn't afford to show mercy, not even once, otherwise the other vultures would end up on your tail. When the team manager congratulated you on a 'good job passing traffic', it really meant that you had been a splendid bastard.

Fast forward to this year, and with an irony that would delight my list of former victims I find myself driving a roadblock with a Ferrari badge. At Silverstone your vision is naturally extended by its long straights and sweeping curves, but the swines still come at you from out of nowhere. Just like in everyday driving, you need to start growing eyes in the back of your head.

I found myself in the unfortunate position of leading the GT race aboard a Ferrari 458 when the rain was trying to decide whether just to cock its leg or summon Noah. Hot on my trail were the factory-run Ferraris driven by a brace of spritely Formula 1 test drivers, James Calado and Sam Bird. I drifted the car out of Copse in fourth gear and groped for an extra lump of steering as the rear tyres spun on the astroturf. While dealing with that little emergency, I remembered to check *all* my mirrors for what must have been the sixtieth time that lap, looking for the piercing white flashes of something rapacious.

Suddenly, two prototypes roared in out of nowhere. The 458 twitched a little sideways as I exited out onto the Hangar straight, the greasy surface affording me some advantage at first as the heavy hooves behind clambered for traction. I felt the thrum of their engines, then the cabin pressure rose as two Prototype missiles skimmed past on either side. The Porsche LMP1 to my right, possibly piloted by Mark Webber or some such rocketeer, shaved me so close that his rear wing amputated my mirror.

The severed limb left a scent of blood in the water. With no way to see what might be attacking my right-hand side, life on a clockwise track became challenging. Sam probed and pushed that area, and when he disappeared into my gaping blind spot during a manly showdown at another fast section, I had to cede him passage rather than risk a collision.

As a poacher turned gamekeeper, I found it fascinating to work the traffic in the opposite direction. Some drivers want to fight the world and waste time and energy defending their position when they get overtaken. In the battle of the classes between GT and LMP1 cars, it pays to help the other side as much as possible. When I see a faster car approaching I gauge its speed by looking two, three or even four times at the mirrors. Those snapshots are the only way to rate its closure in a straight line and decide how best to be 'taken'. If he's close enough, I ease off the throttle to help him pass before we even reach the corner so that both of us can take it cleanly. If my team manager congratulates me this time it won't be for being a hard-ass, but for cooperating and playing well with others.

'These close shaves
would occur up to twelve
times a lap.'

# Night Driving

Picture a section of the most dangerous motorway you've ever seen, loaded with M25-style traffic and no manners – a road that dives down a blind bend, through a fairground, then rushes away towards the horizon, and all the while drivers are crushing past one another, headlights flashing and bodywork ripping.

The tarmac is crowned by years of abuse and littered with bits of gravel. It dumps you into a series of roundabouts without any warning then catapults you along a tree-lined alley where you can't drive slower than 180 mph – and most folks prefer it above 200.

One missed gear shift can blow the engine. Failing to spot a passing car in the mirror can be fatal. And timing your loo break is *essential*. You have to maintain a high level of concentration over an extended period of time just to survive.

The hardest part is undoubtedly driving through the night. Your vision becomes severely limited at the point when your eyelids weigh most heavily. To prepare for a motoring marathon, be it the Le Mans 24 Hours or a late trip home from the office, it's good to know what's taking place in your mind and body so you can develop a diet and sleep strategy to deal with it. This is a rather long-drawn-out way of saying: snack more and take naps.

Our bodies follow a daily routine, known as circadian rhythm. Crudely put, it judges light and dark then pumps hormones around our system to switch our brains and guts off at night and wake them in the morning. That's why jet lag makes you feel sick and dehydrated.

We also follow longer energy cycles during the week. They vary from individual to individual, but don't we all hate Monday mornings?

In addition to the evening sleep there's a secondary dip in alertness after midday, exacerbated by how much and what you eat, because blood flow diverted to your stomach leaves less for your brain. For adults, who have slower metabolisms, this stage of the day is a danger zone for falling asleep at the wheel. The morning period brings on drowsiness amongst teenagers, because they produce more melatonin, the sleep hormone, later in their sleep cycle.

Sleeping at the wheel is the most common cause of vehicles leaving the road. Most sleep-related crashes occur between midnight and 8 a.m. (especially between 4 and 6 a.m.) – and between 1 and 3 p.m.

Dopey accidents are often fatal because the driver rarely decelerates before hitting something solid. Even if you do wake at the last moment, your reaction time and thought processes will totally suck. Eighty-five per cent of those responsible will be male and young, because we do more miles and in our manliness believe we can push through the sleep barrier. I know several racing drivers who met this fate.

Although most normal crashes happen on a Friday, sleepy ones generally occur on Mondays.

This is where *The Le Mans Diet* kicks in:

**Drinks**

Water, little and often.

**Eats**

The Le Mans Diet creates the platform for enduring energy. Maintaining that balance from the beginning of the day is a far more reliable strategy than fighting off fatigue later on.

You can get away with being slightly naughty at breakfast, but by lunchtime you should definitely avoid fatty foods and unnatural sugars.

The overarching principle to maintaining energy is never to feel 'full', hence the old saying: 'Hunt best on an empty stomach.' It doesn't mean wobbling around with low blood sugar and a headache, but consuming less means you save a ton of energy that would otherwise have been expended on digestion. And pound the water like an Olympic athlete, because if you dehydrate you fall asleep. Water also enhances your metabolism, which in turn promotes mental and physical performance.

Breakfast: like a king only if you're about to earn it. Wholegrain cereal, oatmeal, fruit and veg and non-fatty protein. Haddock and poached eggs all the way. Tea/coffee, juice are fine. Never miss the first meal of the day, otherwise your body thinks it's been abandoned in the Sahara and starts storing fat.

Snacking: nuts, dried fruit, & fruit – all day long.

Lunch: good carbs like pasta, rice or potatoes. White meat is best. Veggie soups are good. These slow-burning sugars are complemented by faster burners such as bananas, gingerbread and stewed fruit.

Dinner: treat yourself like a gremlin, only never eat after 8 p.m. Anytime I'm due to drive I follow the light lunch routine. If there's time for a proper sleep after dinner then I might spoil myself with a little extra meat … and some chocolate … foods that are higher in calcium and protein promote sleep. Then it's lights out, phone off and sayonara – always remembering to tell your crew chief where you are in case your shift starts early.

Refined sugars are like rat poison. Throwing sugar down your neck triggers insulin and leads to an energy crash, plus dehydration as your body tries to expel the excess the only way it knows how. And, trust me, you don't want to experience that on the Mulsanne straight where there's no toilets, or the M25.

Good eating and drinking should preserve a balanced energy level throughout the day, but then again we don't live in a perfect world. When your body talks about sleep you'd better listen.

**Sleeps**

Tiredness has a way of creeping up on you unnoticed. The effects include blurred vision, heavily reduced peripheral vision, reduced awareness and therefore reduced ability to react. It also plays havoc with your emotions, which interferes with your decision-making.

Your body will start going into a series of auto-shutdowns. These are known as microsleeps, and last from one to ten seconds. You come to without being able to account for the time that just passed, but you cover about 100 metres in three seconds on a highway, so this is no mini adventure. Micros identify themselves as a head nod, the 'hypnic' knee jerk (usually painful) or suddenly becoming aware of closure with another vehicle or object. Alarm bells …

On a monotonous motorway I've tried pretty much everything to stay awake: windows open, chewing gum, loud radio, self-harm, wrenching out nose hairs and shouting. But before I start looking like a Sweeney Todd victim, I head for the pit stop, because life's too short to arrive dead on time.

Most of us subscribe to the notion that sleep takes place at night in a single six- to eight-hour block. Most animals, babies and our siesta-loving Mediterranean cousins enjoy the benefits of polyphasic sleep, or power napping. The power nap is used by military pilots and sleep-deprived professionals to restore energy levels. A nap of six to ten minutes during times of fatigue throws the brain into a semi-deep sleep, quickly restoring a high level of alertness and cognitive response. Ironically, sleeping longer than thirty minutes can put you into a deeper sleep cycle, and you wake feeling groggy and disorientated. This 'sleep inertia' can last up to an hour, so it's no good for driving.

When I need a boost I set my alarm, down a coffee and fall asleep. The coffee takes longer to digest than the sleep lasts, so you wake up like a newborn warrior. Sleep is cumulative, so it's good to steal it wherever and whenever you can.

The same is true of tiredness; it creeps up on you. Avoid big meals, beware things like cough medicines and other drugs that would tranquilize a horse and try to respect your energy levels.

'When your body
talks about sleep you'd
better listen.'

# Basic Instinct

## It was the night before Le Mans, and I couldn't sleep.

I had forgotten to pack my fireproof lederhosen, my race licence was out of date, and there was every chance that my alarm clock would fail me. It did.

I arrived late for the qualifying session. Other drivers were locked inside their rockets and pounding laps to the delight of the exultant crowds, team owners and sponsors filling the pit lane. The race steward looked me up and down, shaking his head. Everyone was staring, probably because I was bollock naked, and my feet were superglued to the floor.

Then my real alarm went off, and I woke to the relief that it was a month before the actual event. I duly checked the location of my licence, ran an inventory on my fireproofs and noted that I was short of a balaclava, so I ordered one and went through my training regime for the following weeks. My body knows from experience that silly mistakes cost races, mistakes grow from distractions, and distractions are created by chaos.

Forward planning alleviates the chaos and frees the mind to tackle the challenge ahead. That's why nearly every racing driver I know is afflicted by a strong streak of OCD. Everything is neatly stacked in its rightful place, compartmentalized, so that it can be picked up and replaced with the minimum fuss – physically *and* mentally.

Martin Donnelly, one of the fastest men ever to grace Nomex, was notoriously anal about the way he folded his civvies before climbing aboard his race car and flicking a switch inside his brain, the switch that turns off emotion and turns on perception. As he blasted along the pit straight of Zandvoort in a Formula Ford 2000 at 135 mph, his mechanics thought it would be hilarious to dangle his jeans and galoshes over the pit wall as a wind-up. Something in Martin snapped. He lost focus and crashed.

People often ask me what it's like to concentrate for a twenty-four-hour race, where a tiny error in judgement can spell disaster – or worse, someone else might drive faster.

# 'A tiny error in judgement can spell disaster .'

The pit lane gets frantic, nearly sixty crews running around with wheels and fuel hoses and drivers running amuck amidst the mêlée. On track it's much calmer, and you work at your rhythm, in spite of the constant dicing with your competition, until you get to about 5 a.m., when some inconsiderate fellow lights his BBQ at Arnage corner … and throws on the hickory-smoked bacon. The waft of flavour tickles its way up the hairs inside your nose, and an intrusive voice asks, 'Where's breakfast?' By then you've galloped along another 500 metres, which means it's time to take a deep breath and crank the wheel into the über-fast Porsche Curves.

There are two types of thinking going on during these moments: the jungle reflex and the conscious thought. The caveman in me smells food and wants me to pull over to butter up a bun. The human element, the weaker part that I try to think with, orders him to shut up. Thanks to an extensive conditioning programme, the caveman obeys. Usually.

The jungle reflex is powerful. A newborn baby will fling its arms and legs out like Spiderman if it senses it is in danger, or falling. The response is instinctive, pre-programmed and occurs within milliseconds by virtue of evolution, which prepared our ancestors for the real possibility that they might fall out of a tree and have to grab a branch before hitting the deck. Where the hell is Ben taking us with this, you wonder …

There's no way that I can think as fast as my jungle brain can. But cavemen can't be allowed to drive without a responsible adult, though they often do. The jungle brain specializes in identifying threatening behaviour through body language or familiar patterns that suggest danger. This gut feeling is a useful radar for reading traffic on the road or the track, and a honed survival instinct is inventive at coping with tricky situations. However, Jungle Ben is a crude creature at heart: irrational, egotistical, competitive, always hungry, territorial; and he regards any invasion as a threat that should be dealt with aggressively. When someone cuts me up, Jungle Ben takes it personally and wants to teach this enemy a lesson he'll never forget, and his reaction registers first before my intellect kicks in. With a ton of metal in hand, any physical response is likely to lack any sense of proportion.

These basic instincts are hard-wired, so you can't get rid of them, but you can mould them to suit a purpose by cultivating an active thought process. Self-discipline is the only thing separating you from a poo-slinging primate. To harness the jungle power you have to identify and banish intrusive thoughts, which are

Le Mans ... by night, with *dipped* headlights.
For 'full beam' there's a blank white page somewhere.

## 'I fine-tune it in my brain, and do it better.'

usually childish and obvious, and act on genuine instincts. Repetition turns this effort into a pattern of behaviour.

For this process to flourish, the weaker part of the brain, your intellect, needs rest otherwise your body defaults to the stronger jungle mode. Ideally I take twenty minutes to find my inner self and get some sleep before the race starts. I stare at the wall and allow my subconscious to drift and vent its concerns, rather than letting them fester, so that I can address them in an orderly fashion.

In one of my early races at Donington, I knew that I was lining up alongside a rival called Darren Malkin, and we always pushed each other to the edge. Jungle Ben really latched on to this and prepared all kinds of apocalyptic predictions. I visualized all of them in full until I felt that all my bases were covered, including the eventuality of being shunted from behind at a lurid high-speed corner called 'The Old Hairpin'. The lights went green, we both ripped away, and Darren tapped me in the gearbox, the tail end of a single-seat race car, at *exactly* the corner I predicted. My car half spun, and I instinctively swung the steering until it banged into the bump stops, corrected the slide and stayed in front. The mother of all battles ensued, and our fathers even squared up in the pit lane. Like I say, cavemen.

Harnessing the subconscious is extremely powerful for fine-tuning complicated tasks that the human part of the brain tends to 'overthink', or is unable to imagine, and you hear yourself whining: 'I *can't* do it.' You usually can. If you picture yourself performing a task better than you 'think' you can, your subconscious will find a way to make it happen. We call it visualization, which is really active dreaming, focusing on something you want.

Millions of years ago humans mostly wanted to catch food without being eaten, which is why we still dream about running through molasses and being chased by a man-eating Cyclops. Dreaming is deeply rooted in our survival instinct, and it's no coincidence that it connects directly to vision.

I use this technique every time I set foot in a racing car. I imagine what I'm going to do, and then do it, then I fine-tune it in my brain, and do it better. Anybody can do it.

# Visualization:
## *the Perfect Lap*

I always pretended not to care too much about the guests on *Top Gear*, when in reality I loved seeing them realize their full potential.

'What I really needed Billy to do was to think further ahead, even if he couldn't look ahead.'

So when war hero Billy Baxter unfurled a white cane and started tap, tap, tapping it to find his way across the car park, I couldn't help cracking into a massive smile. Billy may have been completely blind, but he had the eye of the tiger if ever I saw it.

He told me that he was prepared to do 'whatever it takes' to achieve his goal of beating a sighted celebrity's lap time around the *Top Gear* circuit. The target was two minutes and six seconds, set by game-show host Richard Whiteley.

Billy's military background gave me the confidence to lean on his self-discipline to help him achieve that goal. I was mean. I barked rapid-fire instructions at him and reprimanded him mercilessly whenever he made a mistake. It was the only way to help him build a virtual picture of his surroundings in his mind and keep him laughing with his foot to the floor.

Billy was hanging on my every word and reacting to my voice so that he could apply the right amounts of steering, braking and throttle as we rolled along. The problem with that was clear. We ricocheted our way from one corner to the next and never followed the same path twice.

By the close of play on that first day we still hadn't negotiated a full lap together without some kind of incident or me diving across the centre console to grab an armful of steering when we veered off course. Whenever we approached the high-speed 'Follow Through' corner at nearly 90 mph, the gap between the tyre wall and the garden was just too narrow to let Billy handle the steering unaided. We were a long way from letting him fly solo. What I really needed Billy to do was to think further ahead, even if he couldn't look ahead.

So … at the end of his first day I created a voice recording of the perfect lap. I used all the familiar vernacular, four-letter warts and all, to paint the picture of the world Billy was trying to imagine, and I timed the recording with a stopwatch to match the circuit corner by corner until we crossed the line within the time I believed he could achieve.

Two weeks later, Billy was standing in the car park. He had memorized the recording by listening to it every day until it was burned into his mind's eye. We climbed aboard the gutless but reasonably priced Suzuki Liana and set off at a steady pace.

To my astonishment we completed our first tour of the circuit without major incident. Billy's hands were shaking with excitement, and I was bursting with pride, but I knew there was a narrow window for Billy to achieve his best before exhaustion set in. We did one more 'sighting' run and then went for it.

Billy gunned the engine and tore away from the start line with a shriek of wheelspin. There's something unforgettable about a blind man doing that.

As we twitched across the finish line, I clicked down hard on the stopwatch. I ogled the figures. It was a moment to savour.

'That felt like a good one. How fast was it, Stig?'

I opened with a confession. Halfway round, I had lied about covering the steering at the 'Follow Through', which meant that Billy had run the entire lap single-handed. Hardman he may have been, but there was more than sweat starting to trickle down that weathered face.

'Your time was one minute and fifty-eight seconds. You've beaten four sighted celebs, you legend.'

The emotion gripped us both, and I'll never forget Billy's achievement that day. To put it in context, Boris Johnson, the mayor of London, barely eclipsed Billy's time by two seconds. To my deep frustration, Billy later had time added to his official score for 'cutting a white line' by a few feet. Bureaucracy knows no bounds.

In a race the most dangerous time of all is the first lap, when the field is tightly packed. You have no option but to run wheel to wheel with all brands of crazies, and there's precious little time to react to signs of trouble.

As the pack of up to fifty machines streams into the first corner at 200 mph, three or four wide, inches apart and jockeying for position, they are dangerously

# 'Buckle up, crack your knuckles and Enter the Dragon.'

close. The varying inputs of man and machine ripple through the field as the speeds reduce unevenly in the braking zones. The drivers' heart rates peak at over 180 beats per minute; turbo-charging the senses with adrenaline and oxygen to *think fast*.

Your eyes are on stalks searching for key indicators – a plume of dust as one car drops a wheel in the dirt, a screech of rubber, a puff of blue smoke from a locked tyre or the sudden convergence of two racers, any recognizable pattern that might lead to a collision – and you're always mindful of what's coming up behind you. It's not a case of whether you might need to take evasive action, it's a question of when and how much.

To cope with information overload and to reduce thinking time, racing drivers visualize things like the first lap many times over before the race begins. When you close your eyes, preferably not while driving, the link between the brain and the eyes is so powerful that you can still form crystal-clear images of real-life scenarios. This isn't quite the same as dreaming, because you consciously control the scene. In the safety of your own synapses you can rehearse how to handle complex situations as many times as you like until your responses start to feel instinctive.

This is a powerful model for conditioning your mind and another way of seeing into the future without even needing the keys to a DeLorean. With your crystal ball in hand, now seems like a good time to pitch you some curve balls …

## Summary

You now have the keys to the freedom of the open road, and on a normal day, in normal conditions, are in control of your car right up to the limit of its capabilities. What follows are the defcon 1 skills and techniques that will keep the beast on the leash when it tries to bite you, from skids and aquaplaning, to the absolute gold standard of Hollywood stunt car control. So buckle up, crack your knuckles and Enter the Dragon.

# 04
# Skidding

# The Limits of Grip

A skid, beyond the reference to brown trousers, happens when one or more of your tyres are pushed beyond their ability to cling to the road surface.

When the bond is broken, you go from gripping to skidding, and it can happen fast.

There are two types of skid: affecting the front tyres, and affecting the rears.

When the front tyres skid, the car has a tendency to go straight on towards the outside of a corner despite your efforts to convince it otherwise. The car understeers.

When the rears let go, the car rotates into the corner far more than you asked it to in terms of the steering angle. It oversteers. This condition is generally also accompanied by a growl from your bowel: '*Fuuuuuuu* …'

Trust me, you will know the difference between understeer and oversteer.

The first thing to say is that preventing a skid is a far better strategy than working to correct one. We are back to the physics of the traction circle (see page 94): if you exceed the forces that the tyres are capable of handling, they will let you know all about it.

The dominant forces at play are longitudinal: braking and acceleration. These will always win the arm wrestle at the expense of the lateral grip required for cornering. That is why you should always apply them carefully. The purpose of the early chapters on smooth driving and cornering technique should put you in good stead on that account.

Nonetheless you arrive here, at the point where the car is out of control, and you'd like to offer a more purposeful response than the airline pilot who lost it in a car at Brands Hatch. He let go of the steering and deadpanned to his instructor: 'All yours.' Then they crashed.

'When the bond is broken, you go from gripping to skidding.'

4: Skidding

200

# 23. Over- and Understeer

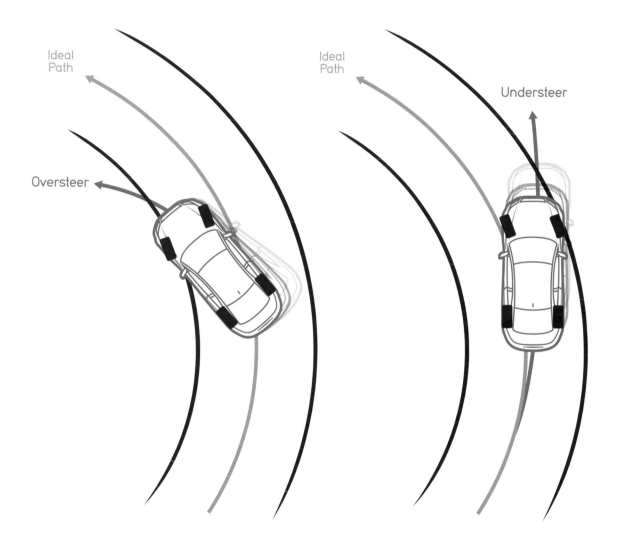

Ideal Path

Ideal Path

Oversteer

Understeer

'Usually *you* create the skid.'

## Common Causes of Skids?

You might have encountered a slippery surface, but usually *you* create the skid by doing something that pushes the tyres beyond their limit such as:

1.  Braking too late and without mercy;
2.  Too much speed for the corner;
3.  Rough or excessive steering;
4.  Accelerating too early/too hard in the middle of the corner.

## Understeer

The good news is that understeer is a piece of cake to deal with, which is why most carmakers design their cars to do it. A front-wheel-drive car is naturally prone to this because the front tyres have to contend simultaneously with the jobs of steering around the corner and accelerating. You flirt around the edges of understeer on a daily basis pulling out of tight junctions.

If you push the gas pedal too hard then you will lose some steering because, as with braking, the accelerator is always the winner in the game of rock, paper, scissors.

If you lose steering ability, the hedge draws closer. You could do what the airline pilot did, or you could just back off the gas pedal, recover some steering and be on your way. Easy. Next chapter anyone … ?

*Hang on.*

There's more to it than that. On a dry, grippy surface you're hardly ever likely to encounter any more drama than point four on my list above – but I will give you chapter and verse on the rest just in case! Bear them in mind when we head out into the rain and snow.

'You flirt around the edges of understeer on a daily basis.'

## Coming Round the Mountain

We're going back to Bathurst, Australia, the road circuit packed with ever frightening and tightening bends, where failure to turn on command results in your immediate introduction to 'the Mountain' on which it is built.

I was halfway through the race, in the groove and swiping round the narrow, double left-hander called 'The Cutting' at 95 mph when a voice inside my head said: *Why won't it go round the corner like I'm telling it to?*

The steering went light in my fingers (see points two and three on my list above) as the front tyres, always the first to encounter anything slippery, broke free of the surface. It didn't take a rocket scientist to realize that, unless something was done sharpish, I had an appointment with the barrier.

The mistake people make when the front skids is to turn the steering more, because normally 'the more you turn the wheel, the more it turns the car.' Once you go beyond the limit of the tyres' ability to grip, however, adding steering makes understeer *much* worse, especially at high speed when the temptation to do so is greatest. Speed is the issue.

I was already off the throttle, which passed weight forwards and added grip to the fronts, but it wasn't enough. I needed to get the speed (point 2) down. I gently applied the brakes (point 1), which made the understeer even worse … but bear with me!

This is a technique I call 'pump and saw', and it's a survival strategy, not a lifestyle choice.

*Pump*: squeeze the brakes to get some speed off – that's the most important thing, then release brake pressure to give it a shot with the steering.

*Saw*: straighten the steering as you brake – that helps the tyres slow you down faster – then saw at the wheel by turning and straightening as your speed reduces.

Each time you steer it reduces your braking performance and vice versa, which is why you try to alternate them to balance the needs of making the corner.

By the final moments of my mini-adventure, my speed was down to a jog, and the steering worked, the tail lurched round, and I slithered past the rock face. As for the helpful guy who had dropped his gearbox oil everywhere, rest assured I thanked him later.

Having dealt with too much speed going *into* the corner, let's have some fun on the way *out* when you give it a bootful.

Some of the longest seconds of my life were spent running away from David Walliams as he turned through the final corner of *Top Gear*'s Dunsfold circuit. He wasn't exactly God's gift to driving, but he certainly wasn't doing it 'like a lady' the day I met him. As I stood beside the track in the line of fire, I noticed the whites of his eyes bulging more than usual. He heaved the Suzuki Liana's steering wheel several times in the desired direction while applying copious throttle, which negated the car's ability to turn. Neither my hand gestures nor the grass and rock

*'Why won't it go round the corner like I'm telling it to?'*

flying across his windscreen convinced David that turning the wheel even more wouldn't save him, and he shot off the track like a torpedo.

I strongly believe that in his mind David was pushing the brake pedal. His only mistake was that he neglected to remove his foot from the accelerator first. The front tyres can only take so much abuse until they reach a limit and stall, like the wing of an aircraft once the angle of attack has been exceeded.

That is why you adopt the quarter-to-three steering position: by fixing your hands there you tend not to add big gobs of steering long after the horse has bolted. An understeering condition becomes obvious because your hands are crossing right before your eyes.

As we dived for cover, David shot past us, steering ever more to the left but heading straight as an arrow. The moment his outer wheels dropped off the shoulder of the road onto the slippery grass, the whole dynamic changed. His rear tyre went light as the road dropped away, then encountered the grass and skidded. All that steering finally found an outlet. The car slewed sideways and spun around like a top.

## Oversteer

Oversteer is predominantly the preserve of rear-wheel-drive cars, where an excess of power through the rear tyres causes them to lose grip. It can occur by virtue of their generally edgier handling characteristics. As David kindly demonstrated, however, it is also possible to destabilize a front-wheel-drive car.

Besides the common causes of skids, here are some more specific examples of throttle-related oversteer.

### Lift-off Oversteer

Applying the throttle has a dynamic effect in the way that it transfers weight within the car. Acceleration plants weight onto the rear tyres and loads them with grip at the expense of the fronts.

In a sweeping corner with the rears squatting, the fronts may reach a point where they start to lose grip. If the driver responds using the corrective model for understeer by lifting off the throttle, it will effect a weight transfer back onto the front tyres. Done gradually, this will restore balance to the universe, and the car will negotiate the curve smoothly.

If the driver snaps his foot off the throttle, the weight lurches forwards, giving the fronts more bite to steer with just as the weight shifts off the rears, reducing their grip and causing them to skid wide. This is lift-off oversteer.

### Power Oversteer

With a rear-wheel-drive car, if you put excessive driving force through the rear tyres they will break traction, and the car will oversteer.

This problem is often compounded by premature acceleration out of a corner, causing the rear to sit and provide grip *at first*. It feels good, so you accelerate harder without noticing that the fronts are skidding slightly up to the moment when the rear tyres spin. The extra steering angle causes the rear to snap sideways *very* quickly.

To counter this, you need to remove the cause by releasing pressure on the throttle and steering into the slide to control your sideways angle, or yaw. If the problem is extreme you can cut all drive to the rears by dipping the clutch. For further detail, skip to drifting (page 258).

Whatever the cause, when your car suddenly rotates more than you're expecting and skids sideways, it will scare the crap out of you. What you do next will either be inspired, or awful.

Here is the recovery technique that covers most bases.

### Opposite Lock

Your instinct, other than to freeze, is to remove lots of steering because the car is turning too much. That's a good start, but most people overdo it. Keep calm and … SHIT!

**S** – Steer into the slide, with catlike reflexes. (Or at least straighten the steering if you run across a slippery surface like Walliams.)

**HI** – Hold It. Let the car recover for a second, no more.

**T** – Turn the wheel towards the corner again. Everybody forgets that part, and it causes all the mess. You have to unwind the corrective steering once the car recovers.

The steering has to be instant and intuitive, otherwise you might spin. If you can find the time and the money, get to a skid-pan. It's as much fun as you can legally have with your clothes on and the best training there is for safe driving.

'Keep
calm and …
SHIT!'

*Addendum*: At the time of writing there is a degree of change regarding skid control and use of the brake. The old rule was that you avoided the brake at all costs during oversteer, because the negative weight transfer this created might worsen the problem or cause a spin. In high-tech cars fitted with the latest ABS and ESP (stability) software, it is no longer the case. These systems may actively cut in and trigger braking to individual wheels on your behalf to control the slide, or become activated when you press the brake during a skid. I've used this in conjunction with steering to recover seemingly impossible slides with Mercedes, Porsches and Audis. It's worth asking the dealer what's under your hood!

### Opposite Lock Explained

When the tail skids out to the left, as would *normally* occur if you overcooked your goose into a right-hander, then you steer left to counter it, and vice versa. All being well the car will follow the curvature of the road, even though you're steering in the opposite direction to the corner.

### Over-correcting

In a small slide the action of the tyres scrubbing sideways can drag enough speed off the car to resolve the situation without much human intervention. In a wider, faster slide, immediate intervention is definitely required.

In a perfect world, where nobody panics in a crisis, you would calmly wind the wheel in direct proportion to the angle of the slide and not a fraction more, then unwind it as the crisis draws to an end.

In reality you counter-steer, almost certainly too much, then hold the slide for a brief and terrifying intake of breath. The duration of this eye-of-the-storm moment varies, depending on how dire things are. The rears recover grip as the speed drops, and this is the instant that separates the men from the boys.

You must reclaim control of your sphincter, which is now twitching faster than a badger's nose, and remember to *straighten the steering* and aim for the corner.

Perfecting that response might require the seat-of-the-pants connection you only find at the *Top Gun* canteen, but you can do it. Counter-steering is natural; just don't overdo it.

'This is the instant that separates the men from the boys.'

**The 'Tank Slapper'**

You overdid it. Turn too far into the skid, lose your place on the steering wheel, and the tail snaps a second time – in completely the opposite direction. All too often, this 'yaw oscillation' is the end of the game. It's like ducking one of Mike Tyson's jabs and planting your face straight into the uppercut.

When the rear balances, the back tyres grip, and so do the fronts (which are now pointing completely the wrong way for the corner). If you fail to straighten the wheel, all the energy in the rear axle rebounds, and the added momentum created by the steering angle causes the rear tyres to skid in the opposite direction. This secondary slide is far worse than the first. Good luck; you're back into SHIT mode.

---

**Hot Tip**

> **Steer properly. Avoid jerky steering that might destabilize the weight of the car and cause a skid. With shuffle steering you lose track of how many times you've turned the wheel. Using the 'racing' method makes it quicker and easier to apply opposite lock and whip the wheel straight at the end.**

---

## Recovering from a Spin

If all your attempts to wrestle your beast away from the jaws of oversteer come to naught, then you will go from sliding sideways to spinning backwards and then … who knows what direction?

The old adage at this point is: 'In a spin, both feet in.'

You hit the brake pedal as hard as you can and put your other foot on the clutch. A maximum brake scrubs off speed in the shortest possible distance, and putting the clutch in will hopefully keep the engine running once the car comes to a stop, should you be lucky enough to drive away from this.

Don't be fooled into releasing the brakes until you come to a rest, because during the spin you will lose all sense of your speed and direction. Rotating on the road is a terrifying and potentially deadly experience, but remembering to floor the brakes could save your life or someone else's.

**Hot Tips**

> In a racing situation, drivers treat spins a little differently.

> In order to do this we deploy a technique known in ballet as 'spotting'. During an intense spin a ballerina fixes her gaze on a spot to prevent disorientation until the rotation of her body requires her to turn her head and refocus.

> In a spinning car you can fix your eyes on your line of travel, flicking your head around as it spins backwards and automatically bringing the car around with your hands until you face forwards again. It goes without saying, this should only be practised on a track with a good instructor!

'In a spin,

both feet in.'

# Driving in the Wet

'There's no such thing as bad weather, just inappropriate clothing.'

*Sir Ranulph Fiennes*

One-fifth of our time on British roads is spent driving in the wet, but it contributes to a third of all daytime casualties and over *half* of all casualties at night.

When it rains, the world changes instantly. You have to change with it. Driving technique in the rain is really no different to dry running, it just requires you to dial your reflexes in to the notion that things take longer, and the driver's inputs need to be slower and gentler to allow the tyres to cope with reduced levels of grip. Put simply, you can't throw as much force around, and the secret to being a wet-weather ace is being silky smooth with the controls and keeping your cool.

The one element that is most different in terms of technique is the way you apply the brakes. In the dry you can be assertive on the pedal and use an initial stab before you squeeze to load the front tyres, plus the car can accept greater forces. This doesn't apply in wet or low-grip conditions. You have to be more gradual with the initial application to create slower weight transfers. Throttle technique is the same, but you effectively have much more power underfoot than normal. Yes, sir, even you in the Cinquecento.

Locking a tyre at the start of braking in the wet can cost you as much as 70 per cent of your stopping power, a problem that ABS is designed to handle. Nonetheless, in the wet, as ever, skid prevention is always better than cure.

I raced an Ascari GT3 car at Mugello with none other than the boss and owner of the company, Klaas Zwart. He's a fast driver and, by his own admission, slightly impatient.

The car didn't make the opening practice sessions, and by the time qualifying started, Klaas' foot was tapping a hole in the ground. As the crew fluttered around us, I insisted they cut air holes into the door for venting. Tempers frayed a touch, but I got my vents and joined one fully soaked circuit.

Forty cars churned the tarmac. Crazy people launched themselves at the track like a demolition derby, and the marshals duly counted them into the tyre

'Walking on
eggshells.'

walls. Clouds of spray added to the downpour already challenging my one-speed windscreen wiper, but the vents worked a treat.

I picked an inside line at the end of each straight, avoiding the usual line, which was caked in glossy rubber, slipped my foot gently onto the brakes and squeezed slowly until I felt the tyre reach its limit. As the tyres squirmed, the feel of grip permeated every sinew of my leg.

Despite walking on eggshells, when I shifted down the gears the rear wheels would occasionally lock over puddles, and the thunder of V8 would be replaced with the deathly chatter of gearbox. I dipped the clutch and released it more slowly than a turtle swimming through Marmite.

As the straight entered the curve, the rubber-coated racing line cut from the outside to the inside of the corner, so I did the opposite; I headed straight across the usual line to the outside of the bend. I released the brakes and, with no throttle, flew around the widest arc to benefit from the most unused, porous stretch of track, steering with only the lightest of touches on the wheel – feeling for a change in asphalt, and then crawling onto the throttle so carefully that I could barely hear the engine picking up.

Down the straights I sought out the shallowest puddles and splashed through dead centre with the tyres straight, wincing as the rears aquaplaned and the tyres spun in fifth gear, but the Ascari never wandered. By the end of the session, this tiptoeing exercise was worth pole position by one and a half seconds.

On the streets there's nothing to be gained by using 'wet' lines because the entire surface tends to be equal in terms of grip, but you can feel the change from one surface to the next. Ah, but puddle watching, what sport.

## After it Rains

The road remains wet, and it's the surface condition that dictates the grip level. After the rain stops the conditions linger, especially on local roads that are sheltered from sunlight. Wooded areas continue to drip water long after the surrounding roads have dried, and a nice coating of wet leaves handles like ice.

Ignore the loonies who want to tailgate in these conditions and keep a longer distance to traffic ahead so that you can see well beyond the immediate.

You have a quarter less grip for stopping and accelerating, 50 per cent less on smooth, slippery roads and *half* the cornering grip of dry running.

## Read the Road

'All that glisters is not gold ...'

In the unlikely event that you get a long period of sun in this country, cars lay down lots of rubber on the road surface. It becomes so highly polished by oily lubricants that it becomes less porous and reflects sunlight. The first droplets of rain sit on top of this layer and create a greasy film, which just sits there, waiting to undermine you. Look out for anything that shines, from manhole covers to cobblestones, and be especially mindful of regular stopping points such as traffic lights, bus stops and taxi ranks; they tend to get doused with slick lubricants, so leave enough stopping distance so you can feather the brake pedal for the last few metres in the wet.

'All that glisters
------------------------------------
is not gold ...'
------------------------------------

## Tyres in Rain

As rain falls, your tyres work hard in a number of ways to support your progress, and their ability to do so varies considerably, as we saw in the chapter on tyres.

Pressure at the tyres' leading edge cuts through the water and displaces it through the channelled grooves, yet traces of water remain. The edges of the sipes and tread blocks dig into the road surface, pressurize it and actually break through the film of water to create *dry* contact.

If the water level rises on the road surface, the fronts of the tyres plough through it, splitting the bow wave. Surface water is channelled away, and this process of cutting and squirting has to disperse the water quickly enough to prevent it building up.

When the pressure of water meeting the tyre's leading edge exceeds the pressure on the contact patch, the tyres lift off the road, and aquaplane begins. You are effectively driving a boat.

## Avoiding Aquaplane

Aquaplane occurs almost exclusively at high speed, so you will experience it most on the motorway or similarly fast trunk roads. All you need to do to avoid it, therefore, is to slow down.

Heavy rain, the stuff that sounds like it's denting the bodywork, creates perfect conditions for aquaplane within seconds. When the road becomes saturated it forms pools in the lower portions, filling troughs and worn grooves made by trucks, and any dips by the roadside. It also creates small rivers that cross slopes in the highway with no thought for your wellbeing. Persistent rain might take a little longer to form puddles, but the point is that you need to read the conditions to anticipate the presence of standing water and *moderate your speed accordingly*. Don't judge your speed by looking at other people, as their vehicles may behave entirely differently to yours.

You scan the ground ahead and search for signs of standing water, which identifies itself by its shine and from the splash of incoming droplets. Noticing these signs in the daytime is hard enough with all the spray, so a healthy following distance helps. At night it becomes harder still. Usually you can make out two black stripes in your lane, which are the grooves from regular traffic filling with water.

'You are effectively driving a boat.'

# 24. Tyres in the Rain

View of the contact patch from below

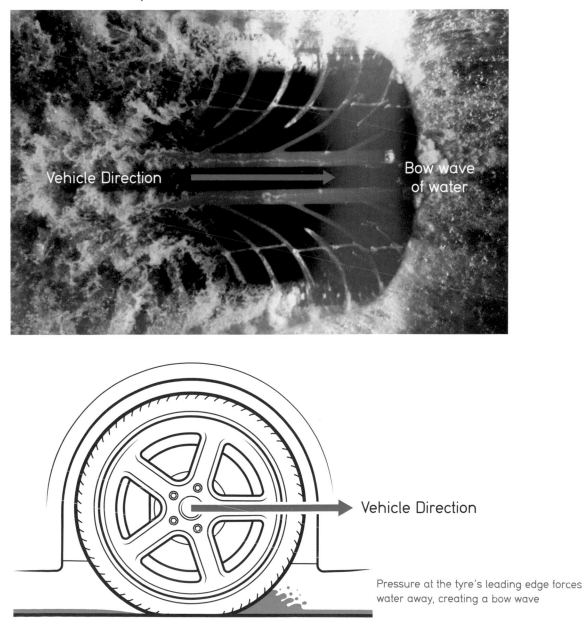

Vehicle Direction

Bow wave of water

Vehicle Direction

Pressure at the tyre's leading edge forces water away, creating a bow wave

Water trapped in the sipes is driven into the tread grooves and channelled away

By running slightly off the centre line you can avoid the worst of it. Lane one is most affected by these grooves, lane three less so, but the right-side verge may be flooded, leaving lane two as generally the safest place to be.

However, situations develop where the whole surface is covered with several inches of water. The tyres become so saturated that they lift off the road.

## Factors Affecting Aquaplane

Aquaplane is directly proportionate to your speed, and a wide tyre has to deal with a much larger flow of water. This feature has been well researched at Bugatti's secret test track in Ehra-Lessien in Germany, where I coached Captain Slow, aka James May, in the finer points of handling a $1 million Veyron. James showcased the one thing it was designed to do best by guiding 1,000 unbroken horsepowers down a 5-mile straight at a speed of 253.81 mph.

The heavens opened as soon as he finished, and it looked like playtime was over, but *Top Gear*'s director, Nigel Simpkiss, had other ideas.

'I'd just like to get some shots of the Veyron whipping up some spray over the top of the Armco. Do you think that would be OK?'

The Bugatti engineer nursed his chin for an answer to this innocently couched question before consenting for us to film 'a couple of runs'.

I strapped into the fitted leather throne, twisted the key and felt sixteen pistons fizzing to life. The engineers checked the tyre pressures, as they did every time the Veyron left their bosom, and I ventured out onto the gigantic highway.

I looped around a carousel and accelerated through a curve towards the straight where Nigel's camera team was stationed by the 12-foot barriers to my right. Even at 60 mph the rooster tail of spray was kicking pretty high, but 'more' is an ever-popular adjective in the film game, so I squeezed the gas.

The bony feeling you get from the Bug on a dry road makes it handle like it's on the proverbial train tracks. It sits on rubbers that are nearly 15 inches across, making them the broadest tyres ever manufactured. Throw in the four-wheel-drive and untold electronic stability systems, and you might be excused for taking a nap on the way to the yacht. So I squeezed some more.

The 8-litre engine promptly replied, and I surged forward into a sea of shiny black tarmac, and a world of pain. All that tight handling evaporated the moment the water crawled under those fat tyres. The Bug flicked sideways, and I

# 'The nightmare was over.'

found myself facing left towards a welcoming grass bank. They say it takes years to build a reputation but you can throw it away in a moment. This was one of them.

The opposite lock went in immediately in an attempt to correct the lurid angle, or 'yaw' as pilots refer to it. Things seemed to be OK, but at nearly 2 tons the Bug was projecting itself into yet deeper waters. I could feel the steering going even lighter, so I pressed the middle pedal to request a little customer service.

The ABS was thus engaged. It could perform the one task I could not, which was to activate individual braking mechanisms on each of the four tyres and by doing so begin the process of addressing the slide sideways.

By adjusting individual wheel speeds and compensating for the tyre that was struggling most, the ABS trimmed out enough of my rate of yaw to keep me from spinning. The speed slowly but surely bled off. Once the tyres landed the Bug snapped back into line, and because I had only applied a modest level of counter-steering I could straighten it quickly, and the nightmare was over.

Nigel crackled over the radio: 'Could we get another one of those from a different angle?'

I pitted.

I mentioned my little moment to the Bugatti engineer, who exhaled and explained that they had lost three Veyrons up the grass bank previously during heavy rain. We agreed we should wait for the track to drain.

*Summary*
- Speed and water level dictate aquaplane severity.
- Tread depth – if the tyres are bald, you're toast. Good tyres dissipate up to 30 litres per second.
- Under-inflated tyres reduce the ability of the tyre to cut the mustard.
- Vehicle weight is a positive factor, unless the tyres are under-inflated.
- The wider the tyre, the more likely it is to aquaplane. It's the only time that driving a 2CV beats a Bugatti Veyron.
- In a rear-wheel-drive, wheelspin in fourth or fifth gear is not for the faint-hearted. Hitting standing water with one side of the car during acceleration can cause you to spin. Lighten the foot.
- Turn cruise control off when it rains. It will try to accelerate when you hit standing water.

Driving in the Wet

'You
recover
control by
effectively
doing
nothing'

## Handling Aquaplane

Aquaplane in a straight line manifests as a tug at the steering wheel, a braking sensation and the sound of water gushing inside the wheel arches. One side of the car might suddenly pull more than the other. If you are accelerating at the time you might hear the engine note rising unexpectedly, as if you pressed the clutch by mistake. That sound is the driven wheels spinning!

• Serious aquaplane only happens at speeds above 50 mph, so you need to reduce your speed, but do it carefully.

• Lift off the gas,

• Keep the steering straight and grip it firmly,

• Stay off *all* the pedals – the force of water hitting the tyres acts like a natural brake, and once the speed bleeds off, the tyres will touch down again. You recover control by effectively doing nothing.

**Hot Tip**

> **Sometimes aquaplane will affect one side of the car more than the other. If you sense it pulling to one side, gently resist by applying a little steering to keep you going straight while lifting off the accelerator as usual. The steering won't actually work until the tyres 'land'. If you panic and wind loads of steering on, it won't have any effect until the tyres kiss the road again, which will cause the car to swerve or spin.**

When a car aquaplanes *in a straight line* I personally prefer not to brake, even with ABS, because it gets confused and drags things out by locking the tyres, albeit slightly, and reducing steering power. I prefer some steering in reserve to handle other problems as required.

Aquaplane in a curve is a different animal. The car becomes possessed, instantly losing steering and then pitching violently sideways as the tyres lift off unevenly, and all this while your ejector seat is still being serviced.

If you do go sideways on standing water and you have ABS, this is the time to use it. Push hard and fast on the pedal, fix your steely-eyed gaze on where you would like to go and put in the requisite opposite lock.

How much you drift across the highway will depend on your speed. Once you slow and the tyres land, locate the nearest service station and dislodge excrement.

If you see a flooded curve coming at the last moment, dab the brakes and try to straighten the steering a little so the tyre can plough better.

## Floods

Near biblical volumes of rain have been turning our towns into Venetian piazzas. There's a temptation to battle the elements. Deep inside, we let rip a silent but deadly Mel Gibson war cry, '*Freeeeedddoommm*', and within seconds the objections of our spouse are drowned out beneath 2 feet of water.

I was sizing up a flooded road last month when a rare moment of Ray Mears-worthy self-preservation gripped me. I waded into the water up to my knees to measure the depth, crucially above the height of my car's radiator, and agreed with another driver it was a no-go. A third man thought better of it.

He reversed his newish Audi Q7 a considerable distance back up the hill, stopped, then gunned it towards the water. He must have hit it at about 50, the equivalent of slamming into a brick wall, judging by the way the bonnet erupted skywards. There was an impressive amount of steam from both engine and driver as he realized the reason the motor died on impact was because the water had taken out the radiator, then been sucked up the air intake. Mucho expensivo.

Avoid floodwater wherever possible, but if you give it a go …

Hot Tips

> It's better to get your feet wet checking the level first than to rinse your wallet at the garage. Walk the full length of the crossing to make sure the road surface hasn't been washed away and confirm where the water level is lowest, which is often in the middle of the road. Ideally you want a depth of no more than 15 cm (the height of the centre of your wheels).

> Don't drive across at the same time as oncoming vehicles, as their wake won't sit well in your lap.

> Take it slow and steady. Select a low gear and head through at a brisk walking pace so that you benefit from the bow wave created in front of the car. That way, if the depth is deeper than you thought you might still reverse out, and it also prevents the water crashing into your engine's vital organs.

> Once you emerge, check the brakes a few times because the water tends to get stuck between the brake pads.

# Seeing and Being Seen

Mr Magoo sees better than most when it rains.
Droplets lash at the windscreen, and spray from other
vehicles outpaces the wipers.

The white noise of water rushing around the wheel arches numbs your eardrums, and before you know it the screen mists up.

Small mistakes that might go unpunished in the dry catch up with you in the rain. There are some technological assets available to counter the elements, as well as some clever driving techniques and strategies.

One of the biggest problems with driving in the rain is simply being able to see through the windscreen when it mists up like a Turkish spa and the Rain God opens its bladder in your face. Some of the biggest shunts on road and track occur when vision is compromised, because people generally don't get a chance to brake for something they cannot see coming.

Rarely, if ever, has a racing driver stepped out of a rain-soaked racing car and high-fived the crew to compliment them on the effectiveness of the wipers

or de-mister. The belts hold you so tightly to the chair that you can't reach the windscreen to clear it. When Guy Smith raced his Le Mans-winning Bentley Speed 8 in the rain, it reached a point where he was gazing through a clear spot the size of a pound coin. The mechanics eventually took pity and passed him a sponge-on-a-stick when he managed to find the pit lane.

De-misting is easier said than done if the inside of the screen has never been cleaned, because the layer of your DNA stuck to the glass surface sucks in the moisture and creates condensation. Your smudgy hand, as you know, does little to wipe it away. A once-over with a cloth and some glass cleaner every decade makes life considerably easier.

You can follow Granddad's advice and keep a dry drag/chamois leather *or* you can line the inside of your screen with a moisture-resistant agent called Rain-X Anti-Fog. Failing that, rub washing-up liquid, or any household soap, across the inside of the screen with a damp cloth, leave to dry, then polish with a soft dry cloth.

Sorted. Vent as required.

### Venting

When it's cold you need hot air to heat the windscreen and vaporize the condensation, then an open window to get rid of it.

Warm air can hold more water vapour than cold. Summer rain fogs up your screen, then you blow hot air at it, which is full of humidity, and wonder why the screen mists up more. Ideally you want to blast cold, dry air (air con works best) with the windows open until the engine has warmed up enough to produce hot air, then heat the screen as quickly as possible.

Race cars use the same heating strips on the windscreen that road cars have on the rear screen, but sadly this hasn't filtered through.

### Hot Tips

>Rain-X, the yellow bottle, for the front screen. Wipe it on, and the raindrops scatter faster than the French Air Force.

### Lights

Headlights on is a good idea – but LEAVE THE FOG LIGHT ALONE. It's illegal to use if visibility is better than 100 metres, and dazzling everyone around you prevents them from seeing your brake lights.

# Winter Driving

If the thermometer in your car reads 7 degrees, you are driving in winter conditions.

At anything below 3 degrees, you should expect ice. Daylight is in short supply during the winter months, road surfaces are 60 per cent more likely to be wet, and, as the cold weather sets in, the chances of ice or snow grow by 35 per cent. The sun's arc tracks 30 degrees lower across the sky, and the grime from salted roads and condensation reduces visibility to a submarine opacity.

The vital ingredient is preparation: five minutes to prepare the car, and with it, your mindset. Muscle memory, the reason you never forget how to ride a bike, lets you down with driving on snow and ice because we do it so infrequently. Grip levels are from a different planet.

At the lowest end of the scale you have ice, which is practically a frictionless surface at temperatures close to zero. Ironically as ice gets *much* colder it offers more grip.

Snow passes through various states depending on the temperature and how much traffic has compacted it. If it looks hard and polished it will behave like ice. Fresh, deep snow provides better grip and as it melts away you approach something closer to a wet road.

The easiest way to transform yourself into the God of Winter Driving overnight is to buy a set of winter tyres. En route to *Top Gear*'s Winter Olympics (car ice hockey, anyone?), our testosterone-charged convoy ventured across a snow-covered Norway to Lillehammer, until we ran into a little local difficulty: a steep, frozen hill at the base of a giant ski jump. Cars in ditches as far as the eye could see, faster than the producer could yelp 'insurance premium', followed by much tyre-kicking and ego-deflation. Then our twenty-four-year-old production assistant drove past the lot of us in her Saab Aero, the only vehicle properly decked out for the prevailing weather conditions.

## Prep the Car

• Start the engine / rev @ 3,000 rpm – crank up the air con/de-mister.
• Unless you're a tank driver, you need front, rear and side vision through the windows, so clearing the snow from these areas is the first order of business. Clear the bonnet too, otherwise you get a faceful of snow as soon as you depart.

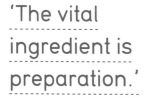

'The vital ingredient is preparation.'

Boiling water can crack the windscreen, but a warm kettle is a quick way to clear ice and be on your way smartly with less misting up.

- Check/replace knackered windscreen wipers. Don't use them straight away; if they are frozen to the screen in the morning the brittle rubber can snap.

- If there's time: use freeze-resistant windscreen washer fluid, which works like Kryptonite on freezing fog/sleet (not engine antifreeze, which strips paint).

- You need a fifty-fifty mix of antifreeze and water in the cooling system. It needs refilling roughly every two years and should be a part of your car's regular service – if your car runs out and it freezes overnight there's a fair chance that vital parts of the engine, like the water pump and the block, will freeze too and then break.

- Leave tyre pressures alone – reducing them does not improve traction on ice, it reduces stability, unless you're on sand!

- Weight: unloaded vans and pickups are tricky in the snow, so it's better to add weight to help the tyres bite into the surface. For rear-wheel-drive cars with a front engine and low-profile tyres … good luck; put something heavy in the trunk.

## Plan a Route

- Unless you love stationary traffic, you want to avoid hills *at all costs*; they will be littered with crashed lemmings. The higher the road, the colder the weather.

- Assuming the roads are open, aim for major roads that will have been gritted, avoiding the tiddly lanes that won't. Allow extra time to get there, and so what if you're late.

- Icy conditions make it easy for the wheels to spin when you accelerate. During a big freeze even the slightest camber or gulley can make leaving a parking space a major extraction.

- I personally prefer to feel the conditions and always use first gear to pull away on ice, but if you find my way too complicated then use second gear to control the wheelspin.

- Using very low revs and hardly any throttle, close to stalling, let the engine torque ease the car forward by gradually releasing the clutch to the biting point so that the car barely moves.

- As soon as you get some momentum the worst is over, and you can feather the throttle until you're clear. Keep your *front wheels* as straight as possible, otherwise they will spin.

Winter Driving

221

# Winter Tyres

## Britons view the fitting of winter rubber as unsporting and a waste of money.

Improvements in the technology mean that you can potentially run winter tyres all year round, decent ones at least, without a major penalty in the summer months. They last as long as summers and are equally fuel efficient.

The secret's in the sipes. Winter tyres have ten times as many sets of teeth and, unlike a summer tyre, their jaws don't stiffen up in the cold. You cannot believe their effectiveness until you try them. Here are some comparisons on braking distances from quite low speeds – the effect at high speed is greatly exaggerated, as you know.

Snow conditions, stopping from 30 mph

Summer tyres: 60 metres

Winter tyres: 30 metres

Ice conditions, stopping from 20 mph

Summer tyres: 46 metres

Winter tyres: 26 metres

Acceleration figures in dry conditions are fairly even between both tyre types, but in the snow you benefit from a tripling in performance with winters when you pull away from low speed, and they work magic on hills.

Whether you fit them or not is a close call. In the far north of England and Scotland especially, there's a ground frost for more than half of the year based on averages across the last thirty years. That means you're definitely better off on winters. For the rest of the country the frost falls to about a third of the time.

We have two cars in the family, one on summers, the other on winters ready for the white-out.

# 25. Summer & Winter Tyres

## Stuck in a Rut

If you're stuck, it's time to deploy some rock 'n' roll!

When snow gets packed around your wheels you may need to dig yourself out. Clear away any ruts around the tyres that will impede progress. Then jam something like a piece of carpet, rags or anything dry underneath/in front of the driven tyre to give it the initial purchase required for forward motion.

Endless wheelspinning only digs you further into the mess. You need to rock the car forwards and backwards until you build enough momentum to creep out. To do this requires timing and deft clutch control.

In first gear, ease forward using the engine torque at low revs up until the point of wheelspin, then let off the gas, or clutch in, to let the car roll back until it meets resistance. And repeat …

It might take ten or more attempts, but each time you roll back, it builds a little ramp behind you, and from that platform you can eventually carry enough forward momentum to drive clear.

To make it a social event you can invite friends to put their weight onto the driven axle. Tell them you'll buy them a drink later, and remember to hose them liberally with slush once they've succeeded in freeing you.

With a front-wheel-drive get someone to sit on the bonnet on the side that is spinning most, and bounce as you accelerate. Weight is your friend on slippery surfaces, and the more you have, the better your traction.

Remember not to run over your saviour in the process.

## Driving in the Snow

Once you get going, make sure there's nobody behind and do a fairly abrupt brake test at low speed to see how easily you can stop. Then try it again without the tyres skidding to tune you in to the available braking grip.

Mud is another element of British life
with a sense of humour.

## '*Always* let your mate get stuck first, then smugly find somewhere else to park.'

Inevitably at some point in your life, someone will invite you to 'park in the field', as casually as informing you that the loo is on the second floor.

I wouldn't dream of insulting your intelligence here, but …

*Always* let your mate get stuck first, then smugly find somewhere else to park.

Aim for the high ground to aid your departure.

Take as straight a line as possible and go in really fast with loads of revs – it'll sound great and you'll look the bollocks, even if you sink straight into a quagmire.

Generally speaking, drive backwards and carry some momentum. By reversing a front-wheel-drive car uphill, it puts more weight onto the driven wheels and provides more traction. And once you've parked you can drive straight out. A proven ice-breaker for the frosty driveway too.

Once stuck – apply the rock 'n' roll method as per snow.

## Braking

Planning ahead is everything. If you enter too fast and try to adjust the speed later, you'll skid. Braking distances are up to *ten times* as long as normal, so although staging a corner feels like putting a date in the diary, it beats ending up in a ditch.

Use low gears to keep the engine rpm high so that, when you lift off the gas, the engine braking instantly reduces your speed without having to touch the brake pedal. If you do use the brakes, use them sparingly so the tyres don't skid. With enough anticipation of junctions and by leaving a big enough gap between you and the cars in front, you can avoid using the brakes almost entirely.

Like the throttle, the brake pedal is super-sensitive on snow. Caress and squeeze it as tenderly as though you were treading onto your own genitals, allowing the wheels enough time to spread away as you increase pressure. A delicate process to be sure.

When you're following other vehicles, a simple calculation of distance is 4 car lengths for every 10 mph. So if you're driving at 20 mph, you allow 8 car lengths between you and the vehicle ahead. At 50, it's up to 20 car lengths.

As a last resort you can use the handbrake, sparingly, to slow down, but only if you're confident enough to do it. There's minimal weight transfer when you brake on snow, which means the rear tyres have braking grip in reserve, so gently applying the handbrake can buy a few metres of stopping distance when you really need it. The idea is not to skid sideways like Starsky and Hutch! And don't try it going downhill …

'Braking distances are up to *ten times* as long as normal.'

## Hot Tips

> Check whether your handbrake attaches to one or both rear wheels. If it's only one, then be aware it will be less stable for the technique described above, and it might not hold you if you stop on a hill (in which case, keep your foot on the brake pedal to avoid sliding backwards – four tyres holding you are better than one).

> If your car has a parking brake in the footwell, it's best not to use it because the rear brakes will lock on until you pull the manual release.

# Pulse Braking

We looked at braking in detail in the first part of the book and established the fastest way to stop in normal driving conditions.

The picture changes when you accidentally cause the tyre to skid under braking, and when driving on slippery surfaces.

Vehicles fitted with ABS are simple in this regard because the computer dictates your options. You press the brake pedal as hard as you can, this activates the ABS, and all you have to do is think about the direction you want to head in and steer towards it.

Without ABS, it gets more interesting. If you lock a tyre at high speed or on a slippery surface, you will slow down eventually, but your braking loss is significant, and you will have no steering ability. You can sit there watching the world go by, or do something called pulse braking.

You quickly release pressure on the brakes to allow the tyres to turn and then reapply them sharply. The tyres lock again, and you repeat the process as fast and often as you can until you slow down.

Pulsing the brake in this way creates small windows of grip during which the tyre takes a bite at the surface as it makes the transition from locking to unlocking, and the more such windows you can create by rapid pulsing the better. Each window also offers an opportunity for you to steer if you need to.

In the case of snow, gravel, and to a lesser extent on ice this method has been proven to stop shorter than ABS because the skidding tyre is able to grind through the slippery surface and latch on to the crunchier stuff underneath.

When it comes to steering around an emergency, such as the moose or another car, you need to time your final release of the brake pedal so that the tyres unlock before you turn the wheel in order for it to respond.

It takes great presence of mind to pulse brake in an emergency, but it's worth it. Just as important is to consider the direction you're taking yourself. I know top drivers who swerved an animal, only to be killed on the other side of the road.

## Steering

Less is more. By turning the steering wheel gradually, you become aware of the point where the tyres start to skid. If you feel the front sliding, *do not turn the steering more*. That's like writing cheques on an overdrawn account. Just wait for the grip to return.

With limited traction to steer around things you need to focus, to anticipate the movements of other road users and pedestrians.

## Accelerating

Don't accelerate into corners, in corners or out of corners. Coast gently through them with the throttle open a fraction to maintain your speed. Wait until the steering wheel is nearly straight and then squeeeeeeze … On snow, your tyres can only do one job at a time, so if you accelerate in a corner you will lose steering.

## Read the Script

Roads exposed to sunlight will thaw first, but areas shaded by woodland, high hedges or under bridges retain freezing temperatures for much longer.

Bridges can be very naughty. They stay frozen the longest, because they have no contact with the ground, just cold air, which forms a lovely layer of invisible black ice. Other practical telltales include pedestrians performing involuntary cartwheels on the pavements, frosty foliage, the whiz of spinning rubber and the crunch of bumper.

Use your local knowledge to pinpoint places where water regularly runs across the road – it will have frozen.

As you cross ice the road noise goes deathly quiet, and you might notice the steering wheel feeling very light. Keep your inputs smooth and to a minimum.

Above all, mind the hills …

## Hills

When I was five years old my mum was driving me to school in her Renault 4, the 'biscuit tin' of myth and legend. We crunched through a few icy puddles before dropping around a left-hander into a steep coppice. At the bottom of the hill lurked a stonewalled bridge across a river, on which was strewn a selection of steaming,

'The car will
be unable
to defy the
effects of
gravity.'

crashed motors. Between them and us was a perfectly laid sheet of black ice. We slid down and joined them.

As soon as my Mum applied the brakes, locked the front wheels and lost all steering, there was little that could be done to avoid that accident *at that point*. Even ABS couldn't have overcome the laws of gravity on a frictionless surface.

Like the men in Lycra, if you find yourself staring down something resembling the Cresta run, once you climb aboard there's no stopping until you reach the bottom. If the road is icy and steep you should avoid it because the car will be unable to defy the effects of gravity.

For gentler descents, bring your speed down early, hold the car with high revs in a low gear and use maximum engine braking to complement the brakes.

## Uphill

When approaching an incline, ensure you have enough speed and momentum to carry you all the way up. If you have to stop part way up, then you may not be able to get going again or, worse, you might start sliding backwards.

It's best to allow traffic to clear in front, for your entertainment as much as anything else. From your vantage point at the bottom you can decide whether to take a run at it or find an alternative route.

## Essential Gear

Even motorways get closed when the weather creates a logjam. It pays to pack a few basics to make sure you're covered:

- food rations – especially water;
- mobile phone, fully charged, kept in a warm pocket to save the battery;
- ice scraper and antifreeze spray;
- trench tool (folding spade);
- foil blanket and high-vis jacket;
- tow rope and jump leads;
- first-aid kit;
- cigarette lighter – in case the door lock is frozen. It's better than licking
  – remember *Dumb and Dumber*;
- hessian sack (to throw the gear in and to place under your tyres when you get stuck).

Winter Driving

231

# Worst-case Scenarios

Here is a series of terrifying situations with remarkably simple solutions. Well… simple as long as you remain calm, think fast and do the right thing.

## Tyre Blowout

Tyre blowout is often cited as a terrifying ordeal – yet it couldn't be easier to deal with, or prevent. You basically do nothing.

The most common cause of a tyre failure is under-inflation, which massively overheats and cuts the sagging rubber until it explodes. If you whack a kerb or something really graunches the wheel then it can weaken the tyre. A fault will reveal itself as a bulge or a cut in the sidewall, assuming you remember to check.

If you didn't check, you may find yourself flying down the highway some weeks later when a sensation similar to the shudder of the rumble strip signals imminent tyre failure.

A tyre blowout at the front or the rear demands pretty much the same response:

- Keep the wheel straight.
- Climb *gently* off the accelerator and let the car's rolling resistance slow you down. *Do not brake* until your speed reduces to at least 50 mph, ideally slower, and then with great care.
- Check your mirrors and ease your vehicle to safety on the hard shoulder using minimal steering.
- Exaggerate your speeds and heroism at the bar later.

If you hit the brakes, the car will want to swivel around the blown tyre and introduce you to a world of pain. The same will happen if you steer sharply. Keep it slow and steady.

A rear blowout in a top-heavy 4x4 or SUV may cause the rear to crab sideways as the proportion of weight higher up in the vehicle acts like a lever, so you may have to work at holding a straight course until the speed drops and you

'Think fast and do the right thing.'

'The car
will want
to swivel
around
the blown
tyre and
introduce
you to a
world of
pain.'

restore control. In the case of a popped front, it may pull at the steering and cause the front to drop on that side. All you need to do is gently resist with the steering to keep it straight.

If you change to a space-saver tyre, remember that they are rubbish, have a speed restriction and a limited range, heat up and don't handle worth a damn. Just saying, change for a real one as soon as you can.

• Keep an eye on your tyre pressures, at least visually if nothing else.

• Check tyres for damage, especially for a long journey with the family (when you double the payload).

• Never buy second-hand tyres. Garages sell them at a tempting price, and though not visibly damaged they were discarded by their previous owners for a reason. Or worse, they might be remoulds.

## Sticking Throttle

This is when the car accelerates all by itself, either because the pedal is jammed or an electronics gremlin tells it to. It is most alarming, and not as rare as you might hope. Between 2009 and 2010, Toyota alone had to recall over 8 million cars; a combination of sticky throttles and ill-fitting floor mats caused them to accelerate against their driver's will, sometimes with fatal results.

A stuck throttle sends your brain into a tailspin because you feel powerless to control the engine – but that's not the case.

In a manual, disconnect the engine by pressing the clutch pedal. Problem solved. In an automatic, shove it into neutral. The engine will scream like hell because the revs will hit maximum – just ignore it and steer to safety

Press the brakes, hard – this will counter the engine while you gather yourself and muster the sense to execute step one.

Passengers take note too – if the driver doesn't select neutral, do it for him.

Common causes of sticking throttle are jammed floor mats or eccentric footwear. *Don't switch off the engine with the key* until you stop – you will lose steering and braking (see below).

## Brake 'Failure'

The most common braking 'issue' is getting something wedged beneath the brake pedal. If your car resembles a rubbish tip, this slumdog might bite you.

Solution: remove the old coke can or copy of *Guns & Ammo* or *Cosmo* that is wedged beneath the pedal and resume business as usual.

Another possibility is that you struck a kerb, pothole or deep water splash. These can knock the brake pads away from the discs, and when you push the brake pedal it goes soft. It's called pad knock-off, and my first lesson was expensive.

I rattled the kerbing at Donington raceway, and the impact knocked the pads from their marks. When I pressed the pedal for the next corner, at 140 mph, it flopped to the floor. By the time I pumped it up and down to restore the system I was airborne, and the brakes weren't much use any more.

Solution: pump up the pedal a few times and restore the brake pressure.

If you service your car regularly, the fluids that feed the brakes' hydraulic systems should be good to go. A quick pump of the pedal when you climb aboard should meet with firm resistance. If it feels increasingly soft or moves further than normal, you have a problem that needs fixing.

## Brake Overheating

Brakes use friction to convert the energy of inertia into heat – and in doing so they can get extremely hot, especially if you drive down a series of bends on a sharp hill. Using engine braking and allowing the low gears to decelerate your rolling mass can alleviate overheating.

However, if you rely solely on the brake pedal during an extended downhill, the brakes might overheat and fade. You will notice that pressing the pedal has diminishing returns and you start cornering with a screech. Assuming you still wish to stay attached to the mountain at the next hairpin, you need to:

Crunch down the gears to force the engine to reduce your speed. Progress down the gears until you reach first, or low in an automatic. This is serious, so buzz the engine if you have to.

Lean on the handbrake all the way, because the rear discs won't be overheated like the fronts. Pull gently at first then apply full pressure, but try to avoid skidding. If you have a modern push-button thing, you're stuffed. American models have a 'parking brake' – basically a handbrake operated by your foot. Get on it.

Park and let the brakes cool down, which might take twenty minutes.

Still not stopping … ?

'Crunch
down the
gears to
force the
engine to
reduce your
speed.'

## Total Brake Failure

This is rare, but could happen if the pedal seizes or the brake lines burst.

If the pedal flops to the floor and pumping it fails to revive it, use the same drill as above for overheating brakes. If you're on a hill or you're still not slowing down, then you may have to come up with a plan B.

Look for an escape route, an incline, an empty street or a gap – you may be able to make a few sharp manoeuvres and thread your way through.

If you're approaching a corner and possess the ability (and mental agility) of Stirling Moss, you might consider doing what he did during the Mille Miglia in 1957. His brake pedal snapped as he slowed from 130 mph for an 85 mph left-hander. He turned the steering wheel several times more than normal and stalled the front tyres. The resulting scrub from the skidding front tyres reduced his speed enough to save his bacon. But for him, after years of similar experiences, it was instinctive.

Crashing to a stop. As an absolute last resort find some gravel, kerbing, hedgerow or – worst case – a wall, or some Armco barrier or a ditch that you can steer into and drag your speed down. Common sense must prevail.

## Parking Brake Failure

Leave the car in first or reverse gear and chock your front wheels against the kerb.

## Steering Failure

Anything that impedes your ability to steer the car in the desired direction is a problem. These days the steering wheel is unlikely to fall off in your hands; nor will the steering column sheer off, unless you've dodged the MOT man for several decades. When it happened to me I felt the wheel lighten and braked before it did anything more dramatic.

Power steering is the principal culprit for what we commonly call steering 'failure' in a road car. Manufacturers these days are designing their vehicles' suspension with phenomenal levels of caster angle in the front wheels – a bit like the extended forks on a Harley Davidson. The benefits include greater fuel efficiency and cornering stability, at the expense of making the steering so heavy that it's practically impossible to turn the wheel without power-steering assistance.

If your power steering fails in a corner then it will be time to test those muscles and drag the wheel to where you want it. Power steering tends to fail in fits and starts, rather than all at once, so as soon as you notice the first heavy hints you should get it fixed.

## Breakdown at a Railway Crossing

Ah, the Swiss Alps … The scent of pine resin, the patter of clogs, the rustle of lederhosen … It's enough to put anyone in the mood to open up a few V12 cylinders. A few years ago we shot Jeremy Clarkson's *Thriller* DVD along the mountain pass at Flüela, and the experience certainly lived up to its name.

On day one, the director shaved a couple of inches off the flank of his Maserati during a close encounter with a concrete barrier. Day two heralded the destruction of a sparkling Alfa Romeo 8C supercar, on loan from Nick Mason of Pink Floyd. And they say that bad luck comes in threes …

I was chewing the fat with Jay Kennedy, our twenty-something cameraman (and my regular co-pilot for anything dangerous) in a brand-new Pagani Zonda Roadster after an exhausting day's shooting. As usual, I had been cajoled into using every last drop of fuel for 'just a few extra shots' and was coasting down the mountain into Davos to find a petrol station with barely a Martini left in the tank.

With the pump in sight, and only a minor incline and a railway track separating us from victory, Jay heard himself saying, 'Wouldn't it be classic if we ran out of fuel in a million-pound Zonda right in the middle of that railway crossing?'

And with that, we did.

As my rapidly pumping foot failed to introduce enough gas to the spark, I noticed a large red train homing in on our right-hand side.

'OH F*** …'

Jay had too.

I popped open the luxurious leather-lined door and looked behind us to see if we could roll back down the hill, but the German parked on our tailpipe was staring blankly ahead. Jay and I somehow summoned the strength of Samson to move the Zonda forward by a crucial two metres. Of course, it started first time after that.

Nobody wants to see their pride and joy become a hood ornament on a southbound freight train, but no car, not even the Zonda, is worth more than your

'The scent of
pine resin,
the patter
of clogs,
the rustle of
lederhosen.'

4: Skidding

legs, let alone life. It's a pressure situation, and time dictates your choice of the following actions:

- Get out and run.
- Clutch in, turn the key *all the way* off and restart the engine, then drive forwards. That usually works.
- Get out and push.

Pressure makes you do silly things like trying to leave the car with the seat belt on or forgetting the person in the back seat. Don't let it beat you.

## Escape from a Sinking Car

More people in Britain drown in cars than on boating lakes. Not many people do drown in boating lakes, but, according to American professor John Hunsucker, about 350 people die every year in sinking vehicles.

RoSPA now agrees that the best survival tip is to get the hell out of it, as fast as you can – rather than following the old-school theory that you should wait until it has filled with enough water to equalize the pressure.

The fact is, your options narrow by the second. You must take quick, decisive action to survive.

As soon as you hit the water:

- Release your seat belt and unlock the central locking (especially if you have passengers).
- Open the door and force it open/wind the windows down if the water is too high already.
- Get out – then you can help attend to others.

What to expect:

- The electrics will fail, which is why you should flick the central locking as soon as possible.
- The windows are also powered by electrics, which is why you can't rely on them and should get the door open quickly.
- Panic. A friend of mine in the Royal Navy had to ditch his helicopter into the sea and despite all his training for this situation was stunned by the pace at which the water invaded the cockpit. 'Frank' (because he used to sound like a yank) got his leg jammed on the seat, grappled with his breathing regulator and finally crawled out. His

# '350 people die every year in sinking vehicles.'

survival made him the first pilot to ditch that particular aircraft and live to tell the tale.

You might run off the road into a river or, with changing weather patterns, be swept off the road in a flash flood. With things happening that quickly, your actions may differ from a situation where there is more time, perhaps if your car rolls down a bank into a lake.

Whatever the situation, if you are in deep water you will have to get out as quickly as possible, but you will need as much energy as possible to swim and, possibly, to fight the cold. If the car has submerged quickly, fight panic by switching on the interior lights (if they work) and breathing deeply.

A few other guidelines might also help:

When you release your seat belts, they might not retract; take care not to get tangled.

If you need to escape through a window and it jams, you need to break it. Unless you happen to carry a window hammer, as I do, you will find it hard to break by kicking. A steering wheel lock might work. If your head rest is removable, pull it out and wedge it down into the door seam of the window, and lever it until it pops the glass. Then smash through. Equally if you have passengers in the back seats this might help get them out.

The car will sink 'heavy end' first (the heavy end is where the engine is). In deeper water it may flip onto its roof.

In a car that sinks front first, there will be a bubble of air in the back, but you should stay in the front … the front windows are often bigger and easier to get out of – for all passengers

The car won't sink immediately, even with the windows open. However, you must use every moment to free yourself and your passengers and get out. Push children out first.

It may seem obvious, but don't try to save anything except lives. Computers, phones, purses, jewellery, etc. can be replaced – you can't!

If you are unable to open a window, there is the equalization option as a last resort. Keep your head. There should be enough air for the minute or two that it will take to prepare to escape. When the car is nearly full of water, take a deep breath and push a door open; you may need to do this with your feet (for extra strength). Note the wait: if you try to open the doors too soon the water pressure will defeat you.

## Bonnet Flies Up/Broken Windscreen

Congratulations on checking your oil, but make sure you closed the bonnet afterwards. I can't remember the last time a bonnet flew up in my face, but the instant blindness and sense of powerlessness came as quite a surprise.

Loose bonnets are mostly a character flaw of an old banger. It's more likely that you will lose your vision from a flying stone or some debris cracking the windscreen and filling the glass with a spider's web that you can't see through. In either event:

- Open the window and stick your head outside so that you can see.
- Hold the steering wheel steady on its original course.
- Reduce speed and casually get off the road.

---

**Obvious Tip**    > Secure your bonnet if it looks loose. If it flies up at speed there will be a
loud bang, the windscreen will probably smash, and you might freak out!

---

Now that your adrenaline is tingling, it's the perfect moment to step into the world of advanced car control and learn to handle a car when it skids.

# Stunt Driving

Once upon a time in the west, men with jaws of granite and Glocks tucked down their Y-fronts developed evasive driving techniques for dealing with mobile assaults by terrorists in parts of the world where you tend not to book summer holidays.

Around the same time, some stunt boys in Hollywood were doing the same thing because it was fun and looked cool on shows like *The Fall Guy*, *Knight Rider* and *The Dukes of Hazzard*. By adopting an aggressive driving style that destabilizes the car, and then bringing in measured amounts of speed, steering and brake, they learned to make a car *dance*.

I've taught some of these skills to law-enforcement operatives, Special Forces and even James Bond himself – but whatever you call them, these moves are only legal on film sets or if you're being shot at. In the real world, you'd only get to have a go on an airfield with an instructor – to do otherwise would be extremely dangerous both to you, and those around you – but they do represent the theoretical outer limits of what is possible and therefore deserve their place in a book called *How to Drive*. So join me, if you will, in a thought experiment: it's your first day on the set of *2 Fast, 2 Furious 27*, you've just been thrown the keys to a brand-new Aston Martin, and the director is about to yell, 'ACTION!' …

## Drive Through

The goal of evasive driving is to evade the threat and flee to safety. Your aim throughout is to *keep moving.* In an ambush your best chance of escape is to drive through it, or spot it early enough to change your route.

In *Spiderman 2* there's a scene where the villain carves through the city with a big towing rig, literally scything through traffic. I was one of thirty cops in hot pursuit, and we had to drive through the mess 'no matter what', while preserving the cars as best we could.

The truck was turning cars into confetti, and squeezing through the maelstrom of flying debris and crashed cars was easier said than done, especially with half of New York's finest trying to fit through the same hole!

When that hole was too small I needed to make it bigger, while avoiding the kind of head-on collision that usually kills radiators, so I would slap the offending blockage with one of the front quarter panels and drive through. One trick I've used before is to lift off the gas or dab the brake pedal just before impact and then accelerate through – it helps to lift the other car out of the way and preserves your momentum. It's still crashing, but with style.

# 'They learned to make a car *dance.*'

# Handbrake Turns

### The Basic 180

If you find yourself in the unfortunate position of actually having the ball during a game of *Top Gear* 'Car Football', then you can expect a visit from one crazy cat by the name of Richard Hammond. For him the ball is like a sack of catnip, and it's best not to get in the way when he speeds towards you with 'that look' in his eye.

In this situation the handbrake turn is a life-saving solution because you can get out of the way fast by spinning the car around and heading off in the other direction. Here's the garden-variety method:

• Slow to a speed of around 20/30 mph – at higher speeds things tend to get messy.

• Pick a spot ahead of you around which to pivot the car on the handbrake, bearing in mind that the car will shift across by roughly its own width.

• *Release the footbrake*.

• Rip the handbrake like you're tearing out a molar and hold it there until it locks the rear tyres and then steer so that the car rotates 180 degrees.

• *Push the clutch in, select first gear*.

• After the car spins around you can brake if you need to, then accelerate away in first.

---

**Common Mistake**   > **Leaving your foot on the brake pedal when you pull the handbrake: it prevents the rear tyres from locking properly. You will just veer off in a cloud of smoke.**

---

### Stunt 180 into a Parking Space

For pulling a 180 into a parking space between two cars I would advise practising with vehicles of the rubber cone variety before attempting it in your driveway.

The goal is to fill the empty gap between two cars, and to do this requires alignment, timing and control. Repeatability is the key to perfecting this move, and that is achieved by using exactly the same speed and turn of the wheel every time. Throughout the move you need to keep your eyes fixed on the parking space.

Line up facing the car you plan to turn away from. That way, when you make your handbrake turn, the car will naturally rotate away from the car you're facing and rotate into the gap.

# 26. The Basic 180

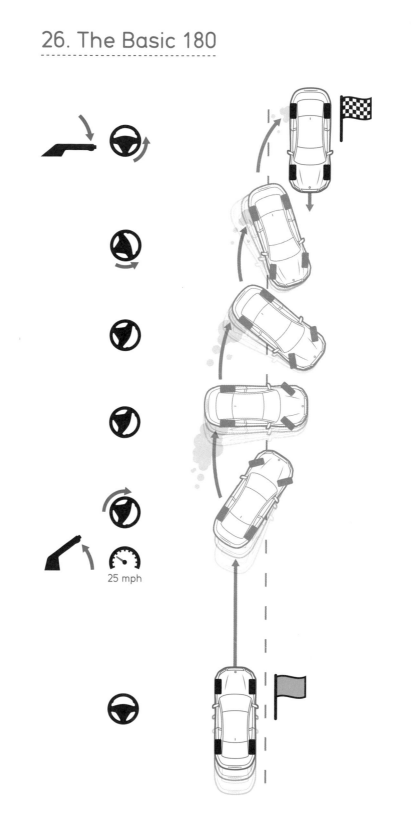

Drive straight towards the outer car and up to your set speed, then flick the car to the right, yank hard on the handbrake and depress the clutch, or flick to neutral.

As the car spins, turn your head in time so that you never lose sight of the parking spot – this helps your hands, which are stupid, follow your eyes which have a hotline to your brain.

A fraction before the car rotates 180 degrees, release the handbrake and straighten the steering to begin reversing. Depending on your distance from the space, you may or may not require reverse gear. As long as you stay off the foot brake the car should have enough momentum to carry itself backwards into the space until you stop on your end mark.

---

**Hot Tips**

> Pick a speed that is fast enough for the handbrake to work, around 40 mph, and still retain enough momentum to keep rolling at the end of the move, but not so fast that you can't control it. Every car is unique and the handbrake will bite differently depending on your speed and surface grip.

> Allow plenty of space between the 180 and the gap until you can repeat it every time without swerving all over the place.

> Try to keep your steering hand in one position on the steering wheel so that you don't get lost and can straighten it the moment you start reversing

---

**Stunt 90 into a Parking Space**

The stunt version of parallel parking is the toughest trick to master, and there is no substitute for practice, practice, practice. To pull the perfect 90 you need to focus on two vital dimensions: the arc of rotation and the landing.

As with the 180, your approach speed will depend on how the car behaves on the surface. The higher the grip, the higher your speed needs to be in order to break traction and skid into the space. Twenty-five mph is about the max.

*Lining Up*

Pick a start point about ten car lengths away from the parking space, offset by roughly three car widths so that you have enough room to steer a gradual arc

# 27. Stunt 180 into a Parking Space

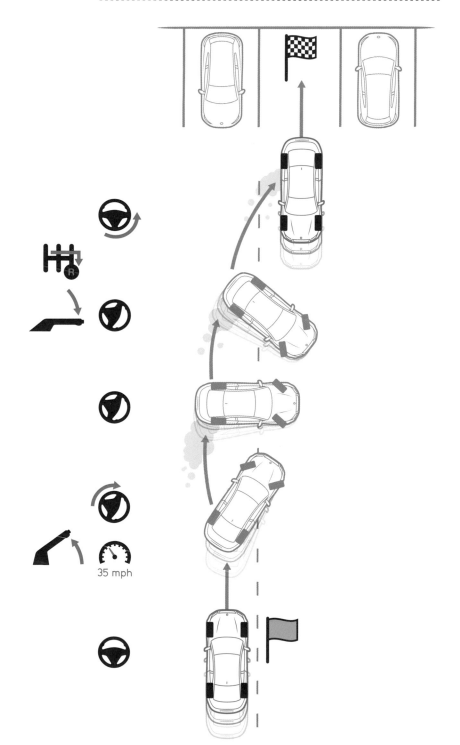

# 28. Stunt 90 into a Parking Space

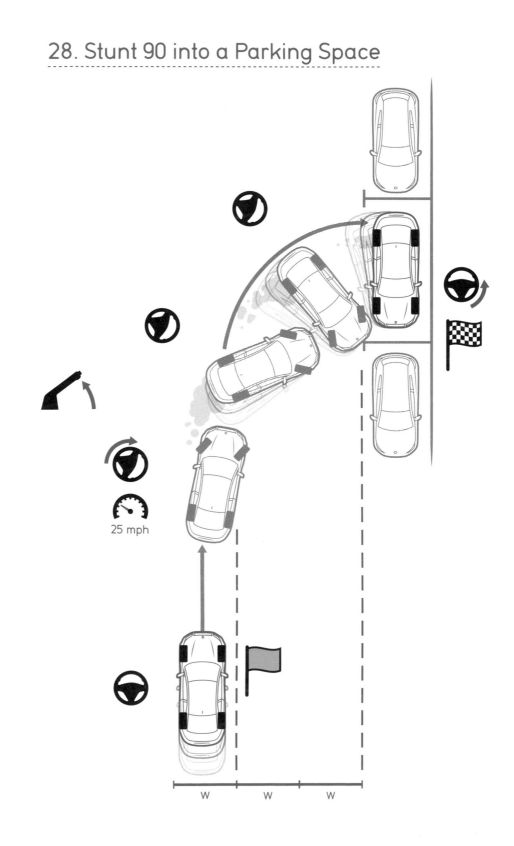

25 mph

W    W    W

towards the space. This gives you a longer arc along which to turn and apply the handbrake so that momentum carries the car into its spot.

The key to this is arriving so that you can aim into the gap at a perpendicular angle. The incredibly hard part to judge is when to steer towards the gap and pull the handbrake.

You need to think everything through in slow motion and remember that, as the car slides, there is a delayed reaction to your inputs.

*Key Markers*

You need to determine an initial pivot point around which to start rotating, and this will vary depending on your style and the grip level. Generally speaking, the pivot point can be found one car length away from the centre of the parking gap.

It is important that you aim towards the centre so that, as the car rotates, it has equal space to fill into at the front and rear, assuming your car doesn't have a vast overhang beyond the rear axle. Your eyeline should draw focus points on the gap itself, as well as your distance from the rear bumper of the car you're about to slide up to.

*Doing It*

Fix your start mark to make the process repeatable, one that gives you plenty of time to get up to a set speed.

Make a few practice runs at low speed to get a feel for timing the steering and pulling the handbrake without actually committing.

Once you're ready to give it a go, drive up parallel to the gap and make your turn. Just before the car is pointing directly at the space, pull on the handbrake and let fly towards the space.

As you enter the gap you should sense whether the car will over-rotate and spill out of the gap if the speed is a little high, or under-rotate if the car isn't sliding on the handbrake. To correct over-rotation as it happens you can ease on the foot brake. If the car isn't sliding enough then pull harder on the handbrake and add a little more speed next time round.

*Break Out*

You could ask someone politely to move the other cars out of the way, but that wouldn't be very sporting.

No, what you need to do is pull the handbrake all the way up and turn the steering as far as it will go in the desired direction. Assuming your car is front-wheel-drive, you select first gear, redline the engine and dump the clutch. With the handbrake restricting forward motion, the front tyres will spin wildly and drag the car's nose out of the gap. Release the handbrake and head off to buy some new tyres.

# J-turn

A J-turn is a reverse 180-degree spin that requires a deft hand and good coordination at each step of the move.

The key to a good J-turn is how quickly you 'whip' the steering through the twelve o'clock position to initiate the spin, and how efficiently you unwind that steering to complete the move.

To achieve both these goals, I hold the wheel at ten o'clock with my right hand and look over my left shoulder (vice versa in left-hand drive), so that I can yank it through twelve with plenty of force and apply enough lock to swivel the nose of the car. At the end of the move it's easy to return my hand to its original position so that I know the fronts are pointing straight again.

*Step 1.* Line-up: stop the car, select reverse and observe the view through the rear screen to check it's clear. There needs to be enough space to accommodate the length of the car when it spins, so you should line up in the centre of that space and fix your sights on an object in the far distance to ensure that you drive straight.

*Step 2.* Position your whipping hand at ten o'clock, or two o'clock for a left-hand turn, and reverse quickly, so as to load the suspension, up to a minimum speed of 20 mph, ideally around 40 mph, to ensure that the fronts will skid when you want them to.

*Step 3*. Whip: once you're up to speed, lift off the accelerator and crank the steering to the right from ten o'clock to about four o'clock and put the clutch in. The car will spin on its axis.

---

**Hot Tip**

> To give it a little extra, I tilt the suspension by gently turning the steering a tad in the wrong direction before throwing it sharply the other way.

---

*Step 4*. Steer through. As the car's nose makes its way past 90 degrees you should be looking *through* the windscreen and steering the wheel *through* to the left. This helps the car rotate a full 180 degrees into its new direction.

*Step 4½*. Gear and go. Calmly move the gear lever from reverse to second and drive away. Failing to do this will result in some disagreement between your transmission and the road over which way each one should be going.

---

**Hot Tips**

> Don't rush the gears. As long as the clutch pedal is pushed in you can take your time moving out of reverse and just drop into second when the car is pointing straight. Autos are even easier. Practise the move from reverse to second whilst stationary; it gets more complicated when you're mobile unless you're an octopus.

---

**Common Mistakes**

> If you don't steer fast enough initially the nose of the car won't spin, it will grip, causing you to head off in a new direction. Brake before you hit something!
> Remember to steer through at the end of the move to prevent the car veering out of control.
> Steering too much. If you wind on loads of steering it's easy to get lost. Keep your golden whip hand in one place throughout the move.

---

Stunt Driving

# 29. J-turn

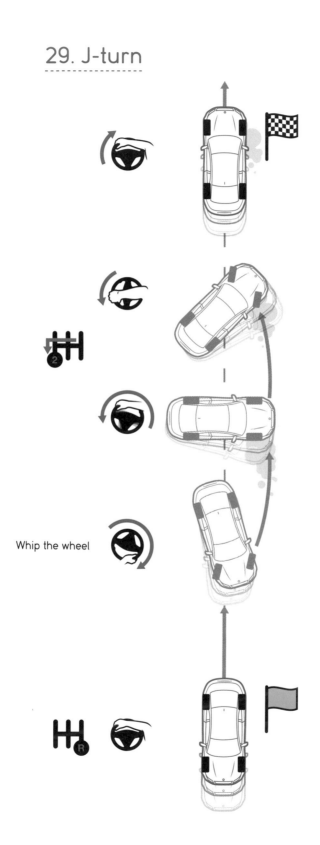

Whip the wheel

4: Skidding

# 30. J-turn Wheel Position

## Doughnuts and Burnouts

To pull off the following manoeuvres you will need a car that allows you to turn off the traction control and stability systems – an endangered species in these times of state intervention and safety Stasi. It also needs to be rear-wheel-drive with a limited slip differential, or 'diff'.

The diff connects the driven wheels together and does two jobs. In a corner it allows the outside wheels, which have furthest to travel, to turn faster than the inside wheels. When you accelerate it also divides the amount of drive transmitting through them.

As the car leans into a corner, the weight bearing down on the outside tyres gives them more grip than those on the inside. This makes the inner tyre more prone to losing traction under acceleration, so in models with a very 'open' diff, all their power slops through the wheel with the least ability to handle it. When the inside wheel spins, no power is transmitted through the other tyre, and you don't go very far.

A 'locking' diff limits the speed differential between the driven tyres and thereby metes out the power more evenly across them, providing better drive and accuracy. There's only one way to know for sure …

### Basic Doughnut

The garden-variety doughnut is as easy as walking out of your front door, as long as you have the space and don't mind abusing your tyres. It's easier using a manual transmission, but still possible with an auto if you have enough power to spin the car around by simply flooring the throttle.

From a static position in first gear, keep the clutch fully depressed, floor the throttle and redline the engine. Let the cacophony sing and don't mind the engine, because the rev limiter will protect your pistons.

Turn the steering hard in your preferred direction and dump the clutch. Dumping means lifting your foot off the clutch faster than if you trod on molten lava. The common mistake people make is to pull away slowly by easing out the clutch, which just fries the clutch plates and accelerates you forwards when you want to go sideways.

When you dump the clutch pedal, the clutch plates grab hold of the engine and instantly transmit all its power to the rear tyres. This overwhelms their tractive

'The controlled doughnut is all about accuracy.'

ability, and they start spinning, which is good. The act of steering causes the car to pivot around its nose, and as long as you keep your right foot planted to the floorboards, you will rotate in a glorious cloud of burning rubber that will cost you around £5 a second.

That part was easy.

**Doughnut: the Black-belt Edition**

This is much harder to do and may take a while to explain, let alone master. With the basic doughnut all you had to do was tramp the gas and turn right, or left, to make the car spin as tightly as possible. The controlled doughnut is all about accuracy around a specific mark, which means keeping the beast on course using some fluid hand-eye coordination.

Before going any further, let's plan some geography. On a live stage with *Top Gear* I used a mark that was about 5 foot 7 inches tall, with chestnut-brown hair, who could do a standing splits, all of which made Chloe Bruce a distinctive beacon to rest my eyes on.

Backstage, behind the blackout curtains, I was mentally visualizing the precise route around which I wanted the car to travel, *the arc*, and agonizing those last seconds before the curtain went up in front of 5,000 pairs of eyes.

The Holden Monaro with its throaty V8 engine and locked rear differential was the perfect car for the job, and I'd wedged a coin into the handbrake button with some duct tape so that it would release immediately after I pulled it.

I must have done that sequence hundreds of times, rehearsed it thousands, but I always felt a deep sense of foreboding. My heart would pound, and my fingers would tingle from the adrenaline, because it was a dangerous sequence. I definitely recommend learning with a rubber cone rather than a human.

The curtain flew up, and a dazzling spotlight pierced the Monaro. I popped the clutch, and the tyres shrieked across the metal floor. I feathered the throttle to moderate the wheelspin and get some drive, then flicked into second gear and skirted the concrete retaining wall.

Chloe's white silk ninja suit entered my peripheral vision as I aimed for a mark one car's width to her left, yanked the handbrake, steered right and swung the Monaro around into its new trajectory.

# 31. Basic Doughnut

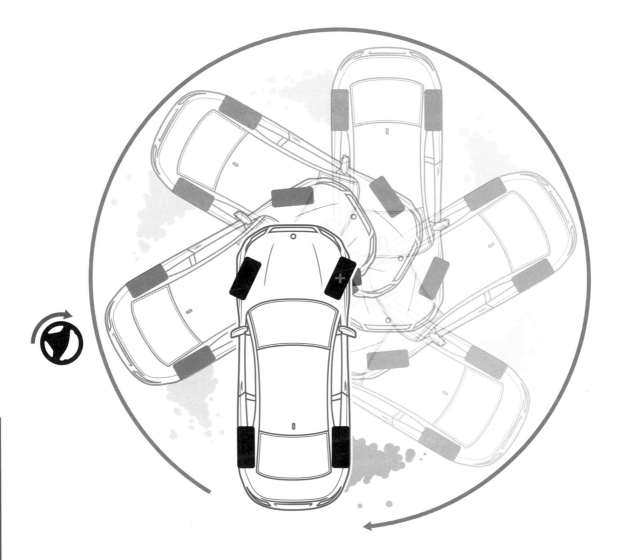

# 32. Doughnut: the Black-belt Edition

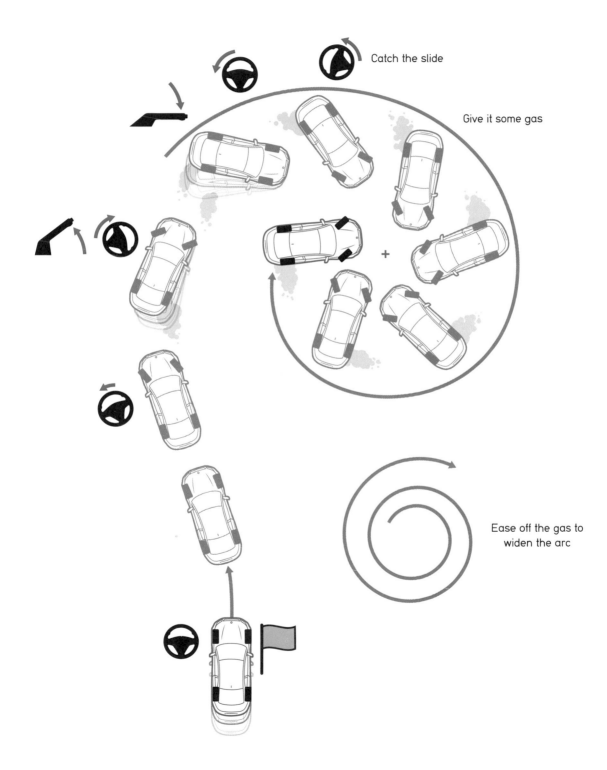

Catch the slide

Give it some gas

Ease off the gas to widen the arc

The handbrake slewed the car around until it reached a yaw angle of around 45 degrees and into a circling arc around Chloe. Thirty-five mph of forward momentum scrubbed down to about 15 mph of lateral clockwise drift.

As Chloe wowed the crowd with her sword-play and high kicks, the Monaro's mouth came perilously close to her immaculately poised leg. Had the car gripped at that moment it would have lurched forward and knocked her down like a bowling pin. Hence the nerves.

At that point I could think about *catching* the slide with the steering, and adding throttle to create enough wheelspin to continue the slide. But not too much. That was the tricky part. Knowing precisely how much of each to use, and when, takes practice.

The first catch usually involved some sweeping movement with the steering to find the correct combination of opposite lock and active throttle until the car *took a set*. At that point the car would balance, and I could trim its progress with smaller corrections of steering and minor adjustments to a fairly constant throttle to keep the rears smoking.

In order to creep the car's nose closer to Chloe and scare the crowd, I had to make it follow a tighter arc, which is just the same as making a sharper turn with a supermarket shopping trolley. You kick the rear out wider so the nose stays put.

I increased the throttle to spin the rears faster and reduce their grip. At first, this made the car want to spin, so I simultaneously added a little more opposite lock to control the additional yaw until it was time to cut back to minimal counter-steering.

The result was a tighter, if busier, circle around Chloe and an unblinking fascination with the distance between my bumper and her knee-cap. Too much throttle at this point and the car would spin; too little and it would grip and shoot forward. Ouch.

If that wasn't enough to think about, the grip level never stays constant in a live arena, so the rear would snap across dollops of water deposited by leaky radiators. I could cope with that, but I needed a back-up plan for when my talent ran dry widening my arc.

To keep the Monaro from taking a bite out of Chloe, I let it drift wide. By steering left more than I needed to control the slide and easing off some throttle, it restored a little grip to the rears, reducing the yaw angle, and the machine obeyed the direction of the wheel. Once I moved out to the left, I increased the power again to spin up the rears and restore the drift.

Step 1. *Walk it*. Walk the route sideways to develop your visual reference on the centre mark and rehearse the relationship between your position and the centre mark. That distance and your rate of yaw dictates the handling.

Step 2. *The throw*. As soon as you turn right, the rear will rotate, and you allow this until the car reaches a 45-degree angle (give or take, depending on the model, subject to terms and conditions) and takes a 'set'. Taking a set is when the rear has swung sideways enough that you can put the steering into opposite lock and catch it, then reduce and modulate the throttle to keep the rears spinning.

Step 3. *The catch*. Once the car reaches 45 degrees, you have to catch it. This is the transition from steering right to create the initial slide, to steering left to maintain a steady ship. The hard part is that the rear floats around pretty fast, and the temptation is to over-correct with steering or spin out. The trick is to back off the throttle the moment you reach 45 so that the rears grip for just a moment as you throw in the opposite lock. Then it's back on with the throttle to maintain the wheelspin, and let the car settle onto a knife-edge. Keep your eye on the centre mark to measure the angle.

Step 4. *The Set*. When you get into the sweet spot, balance the slide with small corrections of opposite lock and throttle. Your aim is to hold your yaw steady and reduce your inputs to the bare minimum. Let the car do the work.

### Arc

On a wider arc you travel faster, and life is actually a little easier, because you have more time to adjust what the car is doing. The higher speed increases your lateral momentum, making it easier to hang the rear out there. If your speed drops on a wide arc, the car will grip, so you need to increase the throttle or turn more tightly. On a tighter arc the car responds more quickly, and your inputs need to be crisp.

'Let the car settle onto a knife-edge.'

*Steering*

Steering is not an infinite resource and if you keep winding it into a skid it will eventually thud into the bump stops, proving troublesome when an extra claw of steering is the only thing keeping you from rotating into the boonies. Pro drifters fit exceptionally wide-angle steering to make the job easier and hold their cars super sideways, but you still need to live within your means.

*Brake*

In the drift universe the brake restricts forward momentum, enabling you to spin up the rear tyres even more and slow the car in general. Yes, this involves left-foot braking. With your right foot busily making music, you creep your left foot onto the brake pedal. This mostly binds the front tyres and transfers weight their way, which allows you to accelerate harder to really light up the rears, increase yaw and all that good stuff.

## Drifting

If you have watched *Top Gear* then you will have seen endless footage of priceless supercars being subjected to a royal pounding. Smoke billowing from the wheel arches as burning rubber churns at the tarmac to a cacophony of screeching tyres and dubbed music. The car yaws perilously sideways but maintains a surprisingly predictable course through the corner, assuming the nut behind the wheel doesn't run out of talent.

The phenomenon of 'drifting' has been the stuff of Hollywood legend ever since Steve McQueen climbed aboard a Ford Mustang in *Bullitt* and proceeded to paint rubber across the San Francisco cityscape.

If you mastered the doughnut, then you're ready to drift, because you've just been doing it. The easiest way to get started is to link two doughnuts together to form a figure 8, but before we get into that, here's some background.

Drifting as a cornering technique developed in rallying during the 1960s after some Scandinavian drivers drank a lot of vodka in the Jacuzzi. They spoke in short sentences, or not at all, and shared their frustration with traditional cornering methods that were painfully inadequate on snow and ice. Their epiphany appeared at the bottom of a shot glass: '*Vee do it sidevays!*'

# 33. Drifting

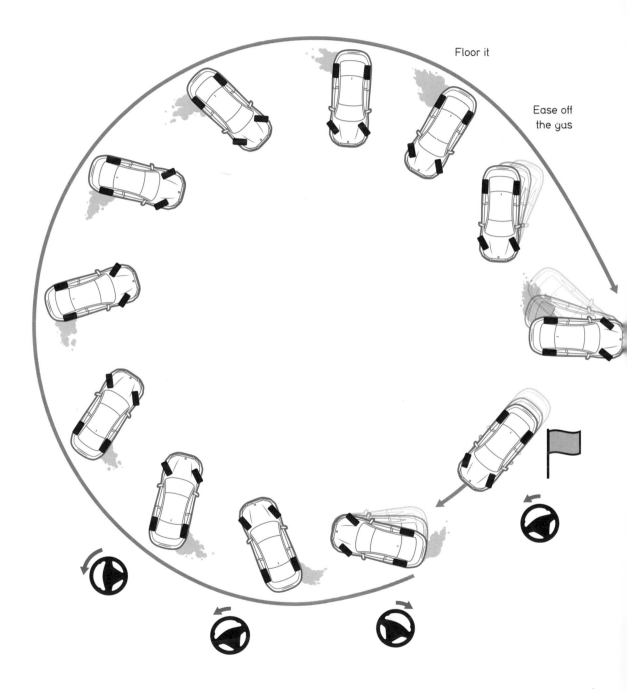

Floor it

Ease off
the gas

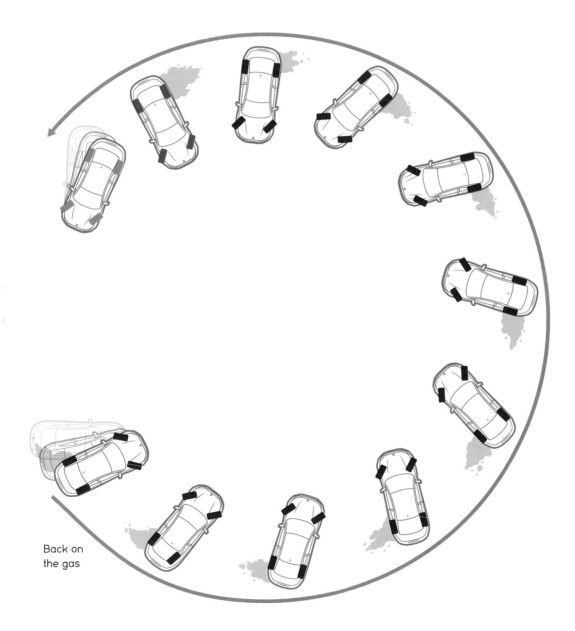

Back on
the gas

Stunt Driving

The conventional style of navigating a curve as quickly as possible had always been to brake in a straight line, get off the brakes and turn in the direction of the corner. The trouble with ice was that the tyres couldn't offer enough traction to overcome the car's forward momentum. The fronts just washed out at low speed, and you missed the corner. There lay the secret.

The Vikings worked out a way to make momentum work for them, and it was as easy, in theory, as swinging an axe. They arrived at a left-hander with the car skidding and pointing in the opposite direction to the corner, the prompt for most people to abandon ship. Then they steered hard left, effectively over-correcting the slide (remember page 207 on car control, 'The Tank Slapper'), and the car's tail swished across to the other side with enough lateral momentum to propel the whole box of frogs around the curve. With the centrifugal forces that previously worked against them during the entry phase averted, temporarily, the car entered the corner at higher speed. Now the problem was keeping it there.

The head of the swinging axe was loose, to say the least. To keep it from falling off and embedding itself deep inside a Swedish pine, the Vikings had to counter the force running down the length of the car's body. The key lay beneath their right foot, and by nailing the throttle to the rug it produced enough driving force to counter the pull of gravity. It also accelerated them out of the corner faster than the conventional cornering method.

Tomi Mäkinen, an early pioneer of the 'Scandinavian flick' (see page 264), explained that perfecting this took 'at least two years, and many, many cars'.

By skidding sideways under braking in the opposite direction to the curve, the tyres dig into the surface and slow the car more effectively until you reach the turning point; then you swing it towards the corner and use the pendulum effect to catapult you around it. Assuming that your face isn't already smeared across the roadside, the car points towards the corner, enabling early acceleration.

This style of driving dominated world rally competition for years. In Japan it developed a cult status, as the heroes hammering the treacherous mountain pass at Touge (*toe-geh*) began tuning their cars to exaggerate the sideways handling way beyond anything performance-related. By that point it was all about style.

## Getting Started

Here are the various techniques for initiating a drift. Each scenario creates an abrupt loss of traction to the rears, and you have to be incredibly fast with the steering to control it. So fast, in fact, that there are times when it's better to let go of the wheel, allow it to spin through your fingers, and catch it again when you have the correct steering angle.

## Handbrake

As you approach the corner, pull the handbrake to lock the rears, aim towards the corner and throw the car into a drift. Once it's sliding, you fling the wheel over and drive on the throttle.

---

**Hot Tip**

> **As soon as you're controlling proceedings with steering and wheelspin, the handbrake returns as a control feature for advanced drifting. When you want to cut power but retain your angle of yaw, you apply the clutch and pull the handbrake in the corner. This allows the driven wheels to stop turning, and the car will drift around a tighter arc. Then you reapply the power to maintain speed and momentum through the corner.**

---

## Clutch

You may remember my emphasis on smooth clutching to avoid upsetting the car. Well, being a meathead is a bonus for drifting. There are two ways to use it.

As you approach the corner, you drop a gear and instead of rev matching or gently releasing the clutch pedal, you deliberately allow the revs to drop and pop the clutch just as you steer in. The sudden take-up of engine braking puts enough shock through the rear axle to break traction and pitch the car sideways as you steer. But this technique can be unreliable, and you lose speed.

The 'clutch-kick' is the best way to get the show on the road. Rather than letting engine braking do the work, you clutch in and accelerate to boost engine revs. With your foot hard on the gas, you steer in, pop the clutch, and the sudden acceleration creates enough wheelspin to send you sideways.

The clutch-kick is used multiple times throughout the corner to maintain wheelspin and yaw angle. You keep the throttle pinned and rapidly kick the clutch in and out as many times as you need to defeat the enemy of grip and trim the drift.

### Scandinavian Flick

If it's got an engine, it can drift. Everything in the book up to this point has been about managing weight transfer to produce maximum stability and grip. Now the objective is to disturb the weight so that it overcomes rear traction and the 'flick' is the primary tool in the drift box of tricks.

You approach the corner with slightly too much speed for a conventional entry, breathe on the brake to shift weight off the rears onto the fronts and then initiate a pendulum turn. That is, you steer towards the outside of the corner and then rapidly twitch it the other way. The rampant weight transfer causes the rear to skid, and then you stamp on the gas to hold it sideways.

### Linking the Chain – Figure 8

So you're sideways ... now what?

Once you've initiated the drift, your attention needs to be drawn to your trajectory. This is very much a seat-of-the-pants vibe and tied to the same technique you deployed in the doughnut to control your arc.

Having made it through one corner without biting the dust, the next goal is to link two corners together. It requires the most careful execution and this is where the figure 8 comes in.

The figure 8 is really a pair of opposing doughnuts with a switchback in the middle. It's the best way to develop a feel, at comparatively low speed, for how the car will cope with a sudden switch of direction whilst sliding.

We call this switch the 'transition turn', and it is the hardest part to control as well as the most satisfying.

As you circle the first doughnut in a clockwise direction, you select a pivot point around which to switch directions and point yourself towards a new arc that takes you anticlockwise around the second doughnut.

You widen your arc out of the initial doughnut, and on approaching that pivot point you create a moment of grip in the rears by over-correcting the slide with additional counter-steering (assuming you have any left!) and by releasing some throttle.

The car obeys the steering, and suddenly the tail swishes across the other way. All the counter-steering has to be passed into the opposite direction in order to catch this new slide and balance your new trajectory.

'The figure 8 is really a pair of opposing doughnuts with a switchback in the middle.'

**Style**

Pro drifters are judged by their angle of attack, speed and the aggression of their transition from one direction to the other as they link two corners. Ideally, you anticipate the turn so that you have enough space and time to really whip the rear across, jump back on the gas and be lined up nicely for the next corner.

With the engine hammering off the rev limiter and your fists banging the wheel into the bump stops, you couldn't be any more sideways if you tried. You release some gas and the tail twitches across faster than an Exocet missile.

You spin the wheel like an LP record to catch the opposing slide. It naturally finds its home for the new angle and you vaporize the scene with smoke as you carve away into the horizon.

This is really making fun of an ordeal that catches so many people out on the road: the tank slapper. And if you can learn to handle this, there's really not much left to teach you.

I guess the only part I left out about drifting is the tandem drift: two cars battling door handle to door handle to see which can hold it the most sideways for the longest and at the highest speed. It's a messy business, and if you spin, you lose, so maybe it's not the best way to end the book. But then again …

# Epilogue:
## *Drifting through London*

### Piccadilly Circus, Saturday, an hour before midnight.

Tucked inside a bald cap, Vin Diesel's leather jacket and his Dodge Charger, my own mother wouldn't recognize me. Alongside, in a modified Jensen Interceptor, British rally champ Mark Higgins was doubling the lead lady, Letty – though with ears like wing-nuts and a long black wig he looked a whole lot more like Ozzy Osbourne.

We were about to drift the V8s around the Circus at up to 70 mph for *Fast & Furious 6*. And we had three minutes to do it in …

Unlike the queues of girls wearing mini-skirts at the peak of an arctic winter, we wouldn't be warming our cockles at the neon-lit bars of China White's. We would be manhandling a pair of recalcitrant beasts around the circus, danger close, and with a Nissan 370Z camera car tracking from just a few feet ahead.

With muscles like mine it's rare to draw comparisons with Vin Diesel, but this was no ordinary occasion. Having spent two hours at the mercy of the girls in the make-up bus, the hairs on my head had been individually water-boarded and locked securely inside a latex bald cap. I spent the time contemplating the best way to pull this gag off without reshaping a famous monument.

Our boss, stunt coordinator Andy Gill, set out his stall of toy cars beside the memorial fountain underneath the vigilant effigy of Anteros. Gill was my hero growing up because he was the stuntman driving 'KITT', the Pontiac in *Knight Rider*. He and his brother Jack jumped, flipped, smashed and blasted KITT across America for four years of what David Hasselhoff called 'non-stop, rock 'n' roll, balls-out fun'. You wouldn't believe a softly spoken gent from Georgia enjoyed such a violent pastime, but Andy has forgotten more about car stunts than I'll ever know.

A few scratches of chalk later and the pavement at Andy's feet was ready to simulate the action with his Matchbox collection. The two 'hero' cars would drive up Piccadilly towards the roundabout, make a sharp left towards Regent Street then switch right to slide onto Coventry Street, finally making another right down Haymarket. 'Sideways all the way, obviously. I want you guys touching door handles. Reckon you can do that?'

Clearly a rhetorical question. We moved off to the cars. My ride was a lowered 1970 Dodge Daytona, so lowered that the front tyres caught inside the wheel arches when you turned them. With a 5.4-litre Chevy V8 under the hood, horsepower was not a problem, and the stripped-out chassis that resembled Frankenstein from the interior made a good power-to-weight ratio.

The similarity between my and Mark's machines ended with the engine. The Jensen would squat on its rear tyres whenever Mark planted his right foot, causing it to grip more and more the harder he gassed it sideways. Meanwhile the 'Bird', as the Dodge was known, kicked like a mule and spun its wheels if you so much as coughed near the throttle. Getting the two cars to match their speeds and rate of slide, which is essential for a tandem drift, would be no mean feat.

When the car travels sideways its footprint naturally covers a wider area, and thanks to Google maps our area was half the size we were expecting. Westminster Council had stuck a bus lane on the roundabout, and to add insult to injury the pedestrian kerb from Shaftesbury Avenue had been extended by about 8 feet. That left a gap on the road of 22 feet, about a foot longer than the Bird in full drift.

Closing one of London's busiest junctions is rare, so we attracted quite a crowd. As is the norm for filming in London, we had a three-minute filming window and then had to release the traffic onto the streets until we were ready to go again. That meant delivering pinpoint accuracy for each of the exclusive takes.

I lined up alongside Mark to his left, and we took turns in warming up the rear differentials to prepare them for the onslaught. The pair of bellowing V8s drowned out the crew's radio chatter and silenced the crowd. With the tyres, engines and gears in tune, we waited for the countdown. Gill called it, and the Nissan camera car took the lead as we rolled along the 30-metre, pulse-hardening run towards the square.

In an ideal world we might have kick-started our drift by flipping the clutch and flooring it. However, this being an American production, we were provided with automatics.

> 'Our only focus was the fire-juggling act of keeping these two broncos close but not touching.'

I reached the roundabout first, turned left and yanked on my soggy handbrake for all it was worth. The Bird's tail sailed out in front of Mark's Jensen as he simultaneously wrangled his ride. Never mind the priceless masonry we might reshape, our only focus was the fire-juggling act of keeping these two broncos close but not touching.

When a car slides into oversteer the slip angle in the fronts reduces to zero for a moment, so the wheel goes light for a fraction of a second. Then the steering torque returns as the car yaws the other way and pulls at the fronts again. As the Bird slewed sideways and the windscreen flooded with four storeys of illuminated advertising screens, I felt the pull returning – so I let go of the steering wheel.

The front tyres effectively stayed pointed where I wanted to go, and the car just rotated around them. Letting go of the wheel allowed it to spin efficiently through my hands. The trick was not letting it spin too far – a skill developed after several weeks of rehearsals on the airfield – and knowing precisely when the rear tyres had taken their 'set'.

With the steering hard over to the right and my foot on the gas keeping the wheels spinning, the Bird was happy to crab through the curve with Mark close alongside. I even had time to notice the jolly expression on Pete White's face through my side window as he drove past in a double-decker bus. 'You stick to those little cars, Benjy, leave the big rigs to the real men,' he had said before climbing aboard. I never said a word. He's a front-row forward and part-time horse dentist with access to tranquilizers; it's best just to keep smiling.

With the Bird and the Jensen parallel drifting we were off to a good start. Since the Jensen was picking up speed at an alarming rate, it was time to flick my old gal into the opposite direction and face it towards the right-hander for Coventry Street. This transition tango slide from drifting one way into another is the traditional occasion for a pile-up.

Unfortunately with the Bird I had no further steering to effect the switch because I was already grinding the wheel arch, so I backed off the gas to let the rears grip a little and kept the steering turned right.

> 'We ran to within inches of the camera lens.'

The Bird's tail lurched across to the left and spewed a handsome volume of rubber dust in my face by way of protest. Mark shot up my right side just as the camera car slowed in front of us to get a close-up. We ran to within inches of the camera lens, and with both of us juggling the steering like hot potatoes we somehow made it through the pedestrian crossing without hitting anything. The first shot of the night was in the can and to the outside world we almost looked like we knew exactly what we were doing.

Cameras relocated to more perilous positions on the pavement, closer to our line of travel, and Pete's bus was brought in later so that he would appear on our front bumpers during our transition turn.

On the next take we swung through the blur of bright advertising, engines screaming and tyres burning, switched direction and our tails flew towards the crowd. I spun the wheel and lost sight of Mark as he dug in behind. I took a deep breath as the long tail floated oh-so-close to the pedestrian barriers and slammed home third gear for the finale.

Our speeds rose to 70 mph. The suspension tramped and bounced all over the bumpy street. The Bird's steering jammed into the wheel arch and for a moment it looked like the Angus Steakhouse on the corner of Haymarket might be receiving a drive-in. I clawed it back and we shoved our rides into Haymarket corner with Greg Powell's words ringing in our ears: 'Don't smash the producer's supercar,' which was parked for beauty directly in our line of fire. We skimmed past, and they moved it after that.

By the end of the night we had filmed every conceivable angle of that part of the chase, and everything had run like clockwork. The crew vanished into the night just as silently and effectively as they had arrived, and the city carried on regardless, the way that it always has.

I circled the Bird out of Smithfield Lane and back to its bed for the night in a derelict car park, still humming with activity as camera mounts were pulled off their special rigs and the grips swore merrily into the night. I gave it a final stroke of the gas to 7 grand, killed the motor, and it shuddered to a still silence.

Life back on terra firma felt considerably slower, but I was grateful to leave the vibrator behind me and climb aboard a modern car. As the door closed on shoot day ninety-six, it dawned on me that I had probably just completed one of the coolest driving capers of my career.

I rolled out and took a leisurely drive home through what felt like a parallel universe. Brake lights flickering and indicators winking, signs flashing and people making their way through the kaleidoscopic canvas of London life. This was no time to rush. This was time to enjoy.

'I had probably just completed one of the coolest driving capers of my career.'

# Index

acceleration, smooth 49
accidents, avoiding 116–27
    knowing your car and its design
        nuances 116–18
    observe, interpret, act 126
    police drivers and 121, 123–5
    speed and 118–21
    statistics 122
    visualize 127
aquaplane 212–7

basic instinct (harnessing the
    subconscious) 190–4
basics, the 26–113
beast, the 36–45
    balance 39–43
    dynamic handling 44
    engine types 45
    light touch 38
braking 65–90
    ABS 79, 80–1, 82, 84, 173, 206,
        209, 215, 216, 229
    brake modulation 83, 85–8
    everyday smooth braking 67
    in the real world 73
    left-foot 90, 258
    on the limit 82–3
    'slip angle' and 65, 69
    stab and squeeze 83–5, 88
    stopping in an emergency 73–9
    thinking and braking distance 73,
        74–9
    trail braking 89–90
    tyre grip area 68–9

Clarkson, Jeremy 55, 57, 70, 91–2,
    95, 117, 124, 236
cornering 91–113
    benefits of 'late apexing' 99

cutting corners 98
filming Fast and Furious 6 and
    112–13
physics of: the tyre vs Isaac
    Newton 95–6, 100–1
premature ejection 99
the racing line 97
the real world 102
rhythm 93
road camber 109–13
road surface 104–9
'slow in, fast out' 98
taking corners 97–9
traction circle 94
types of corner 102, 103–8
viewing the corner 92–3

deaths, car crash 8–10, 18–19,
    118–21, 134 see also accidents,
    avoiding
driving position 28–31, 34–5
driving test 8, 21–3, 153
dual carriageways 150–1
Dunsfold Aerodrome 16, 55, 56, 84,
    203–4

Fast and Furious 6 112–13, 266–9
Formula 1 6, 20, 24, 61, 63, 70, 95,
    180, 184
fuel-efficiency 17, 70

gear changing 50–9
    braking and entering (Ferrari F40
        and Ferrari Enzo testing for
        Top Gear) 55–9
    changing up 51
    common fallacies about 53–4
    common mistakes 52
    down-shifting 54–5

gear selection 50
    how to hold the gearstick 50–1
    skipping gears 54
    slowing down, braking, changing
        down the gears 52–3
grip, the limits of 200–8
    Bathurst circuit, Australia 202–3
    common causes of skids 202
    David Walliams Top Gear
        appearance and 203–4
    opposite lock 205–6
    over correcting 206
    over- and understeer 201, 202,
        204–5
    recovering from a spin 207
    the 'Tank Slapper' 206

Hammond, Richard 169, 170, 172,
    242
history of driving 12–25

ice, driving on 220–1

junctions 128–34
    etiquette 131
    hazard perception 130
    lighter traffic and concentration
        levels 129
    roundabouts 131–3
    rural roads 134

Le Mans 9, 19, 63, 90, 157, 183–5,
    186, 187–8, 190–4, 218
'LMP1' cars 183–5

May, James 214
mindset, your 174–9
    commuting and 175
    distractions and 176–8

drink 'n' drugs and  179
emotional baggage and  174–5
environment and  179
passengers (weight) and  178–9
perceived wrongdoing/rage and
    175
time pressure and  175
motor racing, birth of  19–20
motorways  152–68
    blind spots  161–5
    communication  161
    displacement  156–7
    following distance  159–61
    the game  157–8
    hard shoulder  154
    joining  154, 155
    lane merging  166
    leaving  157
    the pitch  154
    the players  165
    rules  153
    space, time and relativity  158–9
    warm up  153–4
    weather, game-changing  166–8

NASCAR  10, 63, 72, 85, 90, 98,
    117, 161, 164
night driving  186–9

open road, the  110–97
oversteer see skidding
overtaking  135–49
    approaching cars: the second
        most likely cause of accidents
        142–3
    body language  142
    common mistakes  149
    final checks  147–9
    general observations  143
    overtaking line  144–5
    Quantum of Solace filming and
        67, 135–41
    reasons not to overtake  146
    space  142

speed, momentum and
    positioning  145

pulling away  47–8

Quantum of Solace  67, 135–41

road rage  18–19, 175

skidding  198–208
smooth driving  10, 46–9, 70–2, 79,
    200
speed limits  10, 18–19, 70, 118,
    152, 157
Spiderman 2  240–1
steering  60–4
    the push and pull  61
    rotational (also known as
        crossed-hand)  61–3
    the shuffle  60–1
Stewart, Sir Jackie  6, 46–7
stunt driving  240–69
    doughnuts and burnouts  252–8
    drifting  258–69
    drive through (evasive driving):
        Spiderman 2 and  240–1
    handbrake turns  242–51

Top Gear  10, 16, 31, 38, 46, 56–8,
    60–1, 71, 84, 91–2, 125, 169–73,
    195–7, 203–4, 206, 214–15, 220,
    242, 253, 256, 257, 258
tyres, first/invention of  16–17 see
    also under individual area of
    driving

understeer see skidding

vision  180–5
    LMP1 cars and  183–5
    the Mark 1 eyeball  180, 182
    peripheral vision  181–2
    the visual strategy of a racing
        driver  182–3

visualization: the perfect lap  195–7

wet, driving in the  209–19
    after it rains  210
    avoiding aquaplane  212, 214
    factors affecting aquaplane
        214–15
    floods  217
    handling aquaplane  216–17
    read the road  211
    seeing and being seen  218–19
    tyres and  212, 213
winter driving  220–31
    accelerating  230
    braking  228, 229
    essential gear  231
    hills  230–1
    mud  227
    plan a route  221
    prep the car  220–1
    read the script  230
    snow, driving in the  226
    steering  230
    stuck, getting  226
    tyres  224, 225
    uphill  231
worst-case scenarios  232–9
    bonnet flies up/broken
        windscreen  239
    brake 'failure'  233–4
    brake overheating  234
    breakdown at a railway crossing
        236–7
    escape from a sinking car  237–9
    parking brake failure  235
    steering failure  235–6
    sticking throttle  233
    total brake failure  235
    tyre blowout  232–3

# Acknowledgements

Jon Butler, for breathing life into this project, applying your invaluable expertise and for your painstaking edit. Few vegetarians, if any, would so willingly endure a charred meat-feast pizza whilst reconstructing a book with a fine-tooth comb and ten million post-it notes.

Mark Lucas, thank you for your inspirational guidance and for sharing my belief in the merits of driving on eggshells. The loyalty and friendship of the whole team at LAW, especially Alice and Julian, has become an extraordinary pillar of support for which I'm eternally grateful.

Michelin, for providing technical information about their tyres as well as keeping me on the black stuff this season. Thanks also to the FIA Foundation for their research and campaigning for driver safety, and to the team at a²om international for their pioneering work on hazard perception.

Ryan and Andy at Here Design, Julie Martin and James Provost for applying your conscientious craft to my ramblings.

Dusty, Fergus, Laura and the fearless warriors at Team Macmillan for their ingenuity in bringing this book to market.

EON Productions, for kindly allowing me to share a few trade secrets.

The Metropolitan Police Driving School at Hendon, for sharing your impeccable roadcraft with me and generally keeping us safe at night.

My wife Georgie . . . thank you for putting up with endless demonstrations of driving theory, for your proofreading and forbearance, and for generally being such a lovely legend.

# Bibliography

I couldn't have written this book without the accumulated wisdom of generations of driving experts and the talented competitors who shaped my knowledge during many a duel. I also found the following titles particularly enlightening:

*The Technique of Motor Racing*, Piero Taruffi.
*Steering-Wheel Papers*, the Earl of Cottenham.
*Drive to Win*, by Carroll Smith.
*Tune to Win*, by Carroll Smith.
*Jackie Stewart's Principles of Performance Driving*, Sir Jackie Stewart.
*The Art and Technicalities of Grand Prix Driving*, Niki Lauda
*Porsche High Performance Driving Handbook*, by Vic Elford.
*Sports Car and Competition Driving*, Paul Frère.
*Police Roadcraft*.
*The Highway Code*.

# Source Material

The Department for Transport; accident data kindly provided by Charles More of Actuarial Consultants; driver behaviour research kindly provided by Dr Lisa Dorn of Cranfield University.

# Image Credits

All line illustrations by © James Provost; 32: (Volvo S60) with thanks to Simon Atlassi at Volvo & Bill Goodell at Arnold Worldwide; 39 © Alan Welner/AP/Press Association Images; 43 © Drew Gibson; 110, 132, 192 © Daily Sportscar (with thanks to David Downes, David Lord and Peter May); 171 (McLaren F1) © Ben Collins; 136 © EON Productions Ltd; 105, 222 © Alamy; 119 (Ford B-MAX) © Ford Europe/Blue Hive; 213, 225 ©Michelin; 259 © Michal Podemski